Governing
Pleasures

Governing Pleasures

PORNOGRAPHY AND SOCIAL
CHANGE IN ENGLAND, *1815–1914*

LISA Z. SIGEL

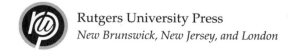
Rutgers University Press
New Brunswick, New Jersey, and London

British Cataloging-in-Publication information is available from the British Library.

Manufactured in the United States of America

Design by John Romer

Library of Congress Cataloging-in-Publication Data

Sigel, Lisa Z., 1965–
    Governing pleasures : pornography and social change in England, 1815–1914 / Lisa Z. Sigel.
        p.   cm.
    Includes bibliographical references and index.
    ISBN 0-8135-3001-6 (alk. paper)—ISNB 0-8135-3002-4 (pbk.: alk. paper)
    1. Pornography—England—History—19th century. 2. England—Social conditions—
19th century. I. Title.
HQ472.G7 S54   2002
365.4'7'094209034—dc21   2001019801

Contents

Acknowledgments

I want to take the opportunity to thank those individuals and organizations who helped me with this project. First and foremost, the librarians and private collectors who saved pornography from the bonfires deserve recognition. Although this might seem like an exaggeration, it isn't. Anthony Comstock measured the pornography he burned by the ton, rather than the piece. The British Library burned duplicates as well as those items that had no "redeeming value." In contrast, private collectors and individual librarians created collections, hid them as needed, and developed an expertise in the area that few academics can rival. Without such efforts I could not have written this work. Current collectors continue the tradition. In particular, Michael Goss in London and Uwe Scheid in Germany allowed me to use their collections and were generous in sharing their expertise. It was extremely awkward to ask if I could come up and see "their etchings," but these collectors treat the subject of pornography with great dignity and professionalism. I would also like to thank the staff of the Kinsey Institute, who went beyond all reasonable bounds in helping me with this project. Staff members at Trinity College at Oxford, the Bodleian, Cambridge University Library, and the British Library have also been most gracious in assisting me with my work.

Millsaps College has been generous in its support of my work. Dean Richard Smith's defense of academic freedom and the Faculty Research Committee's grants to work on this project prove that Mississippi is not what many believe. Millsaps's faculty and staff, including Bob McElvaine, David Davis,

Sandy Zale, Charles Sallis, Eric Griffin, Janice Jordan, and Louise Hetrick, have made the college a thriving intellectual community. The feminist works-in-progress group at Millsaps, composed of Anne MacMaster, Leonora Olivier, Kristen Brown, and myself, made sure that our own writings were as valued as our other activities. If my work speaks to a varied feminist audience, it is because this group vetted my efforts.

Carnegie Mellon University, Temple University, and the Andrew W. Mellon Fellowship for the Study of Objectivity have provided me with financial and intellectual support. The faculty of Carnegie Mellon University taught me how to teach, research, and write, and the school has become my intellectual home—with all the oddities that entails.

Many individuals have read my work and provided comments. Judith Modell, Kris Straub, and Peter Stearns stayed with this project from its initial prospectus stage to today. They read and commented on my plans, my ideas, and my prose, they answered frantic e-mails and phone calls, and they propped me up and sent me back into the ring on a regular basis. When I arrived in Mississippi only to find out that the state had alligators, Peter Stearns advised, "Use alligator skins to make tougher hide." It has become my mantra. Rick Maddox helped me reorganize the project. Mary Lindemann has been more than gracious with her time, her red pen, and her expertise. Gail Savage—in doing a favor for a friend—ended up reading the whole manuscript and providing invaluable input.

A number of other colleagues contributed to my growth as a professional. Jennifer Trost helped me focus on my goals. Tim Haggerty has been a wonderful proofreader and editor. Samantha Fenno helped me think through many vexing issues about the eighteenth century. Liesl Miller has been my role model about how to attend to personal life and still meet professional responsibilities. The graduates and graduate students of my program at Carnegie Mellon University have been good colleagues. Jared Day, Liping Bu, Julie Smith, Tom Buchanan, Susannah Walker, Gina Haimes, John Jensen, Loretta Lobes, and Josh Silverman prove time and again that we are all in this together.

The Journal of Social History has generously granted me permission to reprint chapter 4, "Filth in the Wrong People's Hands," which it published in an earlier form in the Summer 2000 issue. The anonymous reviewers who looked at this manuscript and that article have helped my work immeasurably. The comments I have received have been so consistently on target that I have developed a great deal of respect for the process and the people involved with it.

Leslie Mitchner at Rutgers University Press has been an expert editor and advocate, and I only hope the finished product will repay her faith.

I would also like to thank my family for reading my work. In particular, Bill Pomenti inspired me to lighten my prose when he compared earlier drafts to biochemistry textbooks, and Olivier Lessmann approved the results. Ljubomir Perkovic helped me find the time, energy, and intellectual reserves to complete this project. He read every word innumerable times, and even when my enthusiasm waned, his never did. He has proven himself one of the rare husbands who takes his spouse's intellectual life as seriously as he takes his own. And, finally, I'd like to thank baby Lena for being so very good.

Governing
Pleasures

Introduction

Sexual Imaginings

Who'll bugger the Turk?
"I," said Gladstone, "as Chief of the Nation,
And Premier of England to gain reputation.
I'll bugger the Turk,
And ne'er let him shirk
My prick's Grand Demonstration!"

Obscene verses about Gladstone's buggering prick contradict what we know about the man.[1] As far as historians can tell, Gladstone never buggered any-one, let alone "the Turk." The libelous accusations seem worlds away from the more important matters of the nineteenth century like the formation of the modern state and the emergence of the second British Empire. How, then, can we interpret the ditty? More important, why should we even try? To mull over the implications of Gladstone's prick might be a waste of time for the tradi-tional political historian because the ditty does not tell us about his campaign-ing and policies. It does not tell us about Home Rule for the Irish, nor about trade and diplomacy. However, if we expand our conception of politics from specific policies to the study of political culture and ideologies, then pornog-raphy tells us about the intersection of popular culture and political culture, about attitudes toward state regulation of sexual practices, and about the submerged ideologies of empire. As W. T. Stead, the muckraking journalist,

1

explained over a century ago: "To hear statesmen reckoned up from the standpoint of the brothel is at first almost as novel and perplexing an experience as it is to hear judges and Queen's Counsel praised or blamed, not for their judicial acumen and legal lore, but for their addiction to unnatural crimes or their familiarity with obscene literature."[2] Pornography tells us a great deal more besides. Fears of homosexuality, concerns over foreigners, conceptions of gender and gender-appropriate behavior, hopes for the future, pollution beliefs, bodies formed by work, by leisure, by race and class—all contributed to the formation of Victorian sexual culture, and all appeared in pornography.

Several scholars, among them Judith Walkowitz, Françoise Barret-Ducrocq, Jeffrey Weeks, and Michael Mason, have dug beneath the mythos of Victorian England to explore the sexual behaviors of Victorians.[3] These scholars have differentiated lived sexual practices from Victorian self-descriptions (and self-deceptions). Their work offers insight into the operation of sexuality in nineteenth-century England. The verses about Gladstone, however, do not correspond to actual behavior; after all, he didn't bugger the Turk. The verses speak to another realm entirely—that of sexual possibilities. The phrase "social imaginary" describes the realm of the possible. As John Tomlinson states, "The imaginary is *prior* to the real and the rational: it is the product of an act of cultural creation which is fundamental to any subsequent system of cultural representation."[4] The social imaginary is what the culture sees as "possible." Roger Chartier's discussion of the social imaginary emphasizes its importance as a way of thinking about people's thinking: "The social 'imaginary' of a time is thus constituted as a basic mental structure, as a system of representations whose genealogies must be worked out, and as a reality as real as the concreteness of the relations within a society."[5] The social imaginary allows people a way to organize their culture, to understand the actions, behaviors, artifacts, symbols, and signs among which they live. It acts not only on people but also through people as they continually cast, recast, and reconstitute their milieu in meaningful ways.

Pornography as source material provides insight into the social imaginary of sexuality. Pornography does not state the problems of sex— like disease, prostitution, and bastardy—as some government reports, reformers' tracts, and religious sermons do. Instead, it elaborates the possibilities of sex. Pornography is not tied to the tangible (what people do with their bodies) but to the imaginable (what they can imagine doing). It acts as a mirror—or, more accurately, a series of broken mirrors—that reflects, refracts, and distorts a picture of sexuality. And like people looking into a mirror, those reflected in pornography might change their bearing in response to what they see. Pornography is caught in an intimate relationship with the broader society, even though it remains tied to the realm of possibilities.

This realm of possibilities proves to be extremely adaptable in the nineteenth century; at times it emphasizes female subordination, at other times it centers on the worship of the priapus. Few people today would think of Gladstone or Queen Caroline as a relevant subject for pornographic writings, and even fewer, I suspect, would choose ethnography as their literary form for pornography. But nineteenth-century pornographers wrote about a variety of subjects in wide ranging ways. Some subjects, like maids, Turks, and aristocratic men, retained their allure throughout the period, while other subjects, like incest, gained popularity. Pornographic studies of Indian sexuality appeared alongside the rise of the British Empire in India, while slavery, outlawed in the British West Indies in 1833, only became a popular subtheme in the late nineteenth century. Fluctuations in the popularity of these themes and subjects are less random than one might assume at first glance. The dizzying array of people, positions, sexual activities, and literary styles has patterns and rhythms that relate to society.

In this book, I explore and explain these patterns and rhythms. Like most historians, I examine change and continuity over time. I chart how British society used pornography as a way to communicate and how this communication responded to changing cultural and social relationships. While pornography allows us to look at the social imaginary of a culture, the social imaginary is both synchronic and diachronic. It makes sense as a system at a given time, but it also changes over time—inventing new possibilities, new things to be imaginable. Just as important as what happened in the past is understanding how the realm of possibilities changes, incorporating what happened into the culture and limiting what will happen next. Thus, even though pornography continues to talk about sexuality, it changes form, style, and subject matter over time.

These shifts call for a flexible definition of pornography. Walter Kendrick in *The Secret Museum* has shown that ideas about pornography, both in content and in regulation, have developed over time and that the nineteenth century was the critical period for the contemporary definitions.[6] Only in the nineteenth century does the term *pornography* enter the dictionary as a discrete category of writings. An attempt to impose our current definitions of pornography on artifacts from the past would ignore the historical processes that went into the formulation of these artifacts and the cultural standards that we

use to make sense of them. *The Kama Sutra*, deemed obscene even without illustrations in the nineteenth century (it so seriously alarmed the printer of the
first English translation that he broke off the print run), became semirespect-
able, even with illustrations, in the twentieth.

The shifting formulation of pornography extended to the social position
and social perceptions of the user. The British government did not condemn or
prosecute artists for using photographs of naked bodies, called "artist's studies," but if those same photographs went to the poor, the perception of them
shifted and judges argued that in context these objects were obscene. The
judgment passed on pornography changed based upon where, when, and by
whom it was viewed.[7] In the nineteenth century, the application of labels such
as pornography, obscenity, and indecency hinged upon access. It was pre-
sumed that certain people could look at representations with limited emo-
tional, social, and legal consequences while others could not. Objects became
indecent through the act of viewing or reading. Rather than trying to create a
universal standard of pornography, I demonstrate the socially contingent nature of the definitions as a whole, taking my cues from the nineteenth century.
When asked whether a photograph of the Venus de Medici [*sic*] equaled other
nude representations, the chief constable of Manchester replied, "No, but I
suggest that all the circumstances should be taken into consideration; the photograph of nude women under certain circumstances may be all right, but if it
is placed in the windows and sold to youths and sold on the streets, then I say
it is not for the good of the community, and you should take all the circumstances into consideration when you decide."[8]

Because of the shifting formulation of pornography, I have taken my
definition of pornography from the definitions of the time period. I use the
word *pornography* as an umbrella term to cover a wide variety of representations including literature, drawings, and photographs. A focus on sexuality
ties these diverse mediums together, but in spite of the single predominant
theme, pornography takes a variety of forms and has a wide range of foci and
uses; it does more than just titillate. I consider as pornography works that
people wrote, published, printed, legislated, and collected as pornography.
To the contemporary reader, some of these texts and materials may seem un-
pornographic, unerotic, or downright decent, while others may appear unerotic and downright disgusting. That underscores the point: Pornography
varies as a culture and the symbolic meanings in that culture evolve.

As an aspect of these cultural changes, the language of sexuality shifts as
well. (For my own part, after much trepidation and thought, I have usually
chosen scientific language for clarity, but on occasion vulgar language is

clearer and seems more appropriate for illustrating meaning.) For instance, some of the texts use the word *cunt*. *Cunt* in the eighteenth century had far more bawdy and ribald connotations than it does today. By the late nineteenth century, however, *cunt* began to be used self-consciously as the meaning became "dirty"—an adjective that emerged to describe words and writings in the nineteenth century. "Dirty words" infused ideas of pollution onto aspects of sexuality, and control of purity and dirt is crucial to social organization, as Mary Douglas has shown.[9] Other terms referring to the female body, such as *womb, vagina*, and *reproductive organs*, do not convey what *cunt* implied in the context of the late nineteenth century, namely, the linguistic pollution of the vaginal area for the sake of men's pleasure. *Cunt* brings that connotation to women's bodies, whereas all other terms seem to conceal it. Similarly, the Gladstone ditty uses the word *bugger*, which has gone out of vogue (replaced in the American vocabulary by *butt-fuck*.) During the nineteenth century, however, authors used *bugger* to convey the homoerotic and homophobic desire for domination occurring through penetration. *Bugger* brings those connotations to a sexual act, whereas terms like *anal intercourse* or *anal penetration* hide rather than illustrate meaning. One could talk about having anal relations with the Turk, but why bother?

As this discussion of *cunt* and *bugger* may have demonstrated, pornography— its language, images, meanings— encourages a nearly visceral reaction in many. This reaction has been transformed into a political platform by anti-pornography feminists. Catherine MacKinnon, Andrea Dworkin, Susan Griffin, and others have formalized the position that pornography causes rape.[10] They argue that pornography creates an aggressive masculinity that uses violence to uphold patriarchy. According to this perspective, pornography teaches men to think of women as objects, to subordinate women, and to use violence to control women. As such, pornography not only creates violence against women but is in itself a form of violence.

When Dworkin and MacKinnon developed their positions they were working against the backdrop of the sexual liberation movement. Studies of pornography, influenced by sexual liberation, implicitly and explicitly espoused a linear framework from repression to liberation, which guaranteed that frank discussion would validate both men's and women's sexual desires.[11] In this model, the shift from Victorian prudery to sexual explicitness would benefit everyone; in short, the more sex, the better. MacKinnon and Dworkin have aptly demonstrated that some pornographic treatments of women will subordinate rather than liberate women. Their ideas have been enormously influential in both British and American politics and policies.[12] Questions remain, however, about the validity of these propositions.[13] Numerous works have addressed their propositions from a variety of feminist, philosophical, legal, and sociological perspectives. These accounts make fascinating reading and remain important for anyone researching current approaches to pornography.[14] As a feminist, I appreciate Dworkin's and MacKinnon's desire to make cultural images accountable for the way women are viewed by society, but they lack a historical perspective, which deeply flaws the theoretical underpinnings of their work.[15] By stipulating a universal definition of pornography, "pornography is," MacKinnon and Dworkin in effect ignore the historical process through which pornography as we now know it comes into being. In order to create a strong argument for the present, the antipornography feminists flatten pornography into a monolithic history of the oppression of women.

If we want to consider the claim that pornography teaches people (particularly men) how to think about sexuality, we must first establish which men used pornography and why. Women's historians have nuanced the picture of a universal woman's standpoint and culture; they have shown that class, race, and region matter to women's lives and understandings. Men's culture and cosmologies deserve the same attention.

I use a model of reasoned speculation to consider the historical problem of consumption for a trade in which incomplete documentation, burned evidence, missing subscriber lists, and self-censorship obscure the historical record. Because of its illegality, the trade in pornography is profoundly hidden. As Henry Spenser Ashbee, the most important source on nineteenth-century pornography, states: "The author writes, for the most part, anonymously, or under an assumed name; the publisher generally affixes a false impress with an incorrect date; and the title is not infrequently worded so as to mislead with regard to the real contents of the book. To discover these authors is frequently impossible. . . . To trace the booksellers who have set the law at defiance, who have sometimes made large profits, and at others succeeded at only getting into prison, is a pursuit equally interesting, but quite as difficult."[16] The most basic factors in the creation and distribution of pornography are hard to document. The writers, publishers, printers, vendors, and readers, for the most part, remain hidden from the historian. The pieces of information that are available are suspect; they are partial at best and can lend themselves to overgeneralizing. They are taken from either overfriendly sources who exaggerate the importance of pornography or from unfriendly sources who aggrandize the "problem" as they saw it. Spectators at the time, from the publishers to the police, had every reason to lie and few reasons to tell the truth.

These problems can be surmounted only because of bibliographers, deal-ers, and private collectors, who rarely get the recognition they deserve. Al-though often discounted by academics as mere antiquarians (at best) or perverts (at worst), they have carefully accumulated information, passed down folklore and gossip about the trade, and spent enormous sums of money and great amounts of time putting collections together and reestablishing those that have been broken up. When governments and archives burned pornogra-phy, collectors detailed, compiled, and hid it. Without them, little would be left to study. The Private Case Collection in the British Library, one of the three most important collections in the world, has been accumulated solely through donations made by such collectors.

I build many of my claims from Ashbee, one of the great collectors and bibliographers of the nineteenth century. His bibliographies are an essential tool for anyone approaching British pornography. A three-volume encyclo-pedia of gossip, prices, and information about various texts and editions, Ashbee's work stands as a testimonial to his erudition. Unfortunately, it ends in the 1880s. A remarkable bibliography by Peter Mendes entitled *Clandestine Erotic Fiction in English, 1800–1930* continues where Ashbee's leaves off. His work has been called the best on pornography since Ashbee's, and I rely heav-ily upon it.[17] Only because of these predecessors can I make statements about the audience for pornography. I can specify prices, shop locations, and other methods of distribution. I can piece together which pornographers worked at a given time, what they produced, and how they learned the trade. I can com-pare distribution runs to see if the trade expanded. By correlating factors such as price and availability with broader patterns such as literacy and distribu-tions of wealth, I can make speculative claims about broad patterns of access to pornography.

Access, however, is not the same as consumption. To say that people bought pornography does not say how they consumed the materials, at least not in the sense that Dworkin and MacKinnon mean. The act of consump-tion—the ways that people use and understand pornography—should ulti-mately define the relevance of claims about pornography's effects on men's and women's worldviews. Pornography, like any type of material culture, can be bought and put aside, placed on a shelf for status-value, or glanced at and then forgotten. The different ways of reading (reading briefly, analytically, compul-sively, left-handedly) would form different patterns of consuming these mate-rials. To determine how people consumed pornography, historians would need personal accounts of reading, even though these too are influenced by self-censorship and literary stylization. Unfortunately, the letters, journals, and diaries are not available in necessary numbers. People rarely write of illegal and "immoral" acts, even to themselves.

There are important exceptions. Steven Marcus made a convincing case that *My Secret Life* is a sexual memoir rather than an act of fiction.[18] He thus revealed a source that speaks directly to sexual experiences. According to Marcus, the account of one man's sexual psyche can illuminate specific cultural formations; his classic recreates the worldview of the anonymous narrator and deserves close attention as a psychological reconstruction of sexuality. However, while Marcus demonstrates the synchronic meanings of sexuality, my goal of exploring the diachronic makes the individual account less useful. Because an aggregate of individual accounts does not exist, I employ alternate strategies to make sense of pornography.

To understand the implications of the texts, I return them to their historical context, creating an argument about how they might have been read, rather than what they ultimately must mean. There are a number of steps to this process. First, I look for patterns behind the production and distribution of pornography. Driving this examination are the questions: Who produced pornography? What encouraged them to do so? Were they trying to make money, to disrupt the status quo, to titillate themselves, each other, or a more distant audience? While the products do not necessarily mirror the authors' and publishers' intentions, the intentions might contribute to patterns in the texts, and they undoubtedly give us an understanding of how the producers expected these texts to be read.

Then I link the objects to the audience. Because I cannot say with certainty who read pornography, I begin by asking: Who could read? Who could afford pornography? Who could find it? I can isolate a pool of probable readers only because of the strong tradition of British social history. Social historians have spent the past three decades exploring "history from the bottom up"; they have reconstructed literacy patterns, incomes, costs of living, work structures, and regional differences. Because of this background, I can make reasonable claims about a population's access to materials.

I then explore what might have resonated in the texts for likely readers. The verse about Gladstone's buggering prick would have meant one thing if produced by revolutionary publishers and then sold to a militant and self-conscious working class: It might have been read as a way to dismantle the legitimacy of the liberal platform through political humor. Alas, that reading seems quite unlikely. *The Pearl's* small print run, high price, and limited distribution via mail order make it probable that the lines remained an in-joke among the most privileged in society, those who knew Gladstone, if not his prick, personally. The ditty, while tweaking Gladstone by his familiars, referred more to national aspirations than revolutionary sentiments.

Having established probable readers and likely readings, I delineate literary form and themes in the materials in order to place pornographic reading among other reading and writing practices and locate symbols and meanings within the broader culture of British society. For instance, *The Lustful Turk* (1829) used the form of the epistolary novel, with its inherent voyeuristic attributes, to provide a series of interlocking first-person narratives from women captured by the "Turk." While that form became less important than other methods of narration by the end of the eighteenth century, the pornographic epistolary novel continued into the nineteenth. The first-person narrative in *The Lustful Turk* and other works from the period created an important niche for women's subjectivity, even as these works fictionalized women's voices. Early nineteenth-century pornography saw sexuality as happening through women (not only to women, as later works would do). By locating the form and genre in the historical period, we can nuance the view of women as "objects." [19]

The themes of sodomy, Turks, and the harem also had a broader cultural relevance. *The Lustful Turk,* published against the backdrop of the Greek war of independence, demonstrates a certain ambivalence toward Turks, even though the idea of Turks in this novel is less problematic than in later portrayals. In this early work on Turks, the Turk's ownership of a harem makes him master of fleshy delights: No one buggers the Turk; instead, the Turk gets to bugger European women. When Gladstone metaphorically "buggered the Turk" almost sixty years later, the ditty spoke to a long-term theme that in essence charts the Turks' fall from power. (I am tempted to speak of grace here, given the utopian connotations around early thematic uses of the harem.)

An analysis of the period between 1815 and 1914 can help clarify our current debates over pornography by showing how certain social and sexual formations solidified. Between the end of the Napoleonic wars and World War I, Britain experienced rapid and profound social transformations including the Industrial Revolution, continued urbanization, the formation of the second British Empire, the rise of middle-class hegemony, the development of a strong and vocal working class, the inception of a consumer economy, and the consolidation of the "separate spheres" of men and women. Britain weathered these and many other major changes with surprisingly little social upheaval when compared with France and Germany. The tensions these changes produced in Britain contributed to the richness of nineteenth-century literature as writers argued over new gender patterns, explored the meanings of

mechanization, struggled with the implications of the urban, industrial economy, examined the implications of empire, and responded to new sexual
ideals. The challenges of the nineteenth century were profound, irreversible,
and irresistible, not only to "legitimate" authors but also to pornographers.

Excavating how "minor" writers (what else could pornographers be but
minor?) responded can offer us a more nuanced view of the impact of these
challenges. But the gulf between the realms of sub rosa writings and fine literature diminishes upon closer inspection. A substantial overlap existed between
pornography and the respectable publishing trade for much of the nineteenth
century. William Dugdale published Voltaire, Paine, and works of pornography out of a republican commitment to the broad dissemination of ideas.
Another publisher, John Camden Hotten, worked with Algernon Charles
Swinburne and Richard Burton on both their legitimate and obscene books.
He also brought the works of Mark Twain and Stephen Crane to England.
Writers and audiences, ideas and attitudes, genres and conventions overlapped between the sub rosa and aboveboard, creating a mixture more heady
and potent than either alone. Pornography is not the "underworld" of Victorian literature, and the attempt to segregate it as such does an injustice to the
complicated world of British society and cultural production.

Writers of all types of literature, including pornography, sought not only
to react to their new sexual and social world but also to define it. The same
type of literary foment occurred earlier in France, as Lynn Hunt and Robert
Darnton demonstrate. These scholars tie the growth of pornography to Enlightenment thinking and attacks on the ancien régime of prerevolutionary
France. By combining social critiques with sexual allegations, pornography
undercut the legitimacy of the French monarchy, the Catholic Church, and the
institutions of aristocratic privilege. The French government outlawed both
pornography and revolutionary philosophy, furthering the ties between the
philosophes and Grub Street. As Darnton explains, "A regime that classified its
most advanced philosophy with its most debased pornography was a regime
that sapped itself, that dug its own underground, and that encouraged philosophy to degenerate into *libelle*."[20] The philosophic discussion of politics became saturated with a discussion of sexuality.[21] At the end of the eighteenth
century, as demonstrated by Iain McCalman, the combination of critique and
titillation crossed the Channel, invigorating the English revolutionary world
through the publication of pornography.[22]

The present work begins both chronologically and philosophically where
these works end. Darnton, Hunt, and McCalman follow the rise of pornography as a revolutionary activity that reached its apex in France before the

Revolution and in the 1820s in England. But pornography, as a way of concep-
tualizing the world, continued to change. Chapter 1 charts the permutations of
pornography as revolution quieted into constant tensions and subsequent reforms in England. Chapter 2 follows the new forms of pornography that began to develop in the 1860s based upon the professional, scientistic gaze. The
pornographers of the time, loosely organized in the so-called Cannibal Club,
generated ways of thinking about sexuality that later contributed to the fields
of psychology, ethnography, and medicine. By the 1880s, as chapter 3 shows,
pornography left behind its empiricist roots and developed a new consumer
edge. Marketing and distribution patterns contributed to this development as
a new group of entrepreneurs took over the trade. They allowed consumers to
fetishize the commodity of pornography in the classic Marxist sense (by sev-
ering the product from its means of production); at the same time, pornography established the sexual fetish as a literary and visual form. Finally,
chapter 4 demonstrates that pornography reached the masses in cheap visual
form between the 1880s and 1914. This final phase built upon older ideas of
sexuality and did not offer the masses any greater liberation than earlier pornography had, even though it allowed women, children, the working classes,
and people of color to view their own and each other's objectification for the
first time.

Changes in pornography parallel older models of periodization in British history; any British historian might mark out the nineteenth century as
chronologically defined by the phases of political instability, imperialism, elite
consumption, and the mass market. Pornography, then, offers a new source
to confirm known patterns, even though these appear quite different when
viewed through the lens of pornography. The familiar becomes odd, and the
oddity is well worth thinking about because it disrupts the smooth historical
narratives we have constructed. For this reason alone, pornography would be
worth considering. In addition, despite the similar chronologies, or, more accurately, because of them, pornography raises new questions about the emergence of modern society. State formation and capitalism, in particular, affect
sexuality in hidden ways. A study of pornography insists on a rethinking of
these processes.

During the twentieth century, sexuality developed a complicated relationship with capitalism. Sexuality functions as a lure for capitalism (in advertisements), a reward for success within capitalism (in sexualized leisure), a
counterweight to it (in the affectionate couple who retreat from the harsh
world and "make love"), and as the source of an ever-expanding market (in sex
toys, sexual aids, and sex literature). This convoluted relationship emerged

out of the nineteenth century, and the study of pornography helps explain these developments. Pornography functioned as a leisure activity for consumers, a market for producers, and as encouragement for and critique of the affectionate couple. Pornographers built a demand for their products through advertisements based on sexuality but also used social and cultural patterns such as utopian longings and racialism to sell sex.

State regulation and state sanction of desires further complicated the already elaborate process of the emergence of modern sexuality. Historians, following Michel Foucault's lead, have shown that the campaigns against onanism, prostitution, venereal disease, illegitimacy and bastardy, and sexual inversion all spoke about what they opposed. Examining the negative process of regulation shows only half the picture; desires emerged, whetted by and in reaction against state regulation. Pornography documents the emergence and proliferation of these desires. The longing for pricks and cunts, for combinations more complex than the affectionate couple, for the Turk, and for the Turk's garden of fleshy delights have their own progression related to the regulation and the marketing of desire. The negative attention paid to pornography and the development of licit and illicit desires in pornography looks much like a tango—the smooth evolution interrupted by twists and turns, full of yearning and latent aggression on both sides.

The individual who lives within the tensions among capital, state regulation, and sexuality can be compared to the rose clamped in the teeth of the dancer. Not to overextend the analogy or entirely discount the agency of the individual, but highlighting the long-term forces that affect an individual's options seems central in the study of sexuality, in order to combat the reification of the natural. Against long-term structural demands, the individual adopts patterns to celebrate, subvert, and resist normative pressures. Individuals make the most of options from the limited pool; this study will show the dynamics that create a framework within which individuals exercise this agency. Gay, lesbian, and feminist studies have wrestled with the problems of identity formation in a world that rarely recognizes, and often undermines, the diversity of desires. Feminists and queers ignore, subvert, and reoccupy (with a vengeance) those normative constraints and symbols that hinder their personal happiness. Many of these strategies work. Queers and straights, men and women, recycle these symbols in ways they find meaningful. An examination of these symbols becomes particularly urgent because the symbols we adopt, ignore, or deride have their own hidden histories. John K. Noyes foregrounds his discussion of s/m in *The Mastery of Submission* with a similar problem of symbols.

The thought of an upmarket dominatrix in the old uniform of the South Africa Police [SAP] administering punishment to one of her respectable middle-aged customers was amusing, particularly if I imagined the customer as one who had, in days gone by, occupied the inside of the uniform. But the very idea that such a chillingly *real* scenario, which had been responsible for real deaths, real suffering, could suddenly be reduced to theater for the titillation of sexually bored, upper-middle-class men and women was disturbing to say the least. . . .

And yet, wasn't this a better use of the uniforms and whips than the SAP . . . had found for them? A scenario of consensual sexual pleasure in which no one gets any more hurt than they want to—isn't this the best of all possible scenes of violence?[23]

Fiction and reality, violence and pleasure, merge in ways that demand a recognition of personal identity formed within structural restraints. People make use of available symbols formed by political, economic, and social processes. The symbols that we use have costs and benefits, both recognized and unrecognized. By historicizing these symbols, I attempt to identify the strands of associations that follow from them.

The recognition of economic, political, and social relations codified in pornography might appear to contradict my original statement that pornography forms the social imaginary of sexuality. But the social imaginary is not the "id"—the primordial ooze of wants and needs. In pornography, the realm of possibilities is socially and culturally determined. To return to John Tomlinson's description of the social imaginary: "Individual choices . . . only reflect autonomy within the range of what is 'imaginable' as the attainable 'good life' within a culture." Individual choices of the "good life" or "good sex"—the realm of the possible—are limited by the structural constraints of a given society. This recognition is particularly important because the fantastic nature of pornography has led to a series of false assumptions. Because pornography is so firmly linked to the possibilities rather than the realities of sex, it has been considered both liberatory and oppressive. It has been alternately labeled utopian or dystopian (and in Steven Marcus's account pornatopian), as if it can step out of the milieu from which it is born or provide a fully developed alternative world. Victorian pornography neither fulfilled the promise of liberation nor guaranteed complete subordination; it did not provide the utopia or the dystopia of which people dreamed. Instead, it offered something much more nebulous, flexible, and interesting than most critics acknowledge: a way for people to make sense of and understand their world through the subject of sexuality. That their world was born from the muck of bodies and reflects these lowly origins is not surprising. That individuals spun elaborate fantasies from that matter will also probably not astonish anyone. But, if we inherited our ideas of sexuality from their world, then the sexual relations we can choose from might be far richer and more complex than we believe.

Chapter 1
Revolutionary Pornography

Pornography as a Political Act

The formation of the English working class, as E. P. Thompson demonstrated, happened largely through a network of radical pressmen.[1] Toward the end of the eighteenth century and at the beginning of the nineteenth, the combination of changing work conditions, dire poverty, draconian laws, and an extremely limited political franchise made artisans, laborers, journeymen, and apprentices not only vulnerable but also belligerent. The press became a medium through which these people made demands that would otherwise have gone unexpressed outside of skirmishes of limited political efficacy. Both the French Revolution and the American Revolution demonstrated the effectiveness of the radical press, and while England's 1789 never materialized, the press endowed the working class with a consciousness of its political and economic importance.

Early British pornographers were part of the larger radical movement and saw themselves as political actors. They had a series of specific aims including overthrowing the monarchy, reforming Parliament, separating church and state, and establishing freedom of the press. This was the agenda of a wide range of thinkers, but pornographers between the 1810s and 1850s in England used these goals to create a political platform that attacked old sexual and social standards and promoted new possibilities for society through sexuality.

15

William Dugdale best exemplifies the overlap between politics and pornographic production at the beginning of the nineteenth century. He made his appearance as a radical agitator in 1820 and participated in the Cato Street Conspiracy. He worked for George Cannon, one of the leading pressmen in the Queen Caroline Affair. He published a variety of political tracts between the 1820s and the 1850s that attacked the Corn Laws and workhouses and that promoted Chartism and radical redistribution of land. His bona fides as a radical republican seem beyond question. However, he was also one of the most prolific pornographers of the early nineteenth century, publishing *The Adventures of Sir Henry Loveall* (1830?, 1860), *The Inutility of Virtue* (1860), *The Exquisite* (1842–1844), *The Lustful Turk* (1860 or 1864), and numerous editions of *The Memoirs of a Woman of Pleasure* (1830, 1841, 1850), to name only the best known. While Dugdale's longevity as a leading British pornographer makes him exceptional (he had an almost forty-year reign), the melding of political and sexual radicalism fits into a long and well-established tradition.

Dugdale and other members of the pornographic press adapted the language of the Enlightenment and the impulses of libertinism to argue for a new sexual order. These two strands of thought are not as far apart as it might appear. Both arose out of discomfort with established society, but where one now signifies literary and philosophic ideals, the other became grounded in sexual nonconformity. The historical assessment of one as high culture and the other as low practice disregards the ways libertinism and the Enlightenment nourished each other throughout the eighteenth century.[2]

The word *libertine* (originally meaning freed from slavery) had taken on the connotations of freethinking and sexual excess and was being applied both appreciatively and pejoratively by the seventeenth century.[3] In most appellations, it implied irreligion, cocksmanship, individualism, and a rejection of all restraints. The word was used to describe a style of sexuality, a philosophic position, and an intellectual attitude that defied traditional morality whether defined by the church, the state, or more informal communal mores. David Foxon suggests that libertinism seems tied to the travels of immoral literature emerging from Renaissance Italy, most notably the writings of Pietro Arettino that engaged in anticlerical ribaldry. If so, then libertine erotic literature emerged in an interstitial position that pandered to aristocratic and clerical tastes at the same time it mocked them.[4] Furthermore, as Tiffany Potter shows, over the course of the eighteenth century libertinism became more amenable, focused on female sexuality, and skeptical (rather than outright atheistic).[5] Thus, *libertinism* emerged as a shifting term to describe the sexual nonconformity of the elite.

While literary critics distrust libertinism as cynical, pessimistic, selfish, and manipulative, historians tend to be a bit more gentle in their assessment, linking libertinism to other forms of sexual freethinking (such as the refusal to marry).[6] This divergence arises in part from the objects of study and in part from the perceived consequences of libertinism: Literary critics view the rise of the novel as paramount, and historians tend to see the rise of revolution as more noteworthy.[7] In many ways, pornographers straddled this divide. Pornographers tied up the sexual agenda of libertinism, including cocksmanship, skepticism, rampant individualism, and the refusal to limit sexuality to marriage, with the belief in rationality and the natural-rights philosophy emerging from the Enlightenment.

Lynn Hunt and Robert Darnton have demonstrated the importance of pornography in undercutting court politics in prerevolutionary France.[8] Some of the greatest *philosophes* criticized the government through this medium; by combining social critique with sexual allegation, pornography undercut the legitimacy of the monarchy, the Catholic Church, and the institutions of privilege. Weaving politics and sex together inflamed the populace, by critiquing through titillation and by advocating new ideals for sexuality. The French government's interdiction of both pornography and philosophy strengthened the ties between them, making the boundary between "obscene libel" and "treason" nebulous. As Darnton states, "It no longer seems so puzzling that Mirabeau, the embodiment of the spirit of 1789, should have written the rawest pornography and the boldest political tracts of the previous decade. Liberty and libertinism appear to be linked, and we can find affinities among all the best-sellers in clandestine catalogues."[9]

Pornography and revolution, *Fanny Hill* and *The Rights of Man*, crossed and recrossed the Atlantic, connecting the radical elements in France and England and America. Revolutionary pornography reached a zenith (or nadir, according to contemporaries) in France in the 1780s when the Marquis de Sade blunted the political impact of libertinism by taking the philosophy to its most extreme and exposing its incipient cruelty, but pornography continued to flourish in Britain. Republicans used the language of libertinism but detached the philosophic and sexual freedoms associated with the libertine agenda from the aristocratic social position.[10] The combination of working-class agitation, the radical press, and a rethinking of sexuality gave a new focus to libertinism that has been largely overlooked. John Gillis characterized the period between the end of the eighteenth century and the middle of the nineteenth as "the second great wave of sexual nonconformity." (The first great wave occurred during the seventeenth century, concomitant with the initial rise of libertinism.) This nonconformity constituted itself in a wide variation in sexual practices among plebeians—from sex outside marriage to polygamous unions, from writing one's own marriage contract to choosing common-law divorce through "wife sales"—and gained a theoretical grounding in the writings of freethinkers like Thomas Paine, Robert Burns, and Mary Wollstonecraft at the end of the eighteenth century and a second generation including Robert Dale Owen, Fanny Wright, Richard Carlile, and Elizabeth Sharples between the 1820s and the 1840s.[11] The philosophies of sexual nonconformity nourished a more working-class variant of libertinism that overlapped with other forms of radical agitation, including republicanism, feminism, and incipient socialism. The continued involvement of a core group of radical pornographic publishers, including William Dugdale, his brother John, George Cannon, John Benjamin Brookes, and John and Edward Duncombe, contributed to making sexuality central to political freedom well into the 1840s.

While the connection between pornography and revolution has been well documented in the French context, little attention has been paid to English pornographers as political radicals. That the pornographers whose lives and works are the subjects of this chapter took part in the most radical political movements in England during the first part of the nineteenth century has been generally overlooked. Iain McCalman has quite rightly returned them to the political stage, but he sees a shift in their agenda when they began to peddle pornography. He characterizes their pornographic publications as antithetical to their political platforms: "At best it [pornography] peddled masturbatory fantasies for frustrated upper-class males; at worst it popularized debased versions of the cruelty, violence and perversion of the Marquis de Sade."[12] It is quite possible, however, that the ultra-radicals saw pornography as a political medium. They published it alongside political tracts, and they continued to remain involved in key, working-class political issues. Their publication of pornography should not immediately be discounted; if these pornographers had political intentions, if their pornographic works had politicized messages, and if they reached more than the "debased aristocracy," then pornography advanced their broader political goals.

~

William Dugdale and the Production of Revolution

William Dugdale, born in 1800 in Stockport to a Quaker bookseller-tailor, came to London with the purpose of becoming a radical pressman. He arrived in London at the age of eighteen, already a Paineite and a deist.[13] Within two years he had joined political circles that alternately espoused democratic revolution, violent overthrow of Parliament, full freedom of the press, of association, and of movement, free love, abolition of slavery, utopian landholding schemes, rational religion, and deism. George Cannon, an ultra-radical philosopher-pornographer, employed Dugdale as a bookseller-publisher, and by 1823 or 1824 Dugdale opened his own shop. Dugdale had joined a milieu imbued with contrasts: Enlightenment ideals and bawdy humor, serious political demands and coarse sexual allegations.

Between 1818 and 1820, the first two years of Dugdale's tenure in London, political agitation against the government grew as the radical press advanced republican politics. The press tried to undermine the regime by attacking the monarchy, parliamentary leaders, and other influential members of British society. In response, the government passed the Six Acts, including the Blasphemous and Seditious Libel Acts (1819), and then used them to arrest the publishers of *The Age of Reason*, the *Black Dwarf*, and *The Republican*, among others, attempting to silence leading republican pressmen and break the organization of radicals.[14]

The swell of antigovernment publications, however, did not cease, and popular agitation continued in pornographic and asexual form. It reached critical levels and took a violent turn in the wake of the "Peterloo Massacre" of 1819, in which eleven protestors died as a result of the government's use of force to quell a rally at St. Peter's Fields. Spurred on by an agent provocateur, a group of "fighting radicals" then attempted to assassinate the cabinet and bring down the British government. This failed attempt at violent revolution, the Cato Street Conspiracy of 1819, ended with the trial and execution of the leaders, Thistlewood, Brunt, Ings, Davidson, and Tidd. Although he was not arrested, Dugdale was implicated in the conspiracy.[15]

After Peterloo and the Cato Street Conspiracy, the press, including Dugdale, turned to the scandals of the monarchy in the Queen Caroline Affair.[16] When George IV sought to divorce Caroline in 1820, he instigated a parliamentary investigation to prove that she had committed adultery. The House of Lords heard evidence for divorce and impeachment.[17] The popular press defended Caroline as the wronged wife by publicizing George's own debaucheries, including his drunkenness, his bigamous marriage to Maria Fitzherbert, and his many mistresses. The press had been handed a ready opportunity for political pornography, and they made the best of it.[18] In one print, George IV peeks out beneath the skirts of his mistress Lady Conyngham as she reclines with partially bared breasts. In another, George plays "The Blanket Hornpipe" as his various mistresses toss him on a blanket.[19] Other works included *The Spirit of "The Book"; or, Memoirs of Caroline, Princess of Has-burgh, A Political and Amatory Romance* (1811), written against the background of George's earlier attempts to divorce Caroline, republished in abridgment in 1812 and reissued in 1820, and *Fair Play, or Who Are the Adulterers, Slanderers and Demoralizers?* (1820). Some works focused on the financial and moral corruption of the lords and clergymen who backed George IV. The range of works maligned the monarch's sexual habits, the economics of government, the discrimination of social superiors, and the hypocrisy of the Anglican Church. Although the House of Lords did not find the queen guilty of adultery, perhaps in fear of mob violence if the trial continued, pressmen successfully rallied public opinion. Caroline died shortly thereafter, and the radical press lost a potent arena for subversion, but caricatures and political attacks continued through Victoria's reign. Because Dugdale worked as an employee of Cannon—one of the more prolific writers in the Queen Caroline Affair—he was at the epicenter of popular agitation surrounding the scandal.

Against the backdrop of this wide range of political activities—from armed insurrection to sexualized caricatures—Dugdale emerged as a printer-publisher. His commitments defined him as an ultra-radical who mixed philosophy with indecency, the fight for freedom of the press with scurrilous attacks on authority. Though the spirit of revolution and the Cato Street Conspiracy had turned to respectability and reform by the 1830s, Dugdale was too raucous and bawdy to fit into the culture of reform and respectability that influenced working-class formation in the 1830s.[20] However, he did not abandon his political roots. He used his acumen as a popular agitator to encode a notorious anti–Poor Law tract with the title of *The Book of Murder!* in 1839. This anonymous pamphlet attacked the New Poor Laws—some of the most debilitating pieces of legislation for workers in the nineteenth century—which separated men from women in workhouses, made the poor less eligible for assistance, and shifted the meaning of aid from a basic right to a spur to labor. *The Book of Murder!* "proved" that the new legislation intended to murder the poor. Dugdale's introduction argued that "men have been hanged upon far less strong and conclusive circumstantial evidence, than that which proves that the murderous principle and engine of the new poor law."[21] The book provided step-by-step instructions for smothering babies (from a document supposedly smuggled out of the workhouses) and denounced the new Malthusian regime that insisted that the poor should not marry (or have sex). He also published *An Essay on the Right of Property in Land* (1838), which advocated utopian landholding, and *For General Circulation! A Plea for the Poor* (1842), which agitated against the Corn Laws. In 1843, he offered a new edition of Voltaire's

Philosophical Dictionary that helped inspire the French Revolution. His political and sexual agenda continued throughout the 1840s: "During the political excitement of 1848, a *Times* correspondent commented to Thomas Frost that, judging from Dugdale's shopwindows, the literature of the working classes consisted of 'a mélange of sedition, blasphemy, and obscenity.'"[22] Dugdale might not have fit into the political mainstream of the 1830s and 1840s, but he produced politicized texts that spoke to workers' lives in meaningful ways.

By the 1830s, the radical pornographers had become well established and opened shops (often more than one) rather than distributing their wares through fairs, itinerant vending, or corresponding societies as they had during the 1810s and 1820s. By one estimate in the mid-1830s, there were fifty-seven bookshops dealing in pornography across London.[23] Pornographers clung to artisanal styles of production that utilized family members and apprentices, women as well as men, and family members continued to create and distribute pornography even if one went to jail. The brothers Duncombe printed together and were prosecuted together in 1829; later, when Edward Duncombe was prosecuted, John carried on the family business at five different locations.[24] Similarly, when George Cannon died in 1854, his widow took over his bookshop until her own death in 1864.[25] Dugdale had his entire family working for him, and together they maintained at least five storefronts.[26] In 1852, his brother John worked in conjunction with him and received two years' imprisonment with hard labor for obscenity.[27] When William Dugdale was imprisoned in the 1850s, John Rigdon Thorton, his son-in-law, took charge of the operations; in 1858 Thorton too was prosecuted for possession of obscene books with intent to sell. (He blamed his downfall from good character on his marriage to Dugdale's daughter.)[28]

While the fear of revolutionary disorder encouraged a greater emphasis on the bureaucratic control of political publications with the passage of the Six Acts, no effective mechanisms were in place for the control of pornography. The state left the policing matters of vice to voluntary societies such as the Society for the Suppression of Vice (SSV), formed in 1802. The SSV, an amateur society composed of the gentry, entrapped pornographers by convincing them to sell obscene goods, arrested them, and then paid for prosecution unless the court made the defendant pay for costs.[29] After 1829, the SSV could bring the evidence to the newly formed professional police, who would then be responsible for the arrest.[30] However, out-of-pocket expenses continued to plague the SSV.[31] The problems of amateur policing were compounded by the lack of a coherent legal framework for prosecuting obscenity. An overlapping system of courts left room for the pornographers to operate. The ecclesiastical court could try for obscenity, and common-law courts could prosecute for distribution; however, no systematic procedures were in place to stop porno-graphic or obscene publications.[32] The penalties for printing seditious litera-ture went up with the passage of the Six Acts, but the punishments for printing pornography, while still severe, did not.

The publishers paid fines, suffered under hard labor, and served years of imprisonment for pornographic works. The Crown saw the publication of such pornographic works as attacks on the religious and social order, which undercut the monarch's sovereignty. Edward Duncombe received two concur-rent sentences of imprisonment and hard labor for "being a person of most wicked lewd depraved and abandoned mind and disposition and wholly lost to all sense of decency chastity morality and religion and most unlawfully and wickedly devising contriving and intending as much as in him to vitiate and corrupt the morals of the liege subjects of our said Lady the Queen and to in-cite and encourage the said liege subjects to indecent obscene and immoral practices and to debauch poison and infect the minds of the youth of the king-dom."[33] The Duncombes, Brooks, Cannon, and the Dugdales were imprisoned at least twelve times for obscenity. William Dugdale alone was tried, con-victed, and imprisoned in 1830, 1835, 1852, and 1868.[34] In January of 1858, the secretary of the society reported 159 prosecutions for the past fifty-five years since the inception of the society, or roughly three prosecutions per year, in-cluding at least nine prosecutions of the Dugdales.[35]

Prosecution attempts made little impact on the trade until the 1850s. At that time the SSV gained an ally in Parliament in the person of Lord Camp-bell, who forced the passage of the Obscene Publications Act in 1857.[36] Lord Campbell's Act (as it is commonly known) allowed police to seize and destroy pornography and the means of production such as plates and type, thus jeop-ardizing pornographers' financial well-being by abrogating their rights of property. As Lord Campbell explained when justifying the destruction of pornographic goods, "There is no property in those publications."[37] However, the new legislation proved only slightly more effective than the old.[38] The pub-lishers had been well schooled in evading the authorities in their radical ac-tivities, and they continued to distribute their wares until their deaths. Not until William Dugdale died in 1868 in Clerkenwell Prison, where he had been imprisoned for obscenity under Lord Campbell's Act, was there any lessening of activity by the Dugdales; he had been caught with 35,000 copies of indecent books and pamphlets as well as lithographic stones.[39]

Although the radical pornographers failed to foment revolution, they provided an example of subversive potential that remained antithetical to "respectability." These men linked the notorious underworld of the late eighteenth century to the rise of working-class political activism in the nineteenth. Drunken, licentious, convicted of political crimes and crimes of morals, these radicals were at the center of the political activities that made the English working class.

The Audience: Debased Aristocracy or the English Working Class?

In spite of the widespread belief that pornographers toadied to the debauched aristocracy, the matter of readership is not clear at the beginning of the nineteenth century. Evidence points in contradictory directions, making it seem as if pornography was an aristocratic phenomenon, a worker's phenomenon, or perhaps no phenomenon at all. Cannon began his edition of *Venus School Mistress* (a flagellant novel) by discussing the issue of readership, asserting that "innumerable old generals, colonels, and captains, as well as bishops, judges, barristers, lords, commoners, and physicians" enjoyed flagellation as a practice.[40] Cannon might have mentioned both commoners and lords in an attempt to hawk the novel as widely as possible. At the other end of the spectrum, the *Times* reporter's comment on Dugdale's shop window argues that the working classes alone might have read this mixture of obscenity, blasphemy, and sedition. Contemporary reports point in all directions for good reason. The political inclinations of these radical publishers worked against structural factors such as literacy rates, distribution routes, and prices that affected the parameters of the audience, creating a mixed pattern of access.

While later pornographers did aim their products toward the well-heeled members of society, these early radical printers had a more disparate group of readers in mind for their wares. Because of their political commitments to "the common man," the radical pornographers dispersed pornography across class lines. Radical printers distributed works with abandon at the beginning of the nineteenth century, vending wares by "sending out men from London who periodically visit the different country towns and attend different country fairs, races, and markets to circulate these abominations as their regular trade through the 1830s."[41] Fairs and markets allowed distribution to a variety of potential buyers, including the landless and the landed as well as craftsmen and factory workers. The shift to bookstores in the 1830s no doubt cut into the regional dissemination of these materials, making pornography London a problem. (Later pornographers used the mail to widen the distribution again.) But

FIGURE 1. Anonymous drawing: Cunnilingus. With permission of the Kinsey Institute.

other factors such as illiteracy rates and high prices had a greater impact on the breadth of the readership.

Some pornography of the early nineteenth century featured visual images. Sold as single prints or integrated with a text, these early visuals would allow widespread use of pornography. While some of the period's great illustrators such as Thomas Rowlandson produced obscene images, quite often the drawings remained anonymous and frankly amateurish. The drawing of cunnilingus in figure 1 might have featured a dwarf or merely a poorly rendered man; in any case, the bared breasts, the protruding tongue, and the framed painting of a semierect penis in the background qualified it as obscene.

Although printers could and did produce illustrations using woodcuts, lithographic stones, and copper plates, visuals remained supplementary to the written word. Novels, plays, and poetry formed the mainstay of the pornographic enterprise. This emphasis on the written word eliminated a large proportion of the population as users of pornography.[42] For most of the nineteenth century, the ability to read remained class specific; by 1800, most men of the middle classes could read and write, while the working classes and poor made up the masses of the unlettered.[43] Class distinctions meant that the upper classes had the time and resources for learning. The poor did not have an extended childhood for learning, spare money for books and slates, or the leisure to develop the extensive body of knowledge needed for sophisticated reading practices that much pornography demanded. The poor worked rather than went to schools; even Sunday schools did not end illiteracy.[44] Continued illiteracy on the part of the working classes hindered their use of many types of pornography.

Of course, even if illiterate, individuals could gain access to literary culture through reading aloud and singing. *The Frisky Songster* (figure 2), an

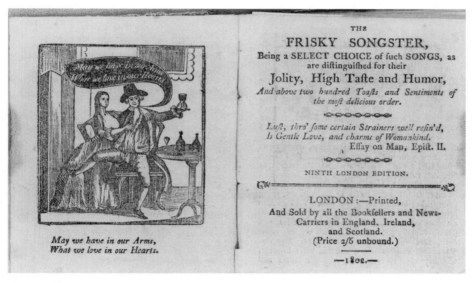

FIGURE 2. Frontispiece: *The Frisky Songster*. With permission of the Kinsey Institute.

early songbook that went through innumerable printings, including one by Dugdale, seems custom-tailored for such uses.[45] The short work included obscene toasts and songs that one can easily imagine making the taverns' rounds. A woodcut showing only a discreet nipple graced the frontispiece; however, the volume included many an obscene verse such as "Little Black Thing," about anal sex, and an obscene version of "Derry Down." The opening toast, "May we have in our arms, what we love in our hearts," was supplemented at the back of the book with the sacrilegious "cunt in a church, and they that won't fuck let them pray." Although songbooks like this could widen access to obscenity, the class-based differentials around literacy meant the middle classes and aristocracy had a far greater chance of using pornography.[46]

Furthermore, few workers could afford a full range of pornography. The cost of the works varied from fourpence for an eight-page serialized magazine like *The Exquisite* to two shillings and sixpence for songbooks like *The Frisky Songster* to three guineas for novels like *The Adventures of Sir Henry Loveall*.[47] Dugdale and other early radical publishers had a commitment to broad radical agitation and dispersal of knowledge, and indeed workers had greater access to pornography during Dugdale's reign than they would for most of the nineteenth century, but the sales of pornography still rested on the economics of social class and wealth. Although some workers could afford the cheaper works, pornography was not a purely working-class phenomenon; the more expensive texts were reserved for the aristocracy and gentry who could afford to throw pounds away on pleasure. Pornography during this period can be described as a cross-class phenomenon that favored the well-to-do.

The cross-class nature of pornography raised concerns, however. The class issues implicit in the early distribution made a particular impact upon the formulation of obscenity as a problem to be regulated. As the Society for the Suppression of Vice stated early in the nineteenth century, "The pernicious effects following upon the distribution of *blasphemous, licentious, and obscene books and prints,* reach equally the rich and poor; but the vendors of them are persons in the lower orders only; and the vendors are the only parties obnoxious to legal punishment."[48]

The desire to maintain control over reading habits of the lower orders was specifically addressed in a later debate in the House of Lords. Lord Campbell, the main proponent of new legislation against pornography, heard two cases as lord chief justice that moved him toward further regulation. One involved William Dugdale, the other William Strange. Strange had published *Singular Misadventures of the Right Honorable Filthy Lucre,* which detailed the seduction of a servant girl by a character named the Right Honorable

Lucre. The low price of the work filled Campbell with "astonishment and horror," and he introduced the Obscene Publications Act to curtail such works.[49] During the debate in Parliament, Lord Lyndhurst asked if such a bill might curtail access to bawdy works like *The Decameron*, which were sold alongside pornography. Lord Campbell responded that "the keeping or the reading, or the delighting in such things must be left to taste, and was not a subject for legal interference; but when there were people who designedly and industriously manufactured books and prints with the intention of corrupting the public morals, and when they succeeded in their infamous purpose, he thought it was necessary for the Legislature to interpose and to save the public from the contamination to which they would otherwise be exposed."[50] The distinction between the reading habits of the well-to-do and of the lower orders indicates that while the upper classes might have had a virtual monopoly on these works, the spillover to the lower orders, no matter how slight, was thought to have a disruptive potential that deserved serious attention.

The Literature: Republican Virtues

Lord Campbell's clear articulation of the issues raised by cross-class access points toward the belief that the spread of pornography could promote sexual excess and radical freethinking. While freethinking alone might alarm authorities such as Lord Campbell, sexual freethinking by the poor promoted action.

The clearest example of the radical program of sexuality comes from Richard Carlile, who was imprisoned under the Blasphemous and Seditious Libel Acts and later wrote *Every Woman's Book: or, What is Love?*. He first published it in *The Republican* and then republished it four times in essay form in 1826. While Carlile was no pornographer, in this work he delineated many philosophic ideals behind revolutionary pornography. In particular, he explained that the corruption of sexuality hindered the natural process of sexual intercourse, which brings beauty and pleasure to both men and women: "If love were a matter of sedate and philosophical conversation, the pleasures arising from it would be greatly heightened, desire would never be tyrannically suppressed, and much misery and ill health would be avoided."[51] According to Carlile, only free discussion would end the tyrannical suppression of sexuality. Religion and hypocrisy caused misery and illness by corrupting honest and honorable sexual passions: "Religion has been a great destroyer of beauty, has greatly deteriorated the healthy character and fine structure of the human body, being a mental disease, that turns love into a fancied sin, and commits dreadful ravages, in excluding due sexual intercourse." The hypocrisy of the church, not sexual intercourse, created mental disease. Only through frank discussion of sexuality, the use of birth control, and the end of marriage—because "the marriage ties in this country are too many for the simple enjoyment of passion that is not constant"—could a free sexuality develop.[52] His philosophy of sex laid out the republican program in both its analysis of contemporary problems and its hopes that through free discussion and the application of reason, sexuality could become a natural and unproblematic right.

This natural-rights philosophy of sex underlay much of the pornography of the early nineteenth century. These works articulated distinctions between passion and sophistication, rationality and religious dogma, and sexual liberation and sexual corruption. The model for narrative structure, characterization, and philosophic implications remained *The Memoirs of a Woman of Pleasure*, or *Fanny Hill* as it was popularly known.[53] *Fanny Hill's* frequent republication—it was published in English alone at least thirteen times between 1800 and 1850—hints at its particular resonance for British society.[54] The potential for subversion in the narrative comes both from the focus on sexuality as an avenue for social transformation and from the combination of bourgeois and artisanal values formed against the upper orders. These two factors could create a crucial realignment in the political order. The continual republication of the text in the politically unstable climate of England in the early nineteenth century made the implications of *Fanny Hill* more problematic than it had been in 1748–1749 upon its original publication.

From the beginning, *The Memoirs of a Woman of Pleasure* was considered an obscene book, even though it picked up on many of the tensions of the eighteenth century.[55] As an early novel, it can be compared to others that explored the adventures of young women exposed to eighteenth-century city life, such as *Moll Flanders, Pamela,* and *Shamela.* At the same time, Cleland was clearly influenced by earlier pornographic works, which had developed certain standard features, including the prostitute as central actor, trips to the brothels, and interlocking narratives. *Fanny Hill* thus fits into the uneasy ground between literary and pornographic traditions. In spite of this marginal place in the literary canon, it set the standard for British pornography throughout the nineteenth century and remained a constant in the pornographic marketplace.

Fanny Hill shows the possibilities and pitfalls of sexuality in eighteenth-century British society. The epistolary novel consists of letters that the main character, Fanny, writes to a female confidant about her sexual adventures. She begins as the tabula rasa, the blank slate, upon which the world acts. "My education, till past fourteen, was no better than very vulgar; reading, or rather spelling, an illegible scrawl, and a little ordinary plain-work composed the whole system of it: and then all my foundation in virtue was no other than a total ignorance of vice."[56] Cleland uses Fanny's naiveté to heighten the reader's expectations of the supposed outrages that will occur.

The innocent country girl, Fanny, journeys to London upon the death of her parents; the enormous rate of migration to the city in the eighteenth century would make this Fanny a familiar figure. There she is preyed upon by Mrs. Brown, a procuress for rich men. Cleland paints Mrs. Brown's person in a manner that vilifies her character: "A more enormous pair [of breasts] did my eyes never behold, nor of a worse color, flagging soft"; her "fat brawny thighs hung down and the whole greasy landskip lay fairly open to my view: a wide open-mouth'd gap, overshaded with a grizzle bush, seemed held out like a beggar's wallet for its provisions."[57] In the brothel, Fanny's passions are awakened in spite of the corrupt, decaying, and decadent circumstances. Thus, from the outset, Cleland legitimizes sexuality even when decrying its social manifestations.

As Fanny negotiates a variety of sexual encounters, natural sexuality, passion, affection, and bodily pleasures are continually pitted against corrupt pleasures and the vices of the upper orders. Fanny escapes the brothel and falls into the arms of her true love, Charles. "We lay together that night, when, after playing repeated prizes of pleasure, nature overspent, and satisfy'd, gave us up to the arms of sleep: those of my dear youth encircl'd me, the consciousness of which made even that sleep more delicious."[58] Cleland describes Fanny's deflowering as if it moved her from one state of nature to another, from the state of natural innocence to the state of natural passion. In this state of nature, Charles and Fanny live in harmony without the disadvantages of marriage. Because the state, religion, and society have no claim on their love, they remain uncorrupted.

Fanny then becomes mistress to Mr. H and lives in a melancholic bond without love. She enjoys material plenty but suffers from a stultifying ennui inspired by a lack of real affection. Fanny and other men's mistresses "visited one another in form, and mimic'd, as near as we could, all the miseries, the follies, the impertinences of the women of quality, in the round of which they trifle away their time, without its ever entering into their little heads that on earth there cannot subsist any thing more silly, more flat, more insipid and worthless, than, generally consider'd, their system of life is: they ought to treat the men as their tyrants, indeed! were they to condemn them to it."[59] When Fanny loses herself to avarice as she does in her relationship with Mr. H, her life becomes as staid and pleasureless as the lives of more respectable women. Cleland contrasts this social and sexual void with a revelation about sexuality's ability to transform. Before the following passage, Fanny has copulated with Will, a serving boy, in revenge for Mr. H's infidelities.

> May I not presume that so exaulted a pleasure ought not to be ungratefully forgotten or supress'd by me, because I found it in a character in low life, where, by the bye, it is oftner met with, purer, and more unsophisticate, than amongst the false ridiculous refinements with which the great suffer themselves to be so greatly cheated by their pride: the great! than whom, there exist few amongst those they call the vulgar, who are more ignorant of, or who cultivate less, the art of living than they do: they, I say, who for ever mistake things the most foreign of the nature of pleasure itself, whose capital favorite object is enjoyment of beauty, wherever that rare invaluable gift is found, without distinction of birth or station.[60]

In the arms of Will, the servant, Fanny finds the truth of passion—limitless pleasure uncorrupted by artifice. The social station, worldliness, and refinements that define the world of the rich fall short of innocent passion, pleasure, and affection among the poor. In *Fanny Hill*, neither man nor woman is born corrupted; instead they learn corruption in the social world à la Rousseau.

Fanny furthers her education in sexuality and social realities by meeting a variety of men who offer lessons on vice and virtue. Mrs. Cole, a second madam, guides her through the process. Fanny "threw herself blindly into [Mrs. Cole's] hands, and came at length to regard, love and obey her implicitly: and to do her justice, I never experienc'd at her hands other than a sincerity of tenderness, and care for my interest."[61] Mrs. Brown and Mrs. Cole function as foils; the former, the embodiment of her ugly intentions, deceives the innocent for the benefit of the rich, while the latter helps the less-than-innocent Fanny, to their mutual advantave, deceive the rich. Together, for instance, Mrs. Cole and Fanny cheat Mr. Norbert of Fanny's faked virginity. Mr. Norbert is "a gentleman originally of great fortune, which, with a constitution naturally not the best, he had vastly impair'd by his over-violent pursuit of the vices of town, in the course of which having worn out and stal'd all the more common modes of debauchery, he had fallen into a taste of maiden-hunting, in which chace he had ruin'd a number of girls."[62] Because he maiden-hunts as sport, Mrs. Cole and Fanny enjoy their game, besides receiving fifty pounds for Fanny's long-gone maidenhead.[63] In another encounter, Fanny meets a dissolute, aristocratic flagellant who needs extra stimulation, having used up his natural vitality. Just as Cleland juxtaposes the two madams, so he provides a counterexample to these displays of aristocratic vice with an example of bourgeois virtue in the character of a sixty-year-old self-made man: "Himself a rational pleasurist, as being much too wise to be asham'd of the pleasures of humanity, loved me indeed, but loved me with dignity."[64] Fanny lives with him until his death, at which time she receives his fortune. The distinction between the bourgeois "rational pleasurist" and the corrupt aristocrats illustrates the divide between the humble lower orders, who act out of pleasure, and the corrupt privileged, who have lost themselves in the quagmire of sophistication.

The narrative closes by returning Fanny and Charles to virtuous passion and then contrasting their natural sexuality with the vices she saw in the artistocratic world. Her experiences with vice, however, did not interfere with Fanny's "remembrance" of honest pleasures or her favorable assessment of fellow adventurers. The sister-prostitutes, the savvy Mrs. Cole, the sweet serving-lad Will, the dignified self-made man, and the true love Charles never renounced passion, affection, or sexuality. Instead, the devious Mrs. Brown, the uncaring Mr. H, the cruel Mr. Norbert, and the decadent sadomasochist— all associated with old-style corruption, rather than the new liberties of free sexuality—deserve scorn because they have lost their passions to worldly vices. Thus the triumph of Fanny and Charles living on the behest of the "rational pleasurist"—who begins to sound like a Carlile-ian revolutionary program come to life—provides a countermorality tale. In this tale, sexuality functions as a fighter on two fronts: one against corruption, the second against sexual prudery. (Here Fanny, and indeed Dugdale and other old-style radicals, differ from the more staid reformers who used the motif of respectability to pit themselves against the old order.)[65]

In the process of criticizing prudery and old-style corruption, Cleland sets up his own sexual agenda, which recognizes nonnormative desires but privileges heterosexuality. The treatment of female intimacy as a prelude to heterosexual intercourse during Fanny's stint in Mrs. Brown's brothel downplays the extent of female-female desire. Furthermore, the disgust Fanny displays at viewing male-male intercourse—a scene excised entirely from most nineteenth-century copies—insists on the prescription of heterosexual desire. Nonetheless, the voyeuristic display of a variety of sexual acts in the text—from flagellation to cross-dressing to public consummations—made room, no matter how problematic, for a wide variety of sexual desires. Julia Epstein demonstrates that *Fanny Hill* has a transsexual, homoerotic quality, by virtue of being written by a man masquerading as a woman for a male audience, and homoerotic overtones in its focus on male sexuality and sexual organs, rather than female sensations and bodies. According to Epstein, the themes as well as the voice leave room for sexual ambiguity and a critique of "conventional novel plots and the sociosexual ideologies they embrace." [66]

If readers did not recognize the transsexual voice, they would interpret Fanny's voice as female, and in the process fictionalize women's sexuality. Imagining the nature of female sexuality became one of the primary fantasies of pornography, even while it further obscured women's own inner lives by making the script stand for truth. However, such fictions allowed women's experience to be the subject of the narrative, rather than the object; Fanny acts in the text, as well as being acted upon, however fictionalized her desires. As in other libertine and radical texts, in *Fanny Hill* the author's use of women's bodies and women's sexuality formed part of an attempt to refocus the social order.[67] Societal liberation would come from within women's bodies. However, this meant that women's sexual acquiescence was necessary for true social reform.

Fanny Hill, with its claims about rational sexuality versus sexual decadence, its democratic vision of pleasures, its fictionalization of the female voice, and its penchant for heterosexual intercourse, remained a model for later pornographic works both in England and abroad. Writers either consciously or unconsciously copied the tropes that Cleland elaborated. Later writers continued the use of the first-person narrative. The device of the epistle, found in cursory form in *Fanny Hill,* and more fully developed in *A Man of Pleasure at Paris, The Lustful Turk,* and *The Seducing Cardinal's Amours,* emphasized the individual's experience through publication of supposedly private material. In these novels, truth could be found in the lived experience of the individual, rather than in abstract discussions or philosophies.

These works pitted pleasure against corruption, real feeling against false learning. *A Man of Pleasure at Paris,* an epistolary novel set in France, summed up the tenets of this distinct form of libertinism by advocating an acceptance of heterosexuality, instinctual passion, and rationality. The narrator, the man of pleasure, writes to his mistress a series of letters about his varied sexual adventures. He begins with an explanation of why his pastime will only bind them more closely together: "You and I understand love in its true, pure, unsophisticated sense, that is, the mutual inclination of the sexes towards each other; that love which pervades, unites, and preserves the whole universe, free from the metaphysical trash with which impotent men and silly women have endeavoured to dull its zest, and curtail its power." [68] The denunciation of a sophisticated sense of love, "metaphysical trash," celebrated tactile pleasures over cerebral and feminized refinements. It was not coincidental that this defense of libertinism was couched in the guise of a man writing to his true love about his sexual exploits with other women. Libertinism fundamentally stood for men's ability to chart their sexual course unencumbered and undiminished by any proscriptions. The heroines of the works became heroic by refusing to stand in the way of progress—by accepting men's sexuality as naturally boundless and unrestrainable. As the narrator states in *A Man of Pleasure at Paris:* "Yes, generous Emily, with unexampled liberality, you reserved this single privilege to yourself, and I have dared to break through it with another!" [69] Though Emily encourages her man to copulate with any and all women, she has reserved the right to be the only woman to fellate him. However, he cannot accept even that small limitation on his liberty and breaks that final proscription. Emily, fashioned as the perfect mistress, of course accepts it. The fiction of a perfect woman rested on her ability to renounce limitations and accept men's full freedom. Women could be the vanguard of sexual freedom, in these formulations, by repudiating social limitations on sexuality and, in particular, their already limited control of it. By unlearning false teachings such as jealousy, modesty, and prudery, women could fulfill both men and themselves.

Bucolic Pleasures and Old Corruption

The zest for pleasure and the critique of false learning were echoed in the works of one of the period's greatest illustrators, Thomas Rowlandson (1756?–1827). Rowlandson juxtaposed sexual pleasure with social corruption through the deterioration of old bodies. "The Old Husband" and "The Star Gazer" mock elderly cuckolds who doze in front of more important matters while their youthful companions frolic with nubile young men. Luxurious furnishings, gilt picture frames, a roaring fire, and a case of gout complete a picture of the self-satisfied but incapable rich man in "The Old Husband." In "The Star Gazer" (figure 3) a wizened, cadaverous old man in a nightcap looks through his telescope while, through the doorway, his wife and a young man copulate under bed-drapes that match the old man's robes.

Rowlandson's attacks on cuckolds mock their wealth and social distinctions and intimate that such old men do not deserve youthful pleasures. In contrast, "The Gallop," executed around 1800, displays a young man and

FIGURE 3. Thomas Rowlandson, "The Star Gazer," circa 1820s. With permission of the Victoria and Albert Museum.

woman atop a horse, with the man entering the woman from behind.[70] A dog runs alongside the couple. The poetic accompaniment reads:

NEW FEATS OF HORSEMANSHIP

Well mounted on a mettled steed,
Famed for his strength as well as speed
Corrinna and her favorite buck,
Are pleas'd to have a flying f—k.
While oer the downs the courser strains
With fiery eye, and loosened reins,

Around his neck her arms she flings
Behind her buttocks move like springs
While Jack keeps time to every motion
And pours in loves delicious potion.

The double meanings of mounting, steeds, bucks, strength, and speed refer to both the act of riding and to sexual intercourse, creating a transference of meaning between Jack and the horse. If Jack was mounted, then Corrinna was doubly so. The transference between a good ride upon horseback and a good fuck moves sexuality into the realm of physical animal pleasures that do not require a higher meaning to be worthwhile. The uncorrupted pleasures themselves matter.

The contrast between learned cuckolds in "The Star Gazer" and the mad romps of the young in "The Gallop" echoes the distinction between corrupt sophistication and pleasure. Pleasures are personified in youth, beauty, and primitive nature. In "The Gallop," the lines of the woman's buttocks mimic the arc of the horse's. Passion in humans, like passion in animals, can remain uncontaminated by worldly pursuits. The dog racing alongside the couple is matched in other Rowlandson prints in which cats copulate, dogs hump, and monkeys lift ladies' gowns. Such representations of animals link the pleasures of sex to an animal nature in which bodies can remain pure and instinctual.

Rowlandson's portrayals satirize the old, the wealthy, the miserly, the religious, and the sophisticated on the basis of their corruption, not sexuality. That is, his satires use sexuality as a means to mock hypocrisy but do not condemn sexuality itself. Sexuality flows freely in the bodies of the youthful sailors, soldiers, maidens, and Turks. The mingling of nature with primitive human sexuality provides the utopian path toward fulfillment. Bestiality and the acceptance of human bodies as repositories of bestial enjoyment stand in a positive light when compared with the hypocrisy of religious sophistication. "The Sanctified Sinner" shows a minister in coat and tricorn hat grimacing in prayer while being masturbated by a pretty young woman. A voyeur watches in horror through the window. The poem reads:

THE SANCTIFIED SINNER

For all this canting fellows teaching
He loves a girl as well as preaching
With holy love he rolls his eyes

Yet view his stout man Thomas rise
Tis sure enough to make it stand
To have it stroked by such a hand
When flesh and spirit both combine
His raptures sure must be divine.

The poem begins with "For all this canting fellows teaching" to underline the hypocrisy of individuals preaching against the pleasures of the flesh when their own flesh cannot comply. The grimace on the minister's face and the look of horror on the voyeur's deepen the contradiction between the enjoyment of sexuality and the abhorrence of it. The attack on the minister's hypocrisy underlines the artificial and arbitrary distinction between holy love and physical love. The critique of the divisions between fleshly and spiritual rapture advocates the worship of a positive pleasure based on rational acceptance of the human state, rather than divine injunction against it. "The Congregation," "Susanna and the Elders," and "The Happy Parson" are based on similar themes. Rowlandson's attacks on clerical dishonesty reach across the spectrum of religions in England to include not only Catholics, Jews, and nonconformists but also the members of the Established Church.

"The Curious Parson" (figure 4), another Rowlandson print juxtaposing the sexual and the religious realms, features an older, grizzled "parson" staring at a young maid's cunny as she kneels on a bed. The aged face of the minister when set against the fresh-faced and fresh-formed appearance of the girl again distinguishes the old from the young. But whereas other images underline religious insincerity, this image displays the parson more sympathetically. Rowlandson drew this parson as singularly naive: He remains fully dressed, including the spectacles he uses to examine the woman's denuded loins. It is hard to tell who is learned and who callow in this image because the title "The Curious Parson" hints that this parson might never before have seen such a sight. In this image, the parson accepts the positive pleasures of the flesh and, in exchange, Rowlandson has omitted the voyeurs' outraged looks that appear in other such images. The contrasts among Rowlandson's many clerics intimates that he did not oppose sexuality or religion per se but instead challenged religion's corruption of life's honest sexual pleasures.

The desire for an unregulated and undifferentiated sexuality cannot be separated from the political roots from which it sprang. The combination of praise for the simple and mockery of the sophisticated served as a potent political protest. The works emphasized a bawdy culture of undifferentiated sex-

FIGURE 4. Thomas Rowlandson, "The Curious Parson," circa 1820s. With permission of the Victoria and Albert Museum.

uality but used indiscriminate sexuality to signal social and political corruption. William Benbow, another radical printer-publisher, was prosecuted by the "Society for Spreading Vice," as he referred to it, for the publication of *The Crimes of the Clergy, or the Pillars of Priest-Craft Exposed*. In this work, he listed the crimes of nonconformists and Anglican ministers alike, including murder, blasphemy, drunkenness, rape, adultery, sodomy, forgery, swindling, whoring, cruelty to slaves, hypocrisy, robbing the poor, injustice, and neglect of duty. For a further bit of irony, the Rector of Ewhurst in Essex was accused of "perverting the minds of his pupils by showing them the plates of *Fanny Hill*."[71] These works revived old scandals to give sexual protest a pedigree. "An Historical ballad" was "supposed to refer to Lady Southesk, mistress of the Duke of York, afterwards James II." The ballad attacked her for lewdness, impurity, lack of discretion, and disease: "Who, though they eternally pizzle her britch/ Can't allay the wild rage of her letch'rous itch/ Which proves our good lady a monstrous b——/ Which they themselves can't deny."[72] James's status as a deposed Catholic king made him a useful and, in many ways, legitimate figure to lampoon. However, the extended focus on the sexual peccadilloes of the monarchy raised questions about the social legitimacy of the governing class. By focusing on the sexual lives of monarchs, aristocrats, and the clergy, the range of works maligned the system of government and the discrimination of social superiors.

These works did not just long for purity but also mocked the same longing with the understanding that pure sexuality would remain impossible as long as sexuality continued to be bound up in other facets of life. For example, in a poem ironically called "The Dream," the exchange of sex for marriage was described as "wedlock fetters" in which a man was encouraged to "sell himself for life" in exchange for simple lust "When ev'ry creature else, but he/ Enjoys the sweets of liberty."[73] The call for liberty became a call for unencumbered pleasure and free love.

The longing for natural pleasures and the attacks on the hypocrisy that stood in their way were echoed in *Ane Pleasant Garland of Sweet Scented Flowers* and *Select Poems on Several Occasions.* Both volumes of poems and songs used critique and scatology to portray a longing for a simplified agrarian past and to attack the hypocrisy that underlay contemporary sexuality.

"Drunck and Sober."

Drunck and sober again,

Drunck and sober again,

But I shall ne'er be merry at heart,

Till I'm drunck and sober again.

I took her about the middle,

And laid her on the grass,

And the wind it blew up her clothes,

That you might have seen her arse.

Drunck and sober again, & c.[74]

The double meanings of *wind* and *laid* reduce sexuality to the ribald; intercourse becomes just another verse between drinking bouts. Pornographic

works used the indifferentiated body—the farting, sexualized, comic body—
to illustrate the protean nature of existence in a sexually complicated culture.

Delight and malice went hand-in-hand in these works to turn the world
upside down. Rather than only creating a sentimental picture of marital pleasures to combat sophisticated excess, these libertine works inverted respectability and took a variety of unrespectable people—the prostitute, the Turk,
the satyr—as the standard-bearers of libertine philosophy. In libertine utopian
representations, the least respectable people were placed at the center of a new
social order. In the Rowlandson print entitled "The Jugglers" (figure 5), the
unrespectable are literally given center stage as three figures on stage cavort
lewdly for the crowd. The carnival of sexuality appropriates the social order of
the world and turns it on its head, making a mockery of respectability. The

FIGURE 5. Thomas Rowlandson, "The Jugglers," circa 1820s. With permission of the
Victoria and Albert Museum.

print features a half-naked woman catching coins in her smock, a rotund man in harlequin costume using his erect penis as a third arm to juggle, and a satyr playing a tambourine with his hands and a horn with his anus; farts make music, the respectable smock catches ill-gotten coins, and the "third arm" juggles better than the other two. Sexuality as a carnival of pleasure offered a perverse vision of society, but one that had long-standing implications, as Robert Darnton points out: "During carnival the common people suspended the normal rules of behavior and ceremonially reversed the social order or turned it upside down in riotous procession."[75] A satyr farting music for the crowds made visible an imagined transformation of society in which a "demon" of sexuality could use an undifferentiated body to enliven the masses. The representation reversed the connotations of satyrs (making them positive), returned the body to its protean roots, and offered a picture of community solidarity formed around pleasure.

Through such early nineteenth-century representations, carnival could be made permanent.[76] By replacing the bottoms with the tops, carnivalesque representations could offer social justice at a time when the traditions of carnival, mumming, and other forms of reverse ritual were losing their socially cohesive functions. According to Robert Storch, "The withdrawal of the upper classes from participation in and patronage of popular culture had an important and closely related political dimension. The English upper classes as a whole became terrified by the French Revolution and the development of a domestic, natural-rights radical movement involving artisans and working men and leery of all plebeian revel[s] that had political overtones."[77] Though the upper classes ceased to participate in them, reverse rituals continued throughout the first half of the century as common folk developed a sense of community defined by social class, rather than region. Reverse rituals allowed peasants and workers to position themselves as dominant in the absence of the gentry and aristocracy, rather than with their temporary consent. Because of the continuous threat of revolution, the ritual overturning of the social order came to be construed as a political act against the upper orders, and reverse rituals came under attack as having political overtones, which explains the stamping out of these long-established customs.[78] Carnivalesque representations in pornography used political overtones to suggest a form of social justice and social leveling through sexuality. Sexuality became an arena for critical focus. It not only was a venue for reviling social superiors but also held possibilities for change. The carnival, the brothel, and eventually the Turkish harem offered representations of the world turned on its head.

The Imaginary Harem and the Problems of Sodomy

A fascination with the Turkish harem in Rowlandson's work exposed a layout of Utopia. "The Harem" and "The Pasha" both depict a lone man surrounded by nubile and eager women vying for sexual attention. In "The Harem" the women, denuded of pubic hair and coverings, stretch into the distance until they become lines and shadows rather than fully fledged figures. The spectator's erect penis testifies to his enjoyment of the parade of female figures. In

FIGURE 6. Thomas Rowlandson, "The Harem," circa 1820s. With permission of the Victoria and Albert Museum.

"The Pasha," the pasha is shown as oversized and overendowed. He has two women between his legs and one woman in each arm while another masturbates in the background. His capacity to pleasure a multitude of women appears indisputable. The placement of women as available and eager for sexual contact contributes to the understanding that sexuality would flow freely, if not for the false standards imposed on human contact. While sheiks and pashas are clearly dark and alien in these illustrations, the willing maidens are not. The harem allowed social proscriptions to be stripped away from Western women and encouraged their return to their supposedly inborn sexual nature.

The imaginary harem as the "garden of delight" became a staple concept in libertine pornography, such as *The Lustful Turk* (1828, 1829, 1860–1864), *The Seducing Cardinal's Amours* (1830), and *Scenes in the Seraglio* (between 1820 and 1830, 1855–1860).[79] The harem, as seen through multiple narrators in each novel, stood for the possibility of sexual abandon. These works went further than *Fanny Hill* in the use of the confessional letter by creating multiple viewpoints and storylines; thus, they portrated women as midway between subject and object. That is, letters narrated by imagined women portray women as actors, while letters narrated by imagined sheiks, deys, and pashas show women acted upon.

The Seducing Cardinal's Amours consistently contrasts the harem with the treatment of women in Western society and its corruption of sexuality. According to the novel, the Catholic Church forced women into decadence, while the Turkish harem allowed them to enjoy their own natural sexuality. Likewise, although women were purchased and abandoned nightly in the brothels of France, they were purchased and then cosseted in the harem. The contrast of women's treatment in the harem—considered by the Western audience as a degraded and degrading institution—with their treatment in the West showed the harem to be superior for women as well as men. The contrast between the West and the harem was not ignored; instead, this contrast formed the crux of the discussion. By showing the West and East as inverted versions of each other, the work built upon the fears of the harem, the Turk, and the decadence of the Eastern potentate, but then made these fears delightful.

> When I was in France the mere mention of Turkish Harem was enough
> to have made me die in fear, (let alone the thoughts of resigning my
> virginity to a Turk;) what a foolish anticipation was this! . . . The habit
> of enjoying a life exempt from cares of every kind soon began to make
> the place agreeable; but when you my dearest lord by withdrawing
> from before my eyes the curtain which had so long blinded my senses;

I mean when taking pity on my state you condescended to teach me the voluptuous joys of love: then your harem, consecrated to pleasure, totally changed its form,! For me liberty has now no charms: now, with you and you only must the rest of my days be spent.

If any young French women with whom you may become acquainted have the same fears as I had deign to shew her my letter; when she sees it, it will render her more sensible of your worth and jealous of a blessing I enjoy.[80]

Contrasting the harem with life in the West illustrated how religious teachings, standards of modesty and chastity, the relentless search for new pleasures, and the daily search to meet human needs had all perverted humanity in the West. The Turkish harem offered a vision of sexuality without jealousies, class antagonisms, or false modesty. Stripping away these impediments allowed men and women to rediscover the strength of natural passions. While Europe diminished men's sexuality, the harem allowed it to grow as rampant as the Dey's organ: "I was safely in her; another thrust finished the job, . . . by Mahomet! Europa was never half so well unvirgined, although love might have had the strength of a bull."[81] In these accounts, Western refinements made men unmasculine and women asexual.

At the same time, though, the sexual possibilities of innumerable women confined for a single male's pleasure exerted a fascination that went beyond the purpose of contrast. The novels began to consider whether limitless control led to despotism or free love. The plethora of women and complete sexual control over them allowed an exploration of a man's capacities for sexual freedom, but only at the expense of women's; these works recognized sexuality as a zero-sum game. Attempts to reconcile the contradiction led to a model in which women desire a loss of freedom when controlled by a good master: "The Dey, indeed had soon discovered my folly [chastity], and like a man of sense, took the proper method to subdue me. In this way, in one short night, you see, he put to the rout all my pure virgin scruples, rapturously teaching me the nature of love's sacred mysteries, and the great end for which we poor weak females are created."[82] If the harem allowed for rampant male privilege, then "poor weak females" were created to fulfill man's natural appetites.

The Lustful Turk illustrates the pleasures of the harem and then undercuts it as a utopia because complete control can lead to degeneracy in sexuality as in politics. The Dey is eventually castrated by a harem slave when he "commence[s] his attack on her second maidenhead." Because he loses all desire as a result, he liberates his harem and sends them home. The narrative concludes with a letter from Emily, an English girl: "As for myself, you well know what my sentiments are. I will never marry until I am assured that the chosen one possesses sufficient charms and weight not only to erase the Dey's impression from my heart, but also in a more sensitive part."[83] While the harem seemed to offer a model for liberation, that model remained tinged with corruption. The castration of the Ottoman Empire because of degeneracy ultimately promised greater sexual rewards for the West. The hatred and envy of the Turks seemed to deride the nature of European male sexuality. Only by invoking sodomy, ruining the Turk, and returning the sexually awakened women to home soil could the utopian possibilities of liberation be achieved.

The vacillation between admiration for the harem as a means to explore primitive desire and condemnation of it for sexual degeneracy framed such stories. The primitive garden of the harem offered both advantages and corrupt temptations. As a counterpoint for "Western" sexuality, the harem was too close for an unproblematic transference. The Ottoman Empire still controlled vast territorial and economic resources in Europe and continued to impede the consolidation of Christian Europe as a distinct social entity. Too many political, economic, and social obstacles between European and Islamic cultures existed for the European imagination to see the harem as purely "primitive." Nonetheless, the imaginative pull that the harem commanded allowed the image of a primitive garden to sit uneasily with the real reminders of the Ottoman Empire. The imagined transportation of British, French, and other "European" women to the harem provided a constant reminder of the links between the regions.

Even the attempt to recreate the harem came tinged with vacillation about the positioning of the Turk. Edward Said argues that "we must continue to remember that novels participate in, are part of, contribute to an extremely slow, infinitesimal politics that clarifies, reinforces, and perhaps even occasionally advances perceptions and attitudes about England and the world. It is striking that never, in the novel, is that world beyond seen except as subordinate and dominated, the English presence as viewed as regulative and normative."[84] Pornographic harem novels, however, allowed the Turk to be at once dominant and subordinate, rampant and castrated. For the English, the existence of real harems, with real deys, beys, and pashas ruling over them, meant that degeneracy needed consequences and that sexuality needed to be balanced with discipline. These novels allowed this imagining and disciplining this degeneracy to coexist.

These novels explored the "limits" of sexuality by transferring the capabilities for socially problematic behavior onto a distinct culture. The Western inability to enjoy rampant sexuality in an unproblematic manner, however, called for the grave repercussions supplied in the text. The Dey's castration because of anal eroticism, and his subsequent circumscription of pleasure, parallel the excision of the scene of anal eroticism in *Fanny Hill*. Both negations of buggery reinforced the privileged position of penile-vaginal intercourse in the concept of pure, inherent sexuality: It was the highest form of natural sexual pleasure. Lesbian sexuality in *Fanny Hill* could remain unexpurgated because it was conceptualized as preceding "real" heterosexual intercourse and functioned only to prime women's desires. Buggery, however, providing an alternative site of sexual pleasure needed discipline.[85]

The Exquisite *and the Failures of Republican Sexual Politics*

Heterosexual relations and activities preceding heterosexual penile-vaginal intercourse became insistently serialized into their components in *The Exquisite*. This work marks the turning point from libertine narratives to later types of pornographic fiction and has elements of both. William Dugdale published *The Exquisite: A Collection of Tales, Histories, and Essays, Funny, Fanciful, and Facetious* weekly between 1842 and 1844. Each issue consisted of an engraving and eight pages of text; the 145 issues together formed three volumes. The initial price of fourpence was raised to sixpence halfway through the series. In fact, Dugdale essentially offered two prices, because the engravings could also be bought in color for an additional shilling apiece.[86] While each issue was cheap enough for the aristocracy of labor to afford, the full volumes, bound and in color, came quite dear. The two-price system fit with Dugdale's republican inclinations: He made his living off the wealthy but served the workers in revolutionary sentiment.

   The Exquisite provided "solid information" on sexuality, ongoing narratives of seduction and copulation, engravings inspired by mythology, primitive places, and dramatic scenes, humorous quips, attacks on religion, poems, stories about the goings-on of the rich and famous, and ironic anecdotes. Its serials offered documentaries on sexuality like "A physical View of Man & Woman in a state of Marriage," which matched humours with sexual needs, offered aphrodisiac recipes, and gave other concrete tidbits of advice for sexual well-being. The narratives came in a variety of forms, including the epistolary novel, the dialogue, and the fictive autobiography.

   The stories were often set at a comfortable distance from contemporary England. This meant, for one thing, that Dugdale could lampoon recognizable persons and offices without committing slanderous or seditious libel. Whereas focus on an Englishman could send Dugdale to prison, as indeed it had, focus on a Frenchman like Richelieu—a member of the clergy and a royal adviser—allowed him to mock the offices through the man without repercussions. Dugdale could also use translations of French works with impunity, which saved him the bother and expense of finding and paying for new material.

While *The Exquisite* used the epistolary form for some of its stories, such pieces were generally reprints of older works like *The Authentic Memoirs of the Countess de Barre*, first printed in English in 1771.[87] The epistolary form gave way to fictive autobiographies, including "The Autobiography of a Footman," "Stolen Pleasure," and "Conjugal Nights." "Conjugal Nights" followed a format similar to *The Decameron* but added the characteristic libertine device of first-person testimonial. Its premise is that each night a husband tells his wife of his past sexual exploits as foreplay for the couple's own sexual encounters. The husband's testimonials to seduction and heterosexual intercourse are matched by the wife's perfect understanding of his need for sexual liberty.

In "The Autobiography of a Footman" and "Felicia, or Follies of My Life," the story of a life becomes the story of sexual adventures, and each novel refuses to justify discussions of sexuality. "The Autobiography of a Footman" describes a man's career satisfying his mistresses. He then becomes a Captain's "Man of Affairs" and continues his sexual pursuits. The work emphasizes the salient details of seduction and heterosexual intercourse. Each installment had at least one successful bout of copulation, and the serialized storytelling encouraged a rapid exchange of female partners; women are introduced, seduced, and sent on their way. "Felicia, or Follies of My Life," by Andréa de Nerciat, a French libertine writer, begins with Felicia's sexual education—a perfect one, unfettered by prejudice and convention—and continues into her life of sexual and social intrigue, equally free and rewarding: "In resisting (which was far from my thoughts) I only beheld obstacles, hatreds, jealousies to remove; in yielding, I beheld, on the contrary, the brightest perspective; instead of rendering myself odious to the chevalier, to Monseigneur, and to Sylvina, I accommodated them all, and accommodated myself."[88] The tenets of libertinism were still present in fictive autobiography, even though descriptions of sexuality and sexual acts were favored over philosophical musings on the nature of sex. The works were pulled in two directions at once—trying to tell a compelling story and trying to tell the same story repeatedly without repetition.

The weekly engravings showed the worlds of sexuality, past and present, which reinforced the emphasis on the sexual possibilities available through the attainment of women. "View in Java," "View in Constantinople," and a variety of views of "The Odalisque" give an around-the-world view of waiting women, while "Expectation," "Before," and "After"—bearing the same names as the prints by Hogarth, but without the negative connotations of the "after"—illustrate similar scenes closer to home. Plates like "Venus and Adonis" and "Le Paradis Perdu" and various scenes of Mars, Jupiter, Psyche, nymphs, and satyrs show sexual antiquity. The basic elements of the world—fire, water, air, and earth—are portrayed in "Fire" and "The Inundation." None of the series exhausted a topic; in fact, topics were picked up and dropped with abandon. Thematically unrelated to the text, the plates provided their own forum for describing the sexual world, which centered heavily on expectation and availability.

The reclining or partially reclining female figure with an oval face and bared breasts became the staple image of sexuality, whether set in the realm of the gods or in Constantinople. While men or animals or cherubs occasionally were paired with women, only women appeared naked or, most often, partially naked. Bared breasts demonstrated women's position as receptive and sexualized regardless of the circumstances. In "The Inundation," four women escape a flood, three with their dresses dipping below their breasts. Though their faces are set in trepidation, their state of partial undress counteracts the flood's biblical connotations: Instead of a purifying inundation, water becomes a backdrop for sexuality. Women's bared breasts became the central token of sexuality in pictorial representations much as seduction became the main theme in narrative representations.

While anecdotes and poems in the magazine attacked the clergy, the wealthy, the foolish, the cuckold, and the social elite, the stories centered on heterosexual penile-vaginal intercourse, which in the process of iteration became privileged. Thus, there was a limited variety of acts and actors in the works. Forms of sexual activity like fondling, kissing, rubbing, and looking became submerged under the process of seduction toward a single goal. Other types of activity like flagellation and anal eroticism were excised completely from the inexpensive magazine and treated in more expensive texts accessible only to the very wealthy. The two-tier system of access limited the poorer patrons to streamlined versions of libertinism. Libertine ideas—the attacks on privilege, the emphasis on revolution through pleasure, the inherent nature of sexuality, and the problems with social corruption—remained in the magazine, but in a truncated form as asides on the way to seduction. This truncation replaced the carnivalesque mode of libertine sexuality with an emphasis on women's availability; thus, satyrs and Turks fit into *The Exquisite* only as backdrops for waiting women. Its stories completed the transformation of the relationship between women and revolution: While *Fanny Hill* offered a vision of revolution by women even though it had been created by a man, *The Exquisite* offered a vision of revolution through the conquest of women.

The Exquisite demonstrated the transformation of libertinism through narrative style, the envisioning of utopia, and the place of women. The deletion of philosophic considerations blunted its efficacy as a movement. The change from the epistolary form to the fictive autobiography excised the justification for sexuality and began to emphasize sexual pleasure as the zenith of the enterprise. The point of the works shifted from a consideration of new sexual and social possibilities to a demonstration of penile conquest of the vagina as a privilege. Increasingly, the visualization of sexuality relied upon a cohesive picture of the world as already sexualized and waiting. Women's availability became the signifier of a sexualized world. Thus, women's place in revolutionary sexuality began to shift from subject/actor to object. While the magazine offered a wealth of information, that information was pointed in a specific direction, away from so-called degeneracy and toward heterosexual intercourse.

New Political Rights on Old Politicized Bodies

In many ways, the deemphasizing of degeneracy and philosophic asides in *The Exquisite* pointed toward the downfall of libertinism as a revolutionary philosophy. Although it sought to unseat the privileged through critique, mockery, and attack, in the process it fed off women, the young, the poor, and the foreign. The restructuring of society needed to occur through their bodies and minds. While revolutionary pornography offered potent protest against privilege, constraint, and hypocrisy, it did so through reconceptualizing the weak.

Although pornography made specific claims for intrinsic sexuality, it did so by making the least powerful the most highly sexualized. The belief that sexual liberty was found in the flesh of young women contributed to the notions that youth epitomized sexual culture and implied naturalness and that sexual acculturation began at the act of defloration. Youth as a sign of purity allowed for continued emphasis on intrinsic nature rather than extrinsic culture. The division between young and old, nature and culture, signaled that true sexuality began with the first act of heterosexual sexual intercourse, which in turn devalued nonpenetrative sexual acts. The hope for uncultured sexuality encouraged a fixation on the seduction of youth, particularly young women, who embodied the height of sexual potential and possibilities. In revolution-ary pornography, women's sexual potential came from their ability to accept men's desires rather than discover their own. The female subject acting in per-fect concert with men's desire to signify liberty, as in *A Man of Pleasure at Paris*, became the female object that is the benefit of liberation, as in *The Exquisite*. This transformation in the narrative form reflected women's place in the con-ception of a free society. Only through accepting the pleasures and the possi-bilities of a sexual utopia could women work toward sexual liberation. Only through the valuation of penile-vaginal intercourse could women's sexual po-tential be fulfilled.

The insistence that "others" —whether women, youths, or foreigners, es-pecially from the Orient—were uncultured and unsocialized, that they existed as "nature," meant that they could provide a blueprint for human sexuality—if science could provide the method for deciphering them. The same people who offered utopian possibilities in early pornography came to dominate later pornographic representations as the objects of study. While the learned, the re-ligious, and the socially privileged had been ridiculed, the powerless became the very matter out of which utopia could be formed. The utopian formation rested squarely on the intrinsic nature of sexuality, which empiricist pornog-raphy tried to document beginning in the 1860s. Increasingly, pornography be-gan to categorize people and acts in an attempt to delineate the objective truth in the natural world.

Chapter 2

Sexuality Raw and Cooked

Empirical and Imperial Pornography

Of Cannibals

Richard Burton promised Frederick Hankey that he would bring back from his next mission to Dahomey, Africa, in 1863, human skin to bind Hankey's volumes by de Sade.[1] Hankey owned other volumes bound in human skin, but Burton promised one stripped from a living woman—"sur une négresse vivante"—so it would retain its luster more readily.[2] In 1863, a disappointed Burton wrote to Monckton Milnes, a mutual friend, that "I have been here for 3 days. . . . Not a man killed, nor a fellow tortured. The canoe floating in blood is a myth of myths. Poor Hankey must still wait for his peau de femme."[3] In 1864, Burton wrote again: "Poor old Hankey, I did so want to get him a human hide . . . and I failed."[4] Even though this mission was unsuccessful, the symbol of Englishmen trafficking in black skin stripped from a living woman captures a certain peculiar logic. The combination of imperialism, sadism, and sexism signaled the emergence of a new relationship between sexuality and society; the word and the flesh became bound together both literally and figuratively to form a new type of pornography.

Burton's later success at forming the so-called Cannibal Club demonstrated his continued fascination with carnal exoticism. "The Cannibal Club" was a nickname for the inner circle of the Anthropological Society of London (later the London Anthropological Society). Along with the Royal Geographic Society with which it shared many members the London Anthropological Society was at the forefront of Britain's imperial ventures.[5] Algernon Charles Swinburne, Richard Monckton Milnes (Lord Houghton), Sir James Plaisted Wilde (Lord Penzance), General John Studholme Hodgson, and Charles Duncan Cameron, among others, joined the club. From the 1860s through the 1880s, these men wrote and read much of British pornography. By examining these men as a group, we can see how their sexual logic intersected with the ideas governing imperial and domestic relations. Their fascination with sexuality and their central place in the production and consumption of pornography delineate an important relationship among science, arts and letters, government, and pornography that has frequently been overlooked. As the name "Cannibal Club" suggests, imperialism was no disinterested enterprise; a prurient interest in the lives of the colonized formed the basis of the club.

Previous scholars have considered the sexual proclivities of these leading Victorians as ancillary to their work as writers, adventurers, scholars, intellectuals, and politicians and have minimized what these men meant to the history of pornography. Conversely, scholars of pornography have ignored the works these men produced because they seemed somehow "too scientific," either too involved with the mechanics of biology or too concerned with rationality to be truly pornographic. However, just as *National Geographic* popularized science and exploration while it functioned as a wellspring of masturbatory fantasies for generations of young men, so too did the writings of the Cannibals simultaneously function as science and pornography.[6] Furthermore, the members of the Cannibal Club recognized that their writings would run afoul of obscenity laws; they hid their authorship behind pseudonyms, had the materials published anonymously, and in at least one case were blackmailed for their writings. They kept no formal records of the club, and those with conscientious executors—like Richard Burton's wife, Isabella—had all references to their erotic adventures and writings burned. By contemporary standards, they wrote pornography and they knew it. Nonetheless, they saw themselves as surpassing mere titillation.

The men who formed the Cannibal Club believed themselves to be radicals, but their radicalism centered on their own personal development rather than widespread political transformations and the revolutionary cross-class agenda of Dugdale's republicanism. While Dugdale used pornography to level social divisions, these men saw the free discussion of sexuality as a radical act in and of itself. Dugdale and his contemporaries used the revolutionary potential of sexuality to disrupt society and politics; the Cannibal Club reinforced the rigid social divisions of Victorian society. The elite social position of the Cannibals, the limited circulation of their texts, and the meanings they drew from the raw matter of sexuality shifted radicalism from an agent of political change to a means of personal definition. These men—who defined themselves by their openness to geographical, physical, sensual, and intellectual exploration—used a scientific platform to justify the need for the free exchange of ideas about their diverse interests.

According to the Cannibals' sexual radicalism, nothing could or should stand in the way of sexual knowledge—not custom, law, or personal preference (although the last seems more of a smokescreen for homosexual and flagellant desires than anything else). Their commitment to knowledge showed in the development of a new narrative voice. Rather than speaking from a place of personal authority through the epistolary novel and fictional autobiography like earlier libertine writers, the new pornographers assumed the voice of an objective, impersonal observer in their formal writings and published papers (although their informal writings retain a certain exuberance). The writers could assume an objective voice because they had no need to disrupt society. Those who produced, consumed, and sold pornography did so from the relative safety of social respectability. The pornography they wrote further stabilized the social order that benefited them in innumerable ways.

The members set themselves apart from society by insisting on their own visions of the world, and they followed these visions in their actions and intellect. In 1873, Burton explained his reasons for starting the London Anthropological Society a decade earlier.

> Many Members joined us with the higher view of establishing a society where they might express their opinions freely and openly, without regard to popularity, respectability, and other idols of the day. We did not tremble at the idea of 'acquiring an unhappy notoriety.' We wanted to have the truth and the whole truth, as each man sees it. We intended to make room for every form of thought, the orthodox and the heterodox; the subversive and the conservative; the retrograde equally with the progressive.[7]

The London Anthropological Society became a forum for delivering papers on hermaphroditism, the effects of incest on offspring, clitoridectomies, the dancing girls of southern India, fertility rituals, prostitution, polyandry, and polygamy.[8] While the society explored a diverse range of interests besides sexuality—including skull size, Mayan hieroglyphics, and early tool use—a fascination with biological and cultural differences in sexuality repeatedly marked their writings. They saw race and sex as central to understanding the rapidly expanding world.[9]

The members of the Anthropological Society used a gavel shaped like a "Negro's head" to call their meetings to order and displayed a human skeleton in their window, much to the dismay of the Christian Union across the street. In opposition to the Ethnological Society, a more liberal, middle-class society that concerned itself with missionary work and humanitarian concerns, the Anthropologicals were mostly Tories from established backgrounds who concerned themselves with finding evidence to support current theories about race and gender.[10] They championed the theory of polygenesis, for example, even after it had been largely discredited, and they supported the racist cause of the American Confederacy. While these reactionary tendencies did not always translate into complete social or political conservatism—Lord Penzance, for example, contributed to divorce reform that allowed women greater abilities to leave their abusive husbands, and Thomas Bendyshe was expelled from the Conservative Club for his support of John Stuart Mill—their political and intellectual iconoclasm contributed to their sense of alienation and fostered a longing for legitimation.[11]

The members of the London Anthropological Society called each other "brother Cannibal" and used the word and its associations to separate themselves from the rest of society; it signified both the study of cannibals and a sense of kinship with these pariahs. A letter from E. Villine, a peripheral member of the club, to Swinburne was addressed to "My dear brother Cannibal," and his laudatory comparisons set the two of them apart from the rest of society: "Un petit mot par charité s'il vous plaît my dear brother and we shall bless you in the name of Voltaire, Sade—and the Devil into the bargain."[12] The substitution of Voltaire, de Sade, and the Devil for the holy trinity mocked respectable society. Swinburne went even further in inverting Christianity in his "burlesque 'hymn' written to amuse Monckton Milnes" entitled "The Cannibal Catechism."[13] In it, Swinburne spoke from the position of the cannibal and playfully constructed a cannibal's cosmology.

1

Preserve us from our enemies
Thou who art Lord of sun and skies
Whose meat and drink is flesh in pies
And blood in bowls!
Of Thy Sweet mercy, damn their eyes,
And damn their souls!

. . .

8

The heathen, whose ungodly lip

Doth in ungodly pewter dip

Curse his gin, whisky, rum, and flip

Strong ale and bumbo!

Scourge him with anger as a whip,

O, Mumbo-Jumbo![14]

This inversion—in which Swinburne damned pewter-toting, rum-swilling, Christian heathens, even though he himself had an enormous taste for alcohol—satirizes the sanctimonious Christian and the omnivorous cannibal. By playing with the Christian catechism, the poet makes both the cannibal and Christian appear equally ridiculous for their presumptions.

Homosexual and homosocial pleasures played a part in these men's dealings inside and outside the club. Other pleasures also emerged, such as flagellation and masochism.[15] In letters to each other they wrote about "swishings" and de Sade and joked about both heteroerotic and homoerotic desires. Swinburne began a letter to Milnes with the salutation "Salus in X Priapo et Ecclesiâ / Sub invocatione Beatissimi Donatiani de Sade": Salvation in Christ Priapus and His Church by the intercession of the Most Blessed de Sade.[16] Simeon Solomon copied an extensive extract from a manuscript for Swinburne:

> I will at once candidly unbosom to my readers, my affections are divided between the boy and the birch; I think it is neither necessary or important here to say which has the greater portion of my swelling heart, perhaps the division has been equal for, although I have always felt an inexpressible and thrilling pleasure in the company and *confidence* of handsome boys, these without that instrument of flagellant delights have not completely satisfied.[17]

Solomon concluded the letter by admitting that he was ashamed of himself, but he then celebrated that shame by including a picture with the caption "The Queen presenting rods to the Schoolmasters of the United Kingdom." In another letter, Swinburne wrote to Milnes (who went by the nickname "Rodin, Inspecteur des Ecoles" in some correspondence) that he had accidentally left behind "the MSS. of our incipient fictitious-biography in Grosvenor Place. Can I write to a maiden aunt rising seventy—'Be kind enough to look over a large portfolio in my bedroom containing autograph studies and sketches in verse and prose, all totally unfit for publication, ranging in date from 1854 to 1862, and forward the more offensive specimens to M. Rodin, I.D.E.D.S.M.I., near Grenoble?'"[18] A tension, among themselves as well as between them and society, emerged through their writings about sexuality, and their jokes did little to dispel it.[19]

In a letter to J. Frederick Collingwood, the assistant secretary of the Anthropological Society and a fellow "cannibal," Swinburne wrote: "Dear Brother, By the Grace of Satan I will be with you—Deo Nolente—*with* a friend—on Tuesday Yours in the faith, A. C. Swinburne."[20] The references to Satan seem part of a conscious pattern of self-exclusion and rejection of the status quo, and the reiteration of *with* underscores Swinburne's longings for Collingwood and hints at his sense of isolation. The recurring constellation of cannibals and Satanism expressed through longing and mockery illustrates how distant these men felt from the rest of society.

They expressed their desires through symbols reviled in the world that trapped them, but one that they themselves created. Rather than ignoring religion, these men subverted it. Rather than exploring an aesthetic relationship to the flesh, they tormented and were tormented by the flesh. The complicated relationships these men had with society and their own sexuality make the salutation "brother Cannibal" more comprehensible. Through their "brotherhood," they established a fictive kinship based upon self-proclaimed mutual alienation. The Cannibal Club attempted to create a standard of male sexuality not tied to either heterosexuality or homosexuality per se. They rejected the strictures of conventionality altogether, and particularly bourgeois calls to respectability. Instead, the Cannibal Club united to create a vision of sexuality that could be both transgressive and masculine. Combining a dash of satanism, a pinch of sadomasochism, a dollop of science, and a portion of imperialism, these pornographers created a new type of sexual adventurer—a world traveler who indulged his pleasures from above the fray.

The Politics of Production and Consumption

At the same time that the working classes became more literate and thus more able to use literary pornography, the works themselves slipped further out of their reach because of rising prices, new distribution patterns, and, most important, a new relationship between privilege and pornography. Pornography continued to be marketed in bookstores, but these bookstores did not cater to the lowbrow. Pornographers cut out cheap publications and felt no need to nest in the working-class warrens of Holywell Street, hidden from authorities. In very real ways, they *were* authorities.

John Camden Hotten, the most prominent publisher of pornography during this period, came to the trade through the literati rather than through politics, and his career demonstrates the shift in pornographic production.[21] Hotten apprenticed with a bookshop owner in London. After an extended trip to America, he returned to London and opened his own shop at 151B Piccadilly. He began writing, compiling, and publishing in the 1850s. When another publisher refused Swinburne's racier poems, Hotten offered to publish them and began an uneasy relationship with the poet, who accused him of unsavory business practices and occasional thefts. However, Hotten himself became a member of the Ethnological Society—no mean feat—which gave him a certain social cachet with his writers and readers. He also left his mark on the literary landscape by publishing the works of Mark Twain, Walt Whitman, and Bret Harte for the first time in England. Intermingled with the cream of American literature were other original publications like *Aphrodisiacs and Anti-Aphrodisiacs* and *The Merry Order of St. Bridget.* He continued to write, publish, and sell both pornographic and respectable literature until his death in 1873.[22] The marketing of pornography in bookstores like Hotten's cut distribution to potential clients by discouraging those not accustomed to shopping at the more exclusive sites of Piccadilly.[23] Even if the curious found Hotten's store, they could not necessarily get access to pornography. The prospective client needed to know of the publications through word of mouth or subscription lists. For instance, as Ashbee explains, *The Index Expurgatorius of Martial* "was never regularly sold to the public, although Hotten and a few booksellers had some copies at ten shillings for the small, and one pound for the large paper."[24] This work, "the joint production of four friends—three of whom had just left Oxford" (probably Sellon, Pike, Campbell, and Swinburne), never reached an open audience.[25]

The prices for these works stayed high, and runs remained limited to under five hundred copies, usually to 250. *A Discourse on the Worship of Priapus* (1865) cost four pounds ten shillings on small paper and ten pounds ten shillings on large.[26] Hotten priced John Wilkes's *Essay on Woman* at four pounds, and the "Library Illustrative of Social Progress" series cost fifteen pounds for the seven-volume set.[27] Even the small version of Martial remained too expensive at ten shillings for the working classes. Other volumes, like *The Kama Sutra* and *The Perfumed Garden of the Cheikh Nefzaoui,* were privately printed through subscription, which kept prices prohibitively high and opportunities for widespread access low.

The exclusivity of distribution reflects a deeper circumscription around who took part in conversations about sexuality. Although the members of the Cannibal Club were not the upper crust of Victorian aristocracy, and more than one of them lamented his "decreased circumstances," each lived a more than ordinary life and came from the better part of society. As a group, they appear to have enjoyed all of the benefits of the Victorian world.[28] A brief return to Frederick Hankey, the least respectable of the lot, illustrates the interconnected privileges of men associated with mid-nineteenth-century pornography. Frederick Hankey lived at number two Rue Laffitte in Paris from the 1850s through the 1870s. Hankey's father had been a general. His uncle Thomson Hankey was a politician and a director of the Bank of England.[29] Hankey knew Burton, Ashbee, and Milnes, whom he supplied with pornography from the Continent. He used a variety of methods to smuggle works from Paris to London. His messengers, like his cousin's valet and Mr. Harris (the manager of Covent Garden), snuck in daguerreotypes and small volumes in their overcoat pockets. Hankey also sent pornography to London via "the bag of a sympathetic Queen's Messenger returning from Constantinople with despatches for Lord Palmerston" and "in a British Embassy bag, addressed to a friend of Hankey's in the Foreign Office."[30] Hankey's methods demonstrate how the consumption and distribution of pornography became bound up in privilege. Hankey, in spite of his self-imposed exile, remained well connected to socially and politically advantageous people. Although he apparently held no job or sinecure, he remained financially secure. He suffered no legal and apparently few social repercussions for his tastes in sadistic and flagellant literature and paraphernalia, even though these were well known in Paris and London. His social position shielded him and allowed him to carve out a self-defined existence, an ability that set him apart from earlier radicals.

The more respectable members of the Cannibals had even greater influence. Monckton Milnes (Lord Houghton) was a member of Parliament and a minor poet. Sir James Plaisted Wilde (Lord Penzance) was a divorce court judge. Charles Duncan Cameron, an officer in the Forty-fifth Regiment turned career diplomat, served as consul to Abyssinia, where he was held captive for almost four years. On his return to England in 1868, he received a hero's welcome and a pension of 350 pounds a year. General Studholme John Hodgson served in Ceylon and Burma. Frederick Popham Pike was a "barrister of standing." Swinburne was one of the more influential, erudite, and prolific (as well as long-lived) writers of the period. Edward Sellon spent at least six years in India. Sir Richard Burton began his career in the British East India Company under Sir Charles Napier, for whom he wrote the infamous report on male brothels that followed him for the rest of his career. In spite of this inauspicious beginning, he became a prolific writer and explorer and a darling of the Royal Geographic Society, which funded his trips to Mecca and Africa. He later achieved consular positions in Brazil, Damascus, and Trieste. Other members of the association included J. Frederick Collingwood, the assistant secretary of the Anthropological Society, Thomas Bendyshe, vice president of the Anthropological Society and senior fellow of King's College, Simeon Solomon, an artist, George Augustus Sala, a writer, and William Simpson Potter, partner in a coal and shipping firm who traveled extensively to India and Japan. Henry Ricketts, Frederick Popham Pike, Edward Vaux Bellamy, George Powell, and E. Villine were also members. These men's collective biography demonstrates how position and relative wealth allowed them the opportunity to think about sexual matters, buy artifacts of their choice, see the world, or as much of it as they chose, and write about what they saw and wanted to see. In addition to their influence on the arts and sciences, they represented the state through their affiliations with Parliament, the courts, the Foreign Office, and the military. They had the capacity to create, administer, and adjudicate social policy both at home and abroad.

Privy to these men's conversations about sexuality and an author of works about pornography, Henry Spencer Ashbee deserves mention as a member of this milieu, rather than as a source hidden in footnotes. Ashbee came from the upper middle class. He began as an apprentice to a warehousing firm in Manchester and soon founded a London branch of a German merchant firm. After marrying well, he worked in Paris, and "having amassed a handsome fortune he devoted his leisure to travel, bibliography, and book collecting."[31] Like most of the men involved with pornography, Ashbee enjoyed wealth, education, leisure, and prestige. Ashbee knew many, if not all, of the Cannibal Club members. Like Houghton and Burton, Ashbee became a member of the Royal Geographic Society.[32] He inherited James Campbell Reddie's notes and manuscripts after Reddie's death, received advanced word from Arbuthnot and Burton about the publication of the *Kama Sutra,* knew Hankey and in fact visited him and his mistress in Paris, and had more than a nodding acquaintance with Milnes.[33] His three-volume bibliography of pornography includes extensive information on authors and publishers, indicating personal knowledge of their circumstances, as well as more standard bibliographic materials. The volumes, published and well known in certain circles during his lifetime, contained excerpts longer and more "obscene" than many pornographic pamphlets of earlier or later periods. That he could publish these bibliographies without repercussion demonstrates the arrival of a new class of producer-consumer.

As a group, they represented a new type of pornographer with new ways of thinking about sexuality. At the same time, they distinguished their pleasures from others' and had little sympathy for artistic or social change or for those who fell afoul of the obscenity laws. Swinburne dismissed Henry Vizatelly's trials and imprisonment for the publication of Emile Zola's *The Soil, Nana,* and *Piping Hot* as mere pornography: "M. Zola and his merry men are artists only in the sense—if such a sense there be—in which the term is applicable to a dealer in coloured photographs of unmentionable subjects." Swinburne went on to suggest "sweeping aside into the gutter such dirty little vermin as know no more of aesthetics than of ethics, of taste or intelligence than of decency or shame."[34] (This came from a man who called the Marquis de Sade "the divine de Sade.") Burton watched the trial from afar and commented in a letter to Leonard Smithers, a young barrister who looked to get into erotic publishing: "As you say these idiots are driving the trade underground to the detriment of every one."[35] He was concerned not about Vizatelly but about the stress the prosecution placed on his own publishing career.

The Cannibal Club formed a community defined by wealth, education, and social standing. They could carve out spaces for shared sexuality while the rest of society grew further regulated by the police, the medical establishment, and the moral authorities.[36] The ability to thwart regulation and to create an alternative system for pleasures stood as an aspect of social privilege. The Anthropological Society of London did not experience the same forces of repression as did the working classes. Older regulatory bodies like the Society for the Suppression of Vice, which entrapped and arrested pornographers, could not investigate the men of the Cannibal Club.[37] Members of the gentry did not look into the reading habits of members of Parliament, even though it was a poorly hidden secret that Milnes had a library well stocked with pornography at Fryston, his estate. In many ways, privilege encompassed not only wealth and skills but also a web of intangible advantages like political power and social rank that allowed Cannibal Club members to create a discourse about sexuality but remain unaccountable to the forces of repression. These privileged few could be expatriates but maintain close ties within the British community. They could receive parcels through the diplomatic pouch like Milnes, they could compel a valet or a respectable manager to perform illegal acts like Hankey, they could donate their obscene works to the British Museum like Ashbee, and they could even be knighted like Burton, in part for the publication of the *Arabian Nights.*

Edmund Gosse, a contemporary literary critic, suspected that a connection might exist between the private life and public writings of at least one eminent member of the Cannibal Club. In his biographical portrait of Swinburne, written shortly after the writer's death, Gosse ended on an ambiguous note: "There is something very extraordinary in the idea of a man writing these noble and impassioned hymns to the Republic on his way to being whipped at a bawdy-house, but may it not throw a faint light on the psychological cause of the practices being described?"[38] Taken together, hymns to Italian revolutionaries, trips to the bawdy house, and a taste for being whipped formed an evocative picture of the overlap between political and sexual culture during this era. Swinburne and other members of the Cannibal Club contributed not only to overt politics and policies in London and abroad but also to the covert politics of the flesh.

The wide variety of literary styles these men employed—from Swinburne's poetry to Burton's heavily footnoted translations to Sellon's imperial ethnographies—makes it hard to pronounce the writings a true "school." Their wide-ranging interests, including bibliography, exoticism, phallic worship, hermaphroditism, and flagellation, appear scattershot at best.[39] Their desires varied from the apparently simple desire for sexual education to the more arcane longings for flagellant discipline. Across this variety of writings, ideas, and desires, however, Cannibal Club pornography created distance between the male and the female and between the British and the foreign, arguing for an intrinsic, natural sexual difference between peoples. These writings insisted that truths about nature—inherent and unchanging—could be found in the body through the study of sexuality and sexual organs. The emphasis on exoticism increased as imperialism provided new arenas for pornographic exploitation and as the world became a backdrop for sexual adventure. The pornography produced and consumed by club members studied, assessed, and organized sexuality. Science did not preclude eroticism; the two went hand-in-glove. In many ways, the diversity of interests demonstrated the nature of the club. They could write about all they surveyed, and from their rather lofty positions they espied a great deal of England and the world.

Ashbee and Scientific Legitimacy

Ashbee, the bibliographer who catalogued every English, American, German, and French work of pornography he could find, demonstrated many of the scientific customs used by pornographers during the mid-nineteenth century. He assumed the scholarly apparatus of the scientist to distance himself from the pornographic voyeur, and he self-consciously pursued objectivity even though his work is rife with myth and prejudice. Ashbee had good reason to advocate the application of the scientific method; because they reprinted extensive selections (like the excised sodomy scene from *Fanny Hill*), his bibliographies were more explicit than many of the obscene works he catalogued. Ashbee recognized this problem, but he emphasized that erotic books had a specific purpose. In the introduction to the *Index Librorum Prohibitorum*, he wrote:

> Improper books, however useful to the student, or dear to the collector, are not "virginibus puerisque"; they should, I consider, be used with caution even by the mature; they should be looked upon as poisons, and treated as such; should be (so to say) distinctly labeled, and only confided to those who understand their potency, and are capable of rightly using them. My idea is thus aptly expressed by the Rev. R. A. Willmott: "Books of which the principles are diseased or deformed, must be kept on the shelf of the scholar, as the man of science preserves monsters in glasses. They belong to the study of the mind's morbid anatomy. But they ought to be accurately labeled."[40]

Collecting, organizing, categorizing, and then labeling sexuality was at the heart of Ashbee's approach.[41] The taxonomical approach to erotica did not just document sexuality, though; Ashbee's phrases for the pornography that he took years to accumulate and study, particularly "diseased or deformed," "the mind's morbid anatomy," and "poisons," reflect a distancing mechanism that tried to separate scientific interest from mere prurience. Ashbee aligned himself with science by creating a rational framework for the discussion of pornography and by clearly articulating an explicit rank-order of access. As Ashbee pointed out, the scholar, the scientist, and the mature (man) could rightly use "poison" for a higher purpose of understanding. Ashbee's competitor, the anonymous author of the *Bibliotheca Arcana*, was so taken with this justification that he nearly plagiarized Ashbee's introduction: "We have said that many, if not most of these works are poisons. But it must be admitted that poisons, rightly used, are of the utmost value in the economy of nature."[42]

The need to distinguish between mere titillation and rational investigation demonstrates the quagmire between pornography and science into which these writers knowingly waded. John Davenport began his *Curiositates Eroticae Physiologiae* by saying that he would *"call a spade a spade"* to distinguish his book from those marked by "overstrained notions of delicacy." However, he quickly stepped back into the fold of science. "Let it not be supposed from these remarks that the author's intention has been that of writing an *obscene* book, or even to employ obscene words. He holds that the grand subject—the Reproduction of the Human Race—which runs more or less through all of the essays in this volume, is, in itself, most pure." (Emphasis in original.) By arguing for the purity of the subject of sexuality, Davenport, like Ashbee, played up the legitimacy of his endeavors. Likewise, Burton and Arbuthnot, translators of the *Ananga-Ranga,* dedicated it to "that small portion of the British public which takes enlightened interest in studying the manners and customs of the olden past." To make the case that their works were not obscene or pornographic—and thus implicitly recognizing that many might think they were—these authors stressed the scientific nature of their bibliographic, physiological, and folkloric studies of sexuality.

Each author used a third-person voice, along with the scholarly apparatus of footnotes, citations, and references, and invoked an objective "nature" and "truth" to bracket and support his discussions. Regardless of the source—translations, medical information, ethnographic data, songs, or older stories—its importance lay, according to these authors, in its success at capturing the natural world. Ashbee himself sought "truth, the extension of bibliographical studies, and the accurate description of the works noticed in the following pages."[43] Truth and accuracy, however, did not preclude Ashbee from including a frontispiece in *Centuria Librorum Absconditorum* (figure 7) that featured a half-naked woman holding a liberty torch who strides over the fallen body of a monk. In the background, a naked cupid with an erect penis is poised over a reclining nude. Finally, an arch bears the names of pornographic writers, and two open volumes record the titles of their forbidden books. This image, provided by Ashbee, belies the notion that his sole focus was bibliographic studies.

While these authors preceded Richard von Krafft-Ebing and Sigmund Freud, many generalizations about early sexologists apply equally well to the Cannibals. The distancing mechanisms that these authors employed, from Ashbee's slurs on the pornography he so clearly loved to the abandonment of the first person for the more "objective" third-person narrative, spoke as much to the conceptual problems and contradictions in contemporary science as they did to complications in pornography. As Jeffrey Weeks later wrote, "The nascent science [of sexology] in the late nineteenth century was centrally im-

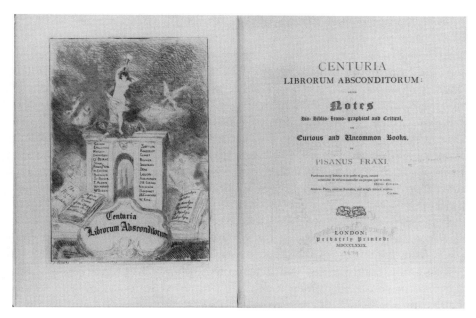

FIGURE 7. Frontispiece: *Centuria Librorum Absconditorum*. With permission of the Kinsey Institute.

plicated in all the debates about gender and sexuality, weaving a web of meaning around the body and its desires through its descriptions, categorizations, definitions, neologisms, and theoretical speculations."[44]

As these authors tried to assume the mantle of objectivity, they avoided examining their own stake in the material. The desire to find deeper truths about sex conflicted with the myths that writers unconsciously relied upon to organize their world. This conflict distorted the writers' formulations of sexuality. As Claude Lévi-Strauss would comment over a century later, the problems arising from empiricists' inability to conceptualize the mythic quality of their own thinking would inevitably confound the process of maintaining objectivity: "You may remember that I have written that myths get thought in man unbeknownst to him. This has been much discussed and even criticized by my English-speaking colleagues, because their feeling is that, from an empirical point of view, it is an utterly meaningless sentence."[45] As they rationally tried to understand their world, these Victorians inevitably stumbled over their own cultural ambiguities. Instead of confronting their desires, they tried to keep them like Ashbee's monsters—under glass and in control.

The Kama Sutra *and the Search for the Exotic*

The scientific approach to sexuality emerged as large parts of Africa, Oceania, and Asia came under British control.[46] The expansion of British interests to include geographic areas that had only peripherally touched the European imagination heightened interest in documentation. The same consciousness that mapped the South American coastline or led to the discovery of Lake Victoria in Africa also encouraged the discovery, collection, and observation of sexuality. Documentation became a way of understanding and controlling far-flung places and their inhabitants, and the Cannibals took part in these endeavors in areas as diverse as Japan, Ceylon, India, Abyssinia, Mecca, Burma, and Brazil.

Not only were Britons going where people had different ideas about the flesh, but they brought those new ideas home with them. A rare, early photograph from Japan (figure 8) testified to such travelers' explorations. In it, two geishas embrace on a cotton mat. The photographer hand-painted the lips and hair ornaments of the women, originally printed in sepia tones, to highlight their sexual exoticism. Such images, imported to the West, contributed to the growing stereotype of geishas as mere prostitutes. Joining the occasional pho-

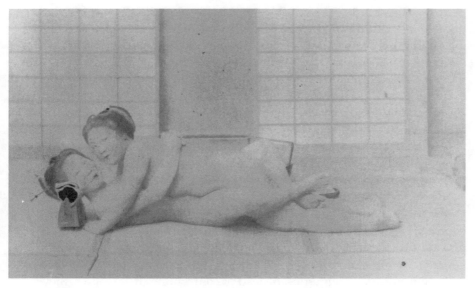

FIGURE 8. Cabinet portrait of geishas.

tograph and pillowbook (volumes of erotic drawings from Japan) were translations such as *The Kama Sutra, Ananga-Ranga, The Perfumed Garden,* and *History of the Sect of Maharajas.* These works, first published in English during the mid-nineteenth century, explored sexuality from non-European standpoints.[47] While the translation and publication of works such as *The Kama Sutra* indicated an awareness of outside cultures and an increased stake in them, this was no disinterested enterprise. Members of the Cannibal Club used documents like these to understand, absorb, and finally govern the sexuality of the colonized. These works snugly fit the imperial and empiricist agenda. The works were "scientific"; they detailed, categorized, observed, explained, and analyzed a diversity of practices. At the same time, the translators made it clear that the sexual practices described in these texts could—and should—be distinguished from British ones.

The *Kama Sutra,* translated by Sir Richard Burton and F. F. Arbuthnot, became pornographic upon its introduction into England. In its original context, it was a step-by-step guide to marital felicity that elaborated the natures of man and woman and the ways in which they could please each other. Brought to London, it was transformed into both an erotic and exotic text. Ashbee noted that the first English publication was disrupted when the printer "became alarmed at the nature of the book, and refused to print off the edition."[48] Its detailed descriptions of sexual practices made it unprintable in the non-pornographic publishing trade. The "Kama Shastra Society," a fictive organization that Burton and Arbuthnot created to distance themselves from their own private printing, published a second run of 250 books in 1883 and this time succeeded in finding printers willing to do the job. The place of publication was "Cosmopoli," a long-standing publishing tradition for prohibited or controversial books. Of course, Cosmopoli was London.

In the preface, Burton and Arbuthnot discuss the authorship of various components of *The Kama Sutra* and highlight the "oddity" of its literary style: "The contents of these works are in themselves a literary curiosity."[49] The antiquity of the work, combined with the "plain, simple, matter of fact sort of way" it described sexual relations, made it curious but also allowed it to function as an important remedy for the obfuscation of sexuality in Britain. According to their formulation, *The Kama Sutra* provided a clarity sorely missed in British discussions of sexuality. "Men and women are divided into classes and divisions in the same way that Buffon and other writers on natural history have classified and divided the animal world."[50] The precision in empiricist explorations like Buffon's *Histoire Naturelle* and *The Kama Sutra* promised to educate the populace in the natural laws of sexuality. For example, *The Kama*

Sutra explained and categorized sexual diversions, positions, and the best "kinds of sexual union according to a) dimensions, b) force of desire or passion c) time." According to the book, "man is divided into three classes, viz., the hare man, the bull man, and the horse man, according to the size of his lingam. Woman also, according to the depth of her yoni, is either a female deer, a mare, or a female elephant."[51] As one would expect, complementary sizes produced the best unions, but for clarity the text provides a small chart to show corresponding types of men and women. Hare and deer match, for example, but not hare and elephant.

The translators viewed this kind of precision as integral to their scientific program. This education was necessary because "complete ignorance . . . has unfortunately wrecked many a man and many a woman, while a little knowledge of a subject more generally ignored by the masses would have enabled numbers of people to have understood many things which they believed to be quite incomprehensible, or which were not worthy of their consideration."[52] According to Burton and Arbuthnot, sexual classification combined with a frank discussion of sexual congress could save the British population from ruined pleasures and wrecked lives.

However, while the model of frank discussion might apply to British society, the sexual practices did not. Ashbee noted of the work that "this is a very remarkable book, containing, among many things almost incomprehensible to a European, much matter which would repay his careful study."[53] The "Hindoo Art of Love" was exoticized into a subspecies of sexuality and rendered "almost incomprehensible" by Ashbee and a "curiosity" by the translators.[54] The incomprehensibility of the work went hand-in-hand with people's interest in it, as Ashbee's summary of chapter 4 indicates:

> Chapter IV on scratching with the Nails is very curious. The marks produced are of eight kinds. The proceeding is of course entirely foreign to our European notions, nor is the practice apparently universal in the East, for the author says: "But pressing with nails is not an usual thing except with those who are intensely passionate, i.e., full of passion. It is employed together with biting, by those to whom the practice is agreeable." The chapter which follows on Biting is equally curious.[55]

Chapter 5 explained that "all the places that can be kissed, are also places that can be bitten, except the upper lip, the interior of the mouth, and the eyes." The book then listed different types of bites, including the hidden bite, the swollen bite, the point, the coral and the jewel, and the biting of the boar, noting that the latter is "peculiar to persons of intense passions."[56] While the book documented Hindu sexual practices and thus fit into the scientific agenda of Ashbee, the translators, and others involved in such examinations, these men still used it to distinguish themselves from Hindus. Such practices might be artful, but they certainly could not be incorporated into the British lexicon. Indians were not monsters, but they were also not like Englishmen. Ashbee's summaries made this quite clear: "The various Postures are carefully considered in the sixth chapter, and many are described which would seem to be impossible of accomplishment by stiff-limbed Europeans."[57] The assertion of difference rested upon a racial dissymmetry. Just as pornographic works could be gathered, organized, and understood in Ashbee's bibliographies, so too could Hindu sexuality be explored even if the dissimilarities of nature and physiology precluded British imitation; Europeans were just not flexible enough, and Hindus liked biting, a pleasure unknown (and apparently unknowable) to Europeans. Hindu sexuality functioned as an "Eastern" version of sexuality that the West could only admire from afar.

Hindu sexuality could remain pleasantly exotic as long as it did not contradict European ideologies about nature, biology, or masculinity. When foreign practices contradicted English beliefs, such acts became offensive rather than opening new avenues for inquiry. The eleventh chapter of *The Kama Sutra* treated the subject of mouth congress, or fellatio, which could be performed by men, women, and eunuchs. *The Kama Sutra* explained fellatio according to its consecutive steps. "The following eight things are . . . done by the eunuch one after another, viz. The nominal congress. Biting the sides. Pressing outside. Pressing inside. Kissing. Rubbing. Sucking a mangoe fruit. Swallowing up."[58] As Ashbee made clear, fellatio—particularly *this* fellatio—stressed his capacity for open discussion to its limits: "The eleventh chapter treats of a subject so disgusting that I would fain pass over it in silence, should I not in doing so be departing from the principle of this work. Its consideration is the more imperative from the fact that the practice undoubtably continues in Europe, although, let us hope, less generally and in circumstances less revolting than in the East."[59] In Ashbee's estimation, fellatio became so disgusting and revolting not only because it made "normal" intercourse unnecessary but also because it demonstrated the fragility of sex organs because of castration. Mouth congress also equalized homoerotic and heteroerotic desire because "men and women irrespective of sex" could perform it. By denying all supposed physiological preconditions for sexual intercourse, mouth congress eliminated the sexual and gendered difference that these writers used to explain their world.

As the British treatment of *The Kama Sutra* demonstrated, pornography reflected the ambiguities of imperial programs more generally. On one hand, the rationale of free inquiry and scientific objectivity demanded a certain flexibility about universal standards for human conduct. Pornographers tried to take a disinterested stance on sexuality to counteract more overt forms of Victorian moralizing. On the other hand, the guise of scientific objectivity masked the coercive relationship implicit in the unidirectional flow of ideas. The British could study, examine, and on occasion deride the sexuality of the colonized because of the unequal relationships implicit in colonialism. John Shortt, in a more empirical paper presented to the Anthropological Society, "The Bayadère, or, Dancing Girls of Southern India," alternated between condemning the dancing girls' virtual enslavement and extolling their charms. He attacked the girls' singing and dancing as "vulgar and lewd" but complimented their "readiness, grace, and ease." Ultimately, he admired the girls' sensuality but insisted that Indian society ruined their lives. Of the Telugu girls, he stated that "I have seen many of these girls in my professional capacity while they lived as mistresses with European officers, and have been greatly surprised at their lady-like manner, modesty and gentleness, such beautiful small hands and little taper fingers, the ankles neatly turned, as to meet the admiration of the greatest *connoisseur*." He concluded, however, that it was not the liaisons with European men that might be problematic but Hinduism itself: "Wherever the Hindu religion predominates, there immorality and debauchery run riot."[60] Only deeper immersion in European culture (no doubt as mistresses and servants) could save such girls. Such scientific inquiries justified British supremacy by legitimating beliefs about the colonized; the freedom to study sexuality in the empire proved that the colonized did base acts with their bodies, further necessitating colonial rule based upon British standards.

Likewise, James Hunt's pseudo-scientific address to the Anthropological Society "On the Negro's Place in Nature" argued that only deepening European rule would help Africans and "Negroes." Hunt compared the physiology of the two and found that "Negroes" were a separate species from Europeans, or, to use his phrase, as different as "the ass is a distinct species from the zebra."[61] Not content to rest on physical data compiled on skull size, leg size, and jaw angles, Hunt proceeded to examine character. "The typical Negro is the true savage of Africa, and I must paint the deformed anatomy of his mind as I have already done that of his body." He continued: "The typical Negro, unrestrained by moral laws, spends his days in sloth and his nights in debauchery."[62] Because of their lack of control, he argued that "Negroes" must be supervised by Europeans: "Scientific men, therefore, dare not close their eyes to the clear facts, as to the improvement in mind and body, as well as the general happiness, which is seen in those parts of the world in which the Negro is working in his natural subordination to the European."[63] According to Hunt, slavery benefited both Europeans and Africans by providing labor for Europeans and civilization for Africans. Returning us to our starting point—Dahomey, from where Burton promised a skin for Hankey—Hunt concluded that the regular export of the excess population would be better than allowing systematic butcheries in that region. Just as Burton saw violence in West Africa as an opportunity to harvest skin, so Hunt saw it as a opportunity to harvest slaves. Scientific men, according to Hunt, should immediately see the efficacy of this solution for all involved. Once again, the lens of "science" allowed race and sex to reinforce each other in justifying the Cannibals' political supremacy.

The Problem with Physiological Explanations

In both licit and illicit writings, authors such as Ashbee, Burton, and Hunt extended their discussions of exoticism into the realm of sexual abnormalcy. Discussions of abnormalities clearly fit within the empiricist agenda by cataloguing the extent of natural variation. Such discussions also allowed the authors to remain comfortably distant from those they studied. But physiological explanations alone could not provide the certainty that these authors demanded, particularly when these writers refused to examine their own cultural stakes in the material. Issues generated conflicting explanations that unraveled as quickly as they were written because the authors could not or would not look at the cultural imperatives behind certain sexual practices. In labored discussions of hermaphroditism, impotence, and mulattoes, these authors tried to tie gender to physiology in unsustainable ways.

Like many other armchair scientists of the time, John Davenport cobbled his theories together from a variety of medical, historical, and ethnographic sources. He developed a functionalist viewpoint of the body that placed human sexuality solely in reproductive organs: "The function of generation is performed by means of two sets of organs, each of which gives origin to a peculiar product capable of uniting with the other, so as to produce a new individual. These two sets of organs assigned to the two different sexes are called *the male and female organs of generation.* The female organs produce a globular body called the *germ* or *egg,* which is capable of being developed in the body of a young female. The male organs produce that which is necessary to fecundate the germ, and enable it to go through its natural growth and development."[64] When Davenport arrived at a discussion of intercourse some fifteen pages later, he examined "which posture is best suited for coition, whether the object be that of begetting children, or that of mere animal gratification," by comparing human intercourse with that of animals. He placed his discussion of sexual positions within natural history, demonstrating the incorporation of new ideas of natural selection: "Our sexual parts indicate that they are not intended to be used in a standing posture like that of a hedge-hog."[65] Instead, "lip-to-lip" or enjoying a woman "as a greyhound bitch" proved the most effective at impregnating the female without undue strain on the male nervous system, which could produce debility, gout, and lassitude.[66]

This functionalist approach, while explaining biological sex in apparently factual ways, had a harder time explaining the cause of sexual abnormality and difference. Davenport's book on sexual curiosities took on the task of exploring these anomalies, but while he described abnormalities such as impotence and hermaphroditism, he could not quite figure them out to anyone's satisfaction. Ultimately, he could not fit these biological "oddities" into his framework and was forced to dismiss them. His definition of impotence, for example, rested on the reproductive capacity of individuals; women, he found, could not actually experience impotency because that would imply they would have no place for the insertion of a penis. He stated that "radical impotence, in fact, results in the female from the complete absence, or the occlusion simply, of the vagina. Now, these cases are extremely rare, and may therefore be considered as exceptions or as real monstrosities."[67] Rather than paying attention to pleasure (which would make female impotence more common) or fertility (which would also raise the number of impotent women), Davenport overemphasized the physiology of biological sex. By doing this, he avoided a contradiction that would undermine his framework of sexuality.

In the case of hermaphroditism, a similar problem arose. First, he introduced a biological standard; according to Davenport, lower animals and vegetables could be true hermaphrodites, capable of both the male and female aspects of reproduction, but humans could not. "In man, and other classes of animals, whose organization approaches the nearest to perfection, this disposition is always abnormal, never offering a character sufficiently decided for hermaphroditism, in the strictest sense of the word, to be predicated of them."[68] Even though he found numerous historical accounts of hermaphroditism and developed a taxonomic and legal model for resolving the problems of sexual identification, he rejected his own evidence and dismissed the issues that hermaphroditism raised. The problems of physiological variation, though articulated clearly with every apparent intention of serious consideration, became insurmountable.

Richard Burton fell into a similar trap. In 1864–1865, Burton sent a brief note to the Anthropological Society on the issue of hermaphroditism, or "anthropological curiosities." While traveling in St. Vincent, in the Azores, Burton had the opportunity to examine a boy: "Antonio de Ramos, as the malformation is called, will be eight years of age in September 1865." (His brutality in the treatment of the boy does not speak well of the distancing mechanisms of science.) According to Burton, a close examination of the child's hips, haunches, and genitals led him to conclude that Antonio was a girl. The hips' shape and the buttocks' width resolved the issue even though there were no discernible testes or nymphae. Burton observed: "It appears, therefore, that the so-called boy is a mere case of deformed clitoris, the feminine apparatus being abnormally developed. It will, however, be interesting to watch the progress of the case."[69] He then promised to send along a sketch of the child's parts to the society so that all could see the curiosity. Like Davenport's, Burton's account raised the issue of hermaphroditism only to dismiss it. The subject of hermaphroditism allowed these writers to separate their own sexuality from others'. They could assume the stance of objectivity because their own bodies and predilections were far removed from those studied. Though physiological explanations brought up unreconcilable issues, they still did important work by masking the cultural components of sexuality.

In keeping with their discussion of "abnormalities," the Anthropologicals made room for papers on "mulattoes"—a central issue in their understanding of the races as separate species. Hindering their arguments was the clear fact that the races could and did breed (unlike asses and zebras). R.B.N. Walker, a fellow of the Royal Geographic Society and a member of the Anthropological Society, focused on the infrequency of impregnation of the women of the Gaboon region in Africa by European men, "although intercourse between Europeans visiting the country and the native women has been frequent." Walker suggested that the native women's lack of "fitness" discouraged fertility and that the few offspring who emerged from such unions were "sickly and weakly" and rarely made it to adulthood.[70] Thus, though blacks and whites could breed, in this formulation, their offspring were not fully viable. While Walker pointed out, however, that the same native women did have children with native men after liaisons with Europeans, the possibility that such women might be exercising a choice to limit their fertility with Europeans apparently did not occur to him. The masking of what must have been a commonplace occurrence allowed Walker to conceptualize the women at the mercy of their "flawed" biology rather than responding to the realities of colonialism.

This willful blindness to the cultural practices and multiple meanings of sexuality hindered the Anthropologicals' ability to observe and theorize about sexuality at its most concrete level. The rejection of cultural explanations—woven through their published and unpublished writings—convoluted their attempts to get at "the truth, the whole truth" (to use Burton's phrase). When they considered the practices they held most dear, this inability to confront culture masked the politics of their own sexual practices as surely as it covered over the sexuality of the natives they observed and bedded. Ultimately, their elaborate explanations ignored the ways that culture forced bodies, including their own, into maintaining a political and social hierarchy.

Reconstructing the Body's Politics: Phallic Worship and Flagellation

The political and social supremacy that pornographers etched onto imperial sexuality becomes ever more clear when placed in the context of how they viewed their own bodies. Victorian pornographers revived an interest in phallic worship and almost unconsciously engaged in unending descriptions of monumental male organs. J. C. Hotten reprinted Richard Payne Knight's *A Discourse on the Worship of the Priapus* (1786) with an additional essay in 1865. Illustrations of phallicism were published separately under the title *The Worship of Priapus* at about the same time. *Phallic Worship* (1888), also called *The Masculine Cross*, a section of John Davenport's *Three Essays on the Powers of Reproduction* (1869), engaged phallic worship, and Edward Sellon's "On Phallic Worship in India," a paper given before the Anthropological Society, contributed to the reemergence of the leitmotif of phallicism. Phallicism clearly crossed the divide between licit and illicit; when broached in the auspices of the Anthropological Society, the topic could be scholarly, but when privately printed, anonymously written, and hidden behind a discreet blue cover emblazoned with a white cross—as was the case with *The Masculine Cross*, which was only intertitled *Phallic Worship*—the topic clearly became pornographic.

Phallic worship, in these authors' minds, had a long and illustrious history that stretched unbroken from ancient Greece to the contemporary world. In these accounts, the phallus united all of the symbols of the Western world: the maypole, British and Greek stone columns, the steeples atop churches across the English countryside, and so on. The symbolic relevance of the phallus crossed art, architecture, religion, and popular culture. Knowingly and unknowingly, people across the world worshiped at the altar of the phallus. According to these accounts, even the cross became phallic, an example of the male T, made of testicles and penis.[71] These authors saw themselves as historicizing an important but overlooked tradition in Western culture.

They built their understandings of phallic worship from smatterings of ancient texts and art. However, the motif of priapism also seemed to reflect the world of male sexuality in particularly nineteenth-century ways. *Phallic Worship* defined phallicism as "the worship of the reproductive powers, the sexual appointments revered as the emblems of the Creator. The one male, the active power; the other the female or passive power; ideas which were represented by various emblems in different countries."[72] In this explanation, the male power acted upon the world, while the female organs and essence could only passively wait. The model of male activity and female passivity reflected the emerging formation of bourgeois gender norms as much as it did ancient beliefs in sex and gender. Of course, wantonness, the flip side of female passivity in bourgeois gender norms, also received its due. In the discussion of Roman priapic worship, John Davenport made clear that women's worship had sexual as well as religious connotations. "Females as superstitious, as they were lascivious, might be seen offering in public to Priapus, as many garlands as they had lovers. These they would hang upon the enormous phallus of the idol, which was often hidden from sight by the number suspended by only one woman. Others offered to the god as many phalli, made of the wood of the willow tree, as they had vanquished men in a single night."[73] In this account, Roman women took on the hypersexualized connotations of the Victorian prostitute. Despite the fascination with the phallus in these texts, the fixation with male organs did not translate into a focus on male genitalia per se. Instead, drawings reproduced motifs such as "goat and Satyr," "Greek sculpture," "Indian Temple, Showing the Lingam," "Celtic Temple, Greek medals, & c," and "Phallic Monuments Found in Scotland." The reappraisal of phallic worship transformed the landscapes of the world into one dedicated to Priapus. The occasional phallus that remained attached to a human figure in these images gained such grandeur that it overwhelmed mere physiology (figure 9). In these illustrations the scale of the phalli guaranteed their glory, dwarfing the men attached and those who sought to attach themselves. Male genitals became ennobled under the majesty of phallic worship, and all worshiped at the altar. The creation of an unbroken tradition of phallic worship that tied English life to the ancient world implicitly justified imperial and biological understandings

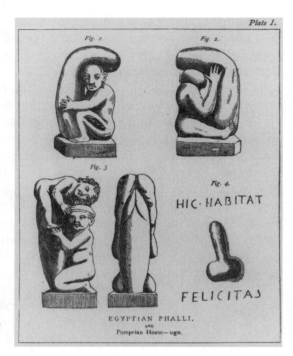

FIGURE 9. Illustration from John
Davenport's *Aphrodisiacs and Anti-
Aphrodisiacs*. With permission of
the Kinsey Institute.

of sex and gender. The authors wrote the phallus in grand symbolic design
across the world so that everyone worshiped from below.

In spite of the aggrandizement of masculinity in the formulation of priapic worship, life within the body as well as the celebration of the symbols of
it did not always proceed so smoothly. Some aspects of sexuality—like the sexual practices of dancing girls, Hindus, and Africans—made it easier to assume
a stance of objectivity because they remained comfortably distant from the
writers' own practices and desires. Others—like phallic worship—made objectivity unnecessary because they reinforced the authors' way of viewing the
world. Some proved more ambiguous. Flagellation was one such issue; while
it was central to the sexual practices of Swinburne, Cameron, Hodgson, and
Powell, among others, it remained an unstable topic because of the authors' refusal to examine the cultural dynamics that made flagellation interesting and
evocative. In spite of an intense focus on flagellation revealed in a surge of new
publications, older reprints, and frequent letters, the Cannibals' approach concealed as much as it uncovered.

Avoiding the considerations that made it deeply symbolic and meaning-ful, the writings about flagellation masked the cultural meanings of masculin-ity, sexuality, and domination. Instead of looking at culture, pornography turned to science—so useful for exploring the sexuality of others—to explain a predilection for flagellation. In *Fashionable Lectures,* the author used a de-scription of human physiology to introduce a discussion of flagellation.

> Now, the loins compose the chief part of the back: for that part of the body takes its rise from the five *vertebrae,* which are placed behind the *vertebrae* of the *thorax,* is continued quite to the *os sacrum.* These parts, muscles, skin and fat, cover outwardly; inwardly they are surrounded and braced by the muscles. These reins adjoin to these, the left and right, one on each side, and take up about the space of four *vertebrae,* and are annexed to the *vena cava* and the large *artery.*[74]

The description documenting the relationship among the bones, muscles, veins, vessels, and testicles continued for an additional page and a half, de-ploying endless scientific details to tie the loins with the circulatory and ner-vous systems and prove that sexual pleasure comes from physiology. Once the author established the physiology of sexuality, he digressed into a series of lit-erary proofs from ancient writers like Juvenal ("When music and when wine to lust conspire,/ Provoke the blood, and set the loins afire") and Martial ("He lets the sun behold his play,/ And brakes his sides in open day"). Eventually he returned to the main point of his essay, which was to "discover the cause why strokes and stripes . . . are incentives to lust."[75] His conclusions finally re-turned to a physiological explanation of this practice:

> Stripes upon the back and loins, as parts appropriated for the gener-ating of the seed, and carrying it to the genitals, warm and inflame those parts, and contribute very much to the irritation of lechery. . . . For it is very probable that the refrigerated parts grow warm by such stripes, and excite a heat in the seminal matter, and that more par-ticularly from the pain of the flogged parts, which is the reason that the blood and spirits are attracted in a greater quantity, till the heat is communicated to the organs of generation, and the perverse and fren-zical appetite is satisfied, and nature, though unwilling, drawn beyond the stretch of her common power to the commission of such an abom-inable crime.[76]

Physiology (the increase of blood to the loins) explained the sexual excitement of flagellation. This physiological approach limited the symbolic by naturalizing it. Thus, excitement was biological rather than a product of culture. According to this viewpoint, sexuality was innately tied to the structure of the human body. By uncovering the physiological structure of the human body, the hidden mechanisms of human sexuality could be revealed.

In these renditions, variations in sexual practice gained merit through their utility in leading toward heterosexuality and reproduction. Overtly, flagellant practices and flagellant literature were valued through the relationship to heterosexual intercourse, although covertly homoerotic desire underscored many accounts. Ashbee panned the seven-part series called "The Social Progress of the Century" because it described flagellation with no heterosexual culmination.

> In a literary point of view they are generally worthless, and insufferably dull and tedious,—one idea—one only—is harped upon throughout all of them, and this is not true to nature. Flagellation, if it has any value, is a preparation for, an incentive to, a higher pleasure (for it can scarcely be called a pleasure itself), a means towards an end, not the end itself. Now, in no single anecdote throughout the series is the flagellation immediately followed by anything else; the chastisement begins and ends each performance.[77]

According to Ashbee, nature caused flagellation to lead to sexual arousal, which in turn led to intercourse. When flagellant representations did not end in heterosexual intercourse, they became tedious. The physiological theory of flagellation, which stated that flagellation brought blood and energy to genitals, allowed the practice to be construed in culturally acceptable ways that augmented heterosexuality, rather than circumventing it.

Nonetheless, the recurrent theme of flagellation, whether with or without heterosexual intercourse, hinted at alternative meanings. "The Social Progress of the Century" exclusively documented flagellation. Although the series explored the practice in verse, monologues, vignettes, Latin quotes, and historical accounts, the descriptions did not extend the possibilities for flagellation. The insistence on only one type—female chastisement of males using a rod or birch—circumscribed the act.[78] By repetitious documentation, the series seemed to exhaust the subject. In fact, they merely limited its possibilities to a single form. Through the insistence on a specific form, these texts focused on flagellation as a way of inducing arousal, rather than the sensations of arousal or the culmination of it. The point became how to animate men's bodies. In this scheme, flagellation allowed the mind and body to work together to control sexual stimulation. These works ultimately accepted a heterosexual order as natural but provided a way for the unaroused to perform within it. They accepted the boundaries of male physiology and allowed men to circumvent nature's vagaries.

The emphasis on flagellation in British pornographic literature has generally been attributed to a homoerotic sexuality established at the public schools, and certainly Swinburne's many notes addressed to Milnes as "Rodin, Inspecteur des Ecoles," uphold this interpretation. The public school system allowed youths to regulate themselves so that they could in turn regulate society. The social structure of the public school replicated society broadly on the basis of age, rank, and ability, and then utilized flagellation to discipline, punish, and control. Flagellation functioned in schools as a means to discipline body and mind. The emphasis on control and self-regulation in school discipline and sexual discipline overlapped at theoretical and practical levels. Flagellation in both areas worked as a pedagogical technique to teach masculine self-control.[79]

This formulation of flagellation insisted that control and discipline become internalized. To maintain the duality of flagellation—that of the dominator and dominated—some authors supplied only half of an apparent dialogue, making readers implicitly supply the other role. In *The Role of Flogging in Venereal Affairs,* the son acknowledges the need to learn control, insists on being disciplined, and learns to like the process. The father's mistress chastises the son: "Do you care for a rod now? do you? do you? do you care for a rod now? You ought to thank the rod and me for whipping your b——so well; here, kiss the rod, and kiss my hand for holding it and making such good use of it."[80] The repetitive questioning and the insistence on kissing the rod and hand heighten the tension between external acts and internal acceptance. The son acknowledges the need for outside control and insists on his own discipline. Such disciplinary tension created a sexually charged space in these fictional and semifictional texts that in many ways was neither heterosexual nor homosexual but based on mastery and submission. Domination and submission stood in for sexual congress altogether in *The Role of Flogging in Venereal Affairs.* Submission mattered more than the sex of the master.

Flagellant literature created a sexual practice that moved the focus from orgasm to the desire for discipline and control. The longing for discipline came through in the prose much more clearly than the longing for intercourse. Swinburne, the least circumspect and the most literary of the lot, rhapsodized over youth and birch in a letter to George Powell (who was clearly aware of Milnes's and Swinburne's fantasies and pseudonyms). His alienation intensified his longings. He saw a landscape waiting to be filled with his desires, but he could not see the culmination. He began by commenting on the beauties of the countryside, in particular the birch trees that had so much symbolic relevance:

> . . . with birch enough at hand for the bottoms of all Eton.
>
> Oh! Monsieur—as our orphan would say—an Atheist might weep to think how the good gifts of God are rejected and where His gracious Providence has been pleased to plant the beneficent materials for so much innocent happiness—never ending, still beginning— to a band of Sadique enthusiasts, this source of healthy pleasure and pure joys unknown to the base vulgar which stimulate at once and satisfy remains thanklessly neglected by a backsliding generation. In these shades might the learned M. Rodin and the venerated Père Severino revel unchecked in the infliction of the most exquisite torture on the loveliest limbs of blooming boyhood—of the most burning shame, the most intolerable suffering, on blushing and writhing adolescence—while Naiads and Oreads, maidens of the mountain and stream stood not far off, to repay the labours and allay the pangs with kisses. Here Pain and Pleasure, twin sisters, might dance hand in hand round the bloody red and rose altar of Love. They might—but alas I need hardly add that they do not.[81]

His rhapsody loses momentum after the Pain and Pleasure dance, although he could clearly see his friends as a "band of Sadique enthusiasts" torturing the "blooming boyhood." He could not envision a sexual practice that moved beyond the initial kiss to allay the pangs, and his altar of Love was left uninhabited by either heterosexual or homosexual fancies. The description denies the end result of heterosexual intercourse. Neither does it provide an alternative in homosexual possibilities. Instead, the focus becomes birching itself and the mingling of pain and pleasure.

The multiple directions for flagellation across these texts—as a prelude to sexual intercourse, as a medical prescription to promote bodily control, as an alternative moment of pleasure—demonstrate the problems of control and desire in the masculine world of the mid-nineteenth century. The physiological explanation in *The Role of Flogging in Venereal Affairs*, the heterosexual culmination in Ashbee's analysis, and the alternative forms of pleasure in

Swinburne's letter competed as ways to explain this practice that many found compelling. All of the explanations played with the idea that control and domination fit bodies into prescribed paths but never really addressed it. The erotics around force and control therefore remain submerged.

The inability to confront the erotics of domination and submission meant that the authors could not challenge the politics implicit in sexuality, even if this omission denied them the possibility of alternative sexual pleasures like homosexuality, pain, and submission. They could not see how their society formed them, just as they could not see how they, in turn, constructed others. Rather than question the myriad relationships between pleasure, pain, and privilege that they enjoyed and engendered, they partitioned off politics in the public sphere even as they wrestled with the play of power on their own bodies. As Gosse noted, there was something revealing about Swinburne's composing odes to Italian revolutionaries before a flagellant session at the local bawdy house. The segregation of overt politics from internalized pleasure, crystallized in that anecdote, allowed Swinburne to celebrate liberties even when he could not fully live out his own desires. The focus on difference, physiology, and rationality obfuscated the very real and very irrational problems these men faced when fitting their own bodies into the social demands placed upon them.

Science and Sexuality

Cannibal Club pornography very neatly laid out the body's politics during the Second British Empire. It distinguished men from women, white from black. It offered a method to legitimize the study of sexuality and provided a scientific rationale for sexual arousal. It justified social and political distinctions between those who studied and those who were observed, and it allowed the observers a means of side-stepping the problematics of their own erotic desires. Club members could write their own belief systems upon the world even when that belief system held its own internal contradictions. As scholars, politicians, scientists, artists, and finally imperialists, their formulations affected the world on both symbolic and practical levels. They contributed to the ethos of British society that argued for immutable difference, and they used this ethos to create the hierarchies of empire. Their fascination with these distinctions helped construct sex and race as biological categories.[82] Working in their own interests, the members of the Cannibal Club found that the pornographic investigation of sexuality did not preclude the scientific; instead, they complemented and intensified each other.[83]

The scientific turn pornography took might have simply been an odd but revealing episode in its history, except that the emerging discourses of anthropology, sexology, natural history, and psychology developed from the same scientific and social platform. Although the Cannibal Club had its dirty little secrets, like a fascination with the "divine de Sade," those secrets ultimately say much more about the cosmology that ruled domestic and imperial policies and the academic disciplines that supported them than they do about individual club members. Just as the empire reached its apex and the human sciences gained legitimacy at the beginning of the 1880s, the Cannibal Club apparently disbanded. The emergent disciplines overtook the club's ways of thinking about sexuality and further legitimized them.

By the end of the 1880s, scientific pornography faltered. Nonetheless, certain elements of it continued to be influential. The unwillingness and inability to confront the politics implicit in eroticism continued. The voyeuristic interest in sexual curiosities lingered. The imperial agenda, with its focus on exotic sexuality, not only remained but gained momentum. Although empiricism left pornography behind, pornographers continued to publish by finding new and revealing ways to sell sexuality.

Chapter 3

The Pearl
before Swine

Fetishism and
Consumer Culture

The verses that asked who would bugger the Turk (and answered: Gladstone) appeared in *The Pearl*, a journal that ran from July 1879 until December 1880. *The Pearl* featured an obscene parody of "God Save the Queen," two flagellant poems by Swinburne, six serialized novels, and a variety of jokes, poems, and songs, including "The State's New Duty," about the passage of the Contagious Disease Acts. The editor and publisher, William Lazenby, offered the following explanation for the journal's title:

> Having decided to bring out a Journal, the Editor racks his brains for a suitable name with which to christen his periodical. Friends are generally useless in an emergency of this kind; they suggest all kinds of impossible names, the following were some of the titles proposed in this instance: "Facts and Fancies," "The Cremorne," "The All Around," "The Monthly Courses," "The Devil's Own," and "Dugdale's Ghost;" the first two had certainly great attractions to our mind, but at last our own ideas have hit upon the modest little "Pearl" as more suitable especially in the hope that, when it comes under the snouts of the moral and hypocritical swine of the world, they may not trample it under foot, and feel disposed to rend the publishers, but that a few will become subscribers on the quiet. To such better disposed piggywiggys, I would say, for encouragement, that they have only to keep up appearances by regularly attending church, giving to charities and always

appearing deeply interested in moral philanthropy, to insure a respectable and highly moral character. . . . Editor of the "Pearl."[1]

Clearly, the editor knew the history of pornography as his references to
William Dugdale and *The Cremorne,* a journal published in the 1850s, demonstrated. Just as clearly, he hated the moral authorities, whom he accused of
reading pornography on the sly. In naming his journal *The Pearl* and metaphorically throwing this "pearl" before "the snouts of the moral and hypocritical
swine," Lazenby vented his fury at the authorities who had arrested him
in 1876.[2]

    Lazenby's accusations about the audience seem to have more than a
grain of truth. The readership of pornography in the late nineteenth century
encompassed, if not the exact moral authorities responsible for his arrest,
certainly members of the same social class. Although Lazenby's references to
Dugdale and *The Cremorne,* his publication of Swinburne's poetry, and the continued exclusivity of the readership point toward long-term continuities in the
history of pornography, there were shifts in the industry that indicated it was
going through a period of intense change. New methods of distribution developed, and a coterie of entrepreneurial publishers emerged to exploit them.
Contemporaries and later critics noticed that the style of pornography changed
as well; between 1880 and 1914, pornographers stripped away characterization, plot, and setting and opened up room for an intense formulaic focus on
specific sex acts. Literary critics have lambasted these works for diminishing
the artistry of writing about sexuality and for the growing perversity they displayed. These critics have ignored how these works functioned as narratives,
however, just as they have avoided exploring changes in literary style in relationship to an altered marketplace. While luxury goods had always been served
up to the leisured classes, entrepreneurial publishers exploited this trend by
providing specialized texts for specialized tastes. The so-called perversity of
modern pornography seems innately tied to these new market trends.

Publishers and Distribution Networks

Edward Avery, Leonard Smithers, Harry Sidney Nichols, William Lazenby,
and Charles Carrington formed a tightly knit group of publishers involved in
the production and sale of pornography from the 1880s through 1914. They
knew each other, used each other's skills, and passed down strategies in a

chain that went from Lazenby to Nichols to Smithers to Carrington and from Carrington to the quite recent Olympia Press. Each man learned the craft in England, and each ended his life in exile, notorious, and broken.

According to Peter Mendes, Lazenby (alias Duncan Cameron and possibly Thomas Judd) became the main publisher of pornography between roughly 1873 and 1886.[3] Some of the classic works of the period came from his presses, including *The Romance of Lust* (1873–1876), *The Story of a Dildoe* (1880), and *The Pearl*. He built an enormous enterprise; when the police arrested him in 1886, they found "16,000 books, photographs, stereoscopic slides, and prints" at one location; ultimately they found "five cab loads" of books at his locales.[4] Lazenby was imprisoned, tried, found guilty, and sentenced to two years of hard labor. He disappeared from public view before serving his sentence, however, and apparently fled to Paris. Avery—his associate—continued the business until he, too, was caught and given nine months of hard labor, sometime during the 1880s.[5] In spite of this sentence, Avery appears to have stayed in the business.

In 1888, Avery pulled in H. S. Nichols to distribute his works in Sheffield and then, by 1892, in London; together they published *Teleny* in 1893. During his time in London, Nichols branched into publishing with works like *Priapeia* (1888).[6] A decade later, he not only published and ran a bookstore, he also speculated on the stock market. In 1898, Nichols declared bankruptcy because of unredeemed debts, illness, and unprofitable speculation.[7] Two years later, he returned to publishing and opened the Walpole Press at a new location. Scotland Yard raided his premises after sixty-three complaints about prospectuses for "Kalogynomia" sent "to people of all professions in all parts of the world."[8] The authorities arrested him and destroyed his stock. Nichols jumped bail and fled to Paris until 1908, when he emigrated to New York.[9]

Leonard Smithers went into partnership with Nichols well before the latter's arrest in 1892. Smithers began his career in pornographic books through translation and publishing. Unlike his fellow pornographers, Smithers embraced public scrutiny. He helped make Aubrey Beardsley a cause célèbre and linked Beardsley's name with Oscar Wilde's by encouraging their joint work on *Salome* (1894). Although he sought the limelight, his publication of their works finally cost him his tenuous hold on respectability after Wilde's trials in 1895. Poverty soon overtook him, and he began pirating Wilde's works and selling forged copies of Beardsley's deathbed note that asked for the destruction of *Lysistrata* (1896).[10]

Last, the infamous Charles Carrington (originally Paul Ferdinando) was born in Bethnal Green in 1867. By the 1890s, he worked as a courier and general dogsbody for Smithers and Avery, eventually setting up his own shop in Paris in 1895. Carrington made his place in the annals of erotic publishing by exploiting the new mail order trade, eventually outdoing his mentors in both volume and notoriety. Printers in Amsterdam produced his works, which he then sold through catalogues and intermediaries in London. His works included *Untrodden Fields of Anthropology* (1895), *Sweet Seventeen: The True Story of a Daughter's Awful Whipping and its Delightful if Direful Consequences* (1910), and *Memoirs of a Russian Princess* (1890). Carrington continued to publish and sell until his death in 1921.

These men came to the trade with particularly middle-class skills, and they made the most of them; certainly, working-class activities did not include dabbling in the stock exchange as Nichols did, roaming the Continent with the intelligentsia as Smithers was wont, and translating from French to English like Smithers and Avery. These men were adept at avoiding the authorities, and they matched each move by the Home Office and Scotland Yard with a countermeasure of their own. After the National Vigilance Association absorbed the Society for the Suppression of Vice in the 1880s and developed the strategy of working for legislative changes rather than arrests, the police force and New Scotland Yard took over the curtailment of pornography and soon proved themselves more successful.[11] Lazenby, Carrington, Nichols, and Avery shifted their enterprises to Paris because of the English authorities' success at harassing the trade. The combined forces of the police, New Scotland Yard, and the NVA successfully eradicated the *production* of pornography in England. However, they did not eradicate pornography; pornographers just began shipping the materials from abroad to escape prosecution.

The authorities tried to crack down on the shipping of works from overseas, but this program proved unsuccessful. The Post Office (Protection) Act of 1884 made it illegal to send obscene or indecent materials through the mail. Under the act, a violator could be liable for up to twelve months in prison with hard labor as well as fines up to ten pounds.[12] While the government used the law to prosecute both pornographers and disseminators of birth control, the act did not make it possible to prosecute those who remained abroad.[13] Nichols, Lazenby, and Carrington set up shops and mail order enterprises overseas.

By 1900, Paris had become the distribution center of pornography intended for England (as well as the Continent and America). Wealthy tourists could easily go there to browse the obscene, bawdy, and pornographic works of the time, and the city became a mecca for vendors and distributors of obscene wares.[14] A fairly complex international trade had sprung up involving many of the major European cities, notably Amsterdam and Rotterdam, but also Antwerp, Budapest, Barcelona, Berlin, and Genoa.[15] New distributors operating out of Amsterdam and Rotterdam set up their own independent mail order companies (like the vaguely euphemistic "Graphic Toy Company") augmenting the more established dealers out of Paris.[16] The traffic between London and the Continent became voluminous, despite legal attempts to stem the flow, and showed no signs of diminishing.

Dealers shipped mail order catalogues to prospective customers who perused the wares in the comfort of their own homes or, in the case of schoolboys from Winchester and Eton, their rooms. Clients would pay for their goods with cash, stamps, checks, and money orders. At first, the pornographers gave their own addresses, but when they realized that the Post Office had begun confiscating their mail, they developed a system of postal drops.[17] Pornographers also used middlemen in England to transmit orders and send packages on to clients. For instance, Dolly Ashford, the widow of a distributor in Paris, continued the business after her husband's death. She had materials, including obscene books and "some really hot photos," shipped to a friend, Mrs. Mason of London, supposedly a respectable woman above reproach. When police opened the packages, Mrs. Mason was suitably "shocked" to find such goods under her name, and no charges were brought against her.[18] In a similar maneuver, Carrington "was known to be employing an agent in this country to whom he was sending the matter in question for distribution, and it was undoubtedly for the purpose of sending them in large quantities in bulk, to be posted in this country to save the expense of being posted abroad."[19] The use of middlemen, false monikers, and dummy companies indicated the sophistication of these entrepreneurs and the profitability of their ventures.

From the 1890s until 1914, this international pattern of production and distribution continued despite further attempts by the police, Home Office, and Foreign Office to curtail them. These organizations tried to address the influx of pornography when catalogues fell into the wrong hands—the headmasters at Winchester and Eton, rather than the students for whom they were intended. The headmasters complained to the Home Office, which subsequently took a series of actions. First, the Home Office asked the Foreign Office to contact the governments in the countries where the pornographers resided and push for obscenity prosecutions there. However, indifference in France, Belgium, and Holland guaranteed limited success.[20] Second, the Home Office and the Post Office made a list of names and addresses of known pornographers and began to "arrest" packages from them as they entered the country. This policy worked marginally better; they confiscated over twelve thousand packets from Carrington alone.[21] The policy gained momentum through

World War I, and "warrants" for the mail from as many as thirteen pornographers were issued at a time.[22] However, the authorities recognized that pornography still slipped into the country through dummy corporations and false fronts.

Because they could not control the supply of pornography, the Home Office and the Post Office turned to demand. The Post Office began tracking letters addressed to pornographers, opening the letters, and compiling files on those who placed orders. One man, John Flewelling, ordered a number of pornographic photographs from Adolf Estinger, who operated out of Hungary and Amsterdam. Flewelling's taste ran to young girls aged eight to twelve, young boys and girls in interesting positions, and "ballet girls."[23] Flewelling avoided prosecution, but his name was bandied about the Home Office. Similarly, a Mr. Webb from Reading and an L.B. from Holloway also had their outgoing mail opened and scrutinized.[24] After the postal authorities inadvertently opened a young member of Parliament's mail and made his name known to the Home Office, the Home Office abandoned the policy of opening and examining outgoing mail to pornographers, but not before the Post Office had opened and scrutinized 3,724 outgoing letters.[25] After accidently catching the MP, the government closed its incipient files on users because of the power and privilege some of them wielded. Thereafter, the postal service returned to confiscating only incoming catalogues and packages. By 1914, the pornographers and authorities had reached a detente. Few pornographers were persuaded to abandon the trade, however, the authorities could do little but beleaguer them. When the authorities got too near, the pornographers would simply move to another location, another town, or, as a last resort, another country.

Partially from this intensified crackdown against pornography and partially from the professionalization of the trade as a discrete moneymaking enterprise divorced from politics and science, the pornographers moved to the margins of society. These later pornographers refused to accept their marginality. They did not emerge from the world of radicalism like Dugdale, nor did they seem to overlap with respectable publishing as did J. C. Hotten. They seemed to occupy precarious positions as members of the petite bourgeoisie who came to the trade with some middle-class skills, little capital, and a great desire to enlarge their lots in life. Their aspirations, their strategies, and even their conceits marked them as social climbers. Carrington not only adopted a plumy name to appeal to his readership when he abandoned "Ferdinando" but also adopted an upper-class literary voice styled after Ashbee's.[26] Frequent false imprints identified the place of publication as Oxford and the author as "a gentleman for his friends," indicating the imagined alliance. Instead of working *from* a tradition of political agitation, or working *with* the developing professions, these pornographers worked *for* the aristocracy and upper middle-class. But a relationship based on service did little to resolve the tensions between publishers and their clientele. As Lazenby made bitterly clear, the pornographers lost their bid for a rough equality when they were pushed out of semirespectability, out of the country, and into the forefront of the international market.

Audience

By the end of the nineteenth century, most people in England could afford basic commodities and leisure. Most Britons bought standardized footwear, ready-made clothing, second-class tram tickets, tabloid newspapers, and seasonal fruit. Only a small minority of Her Majesty's subjects could cultivate more exotic tastes. Eric Hobsbawn highlights the distance between the rich and the rest of society by noting that "the situation of the upper classes was very different, and the immensity of the gap between the top and bottom of society was merely underlined by the orgy of conspicuous waste into which a section of the rich threw themselves." [27] Pornography exemplified these luxury goods.

The upper echelons could concern themselves with exclusivity, authenticity, and artistic integrity, and pornographers did their best to speak to their desires. One catalogue listing the fairly common work called "Aretino's Postures" in 1889 justified the exorbitant price of three pounds with the following description:

> These celebrated Ragionamenti, of which we now offer the first complete and literal English translation, are altogether different from the insipid, unwitty, trashy little books published within the past two or three hundred years under the name of Aretino. They are the offspring of one of the greatest and best satiric writers. Every impartial scholar will, on reading them, be easily convinced that the Devil is no so black as people would fain paint him.
>
> Aretino possessed such a capacity for handling no matter what subject with the utmost elegance, that on this account he received the surname of the Divine: and amongst all of his writings the most worthy of esteem and admiration are the Ragionamenti. [28]

The editorial description elevated this *Ragionamenti* from others for the status-conscious buyer. This translation was elegant, complete, and historic, whereas others were "insipid, unwitty, trashy." This version would appeal to the most "impartial" judge, who would elevate the text from the merely prurient to the aesthetic. The pornographers wanted to make money, and they did so by skimming the cream of the market.

They produced fine articles, for only the fine members of society that could afford such indulgences. Small distribution with a high return per volume fueled the profitability of the pornographic endeavor. Pornographic booksellers charged whatever the market would bear, and prices remained extremely high. *Frank and I,* a three-volume work of 244 pages, cost five pounds or twenty-five dollars in 1902, the first year of its publication.[29] (Catalogues listed prices in both dollars and pounds as befitted the new international parameters of the trade.) The price continued to rise, reaching five pounds five shillings in 1910.[30] *The Mysteries of Verbena House, or Miss Bellasis Birched for Thieving* began its printing history with a price tag of four pounds. However, the price of the work soon settled down to two pounds and stayed within that range.[31] Length was a factor in the price; *The Romance of Lust,* a four-volume set of roughly six hundred pages, cost between four and twelve pounds. Even very short works such as *Kate Handcock,* which would be considered a pamphlet today, went for three shillings.[32] *The Pearl,* in a complete set, cost eighteen pounds, and *My Secret Life* came exorbitantly priced at forty to one hundred pounds.[33] No other work can compare with *My Secret Life* for length, rarity, or price. Supposedly, six copies of the eleven-volume set (three hundred pages per volume) were published in Amsterdam and then smuggled back into England. While *My Secret Life* is an exception, the magnitude of the outlay for such a work sets the outside boundary for prices. Pornography revolved around high-end goods meant for the luxury classes. The gulf between working-class wages and pornography prices made even the shoddiest pamphlets unobtainable for the majority of workers. The middling classes could afford such pamphlets easily, but, given budgets of five to eight pounds for books and newspapers per year, the longer, illustrated works still represented a financial sacrifice.[34]

As illustrations and photographs became more available, they supplemented the already established market. Buyers could purchase pictures to accompany the literary works, but the illustrations typically added 50 percent to the original price. The book *Child Love, or, Private Letters from Phyllis to Marie* cost two pounds twelve shillings, and the eight accompanying aquarelles cost one pound ten shillings.[35] Watercolors and etchings could also be bought individually. Sets of four hand-colored etchings entitled "Four Ages of Life," "The Mystified Peasant Girl," and "By Operation of the Holy Spirit" were priced at two pounds, while a set of twenty-six etchings representing the various letters in the alphabet cost only four pounds. Individual watercolors such as "Artificial Impregnation," "Between Brother and Sister," and "The Human Pyramid" cost one pound apiece. Clearly, illustrations went to the same exclusive audience as had literary works.

Photographs followed the same price limitations. "Pissing Women" came as a bargain at eighteen cabinet portraits for under a pound, but most were more expensive. For instance, twenty cabinet photographs showing "The Negro's Revenge. Young wife violated by Negro in revenge for cruelties by master" cost $6.25, or over a pound.[36] Twenty cabinets of "Green Fruit," which featured two girls aged eight and nine, cost fifteen shillings.[37] Twenty larger photographs of "Flagellation" cost one pound ten shillings, while the smaller *cartes de visites* could be bought at bargain prices because of their reduced size. While it could have created new markets by offering sexual commodities to the decreasing portion of society that remained illiterate, the price kept visual pornography from all but the wealthy.[38]

Even the development of mail order pornography did not alter patterns of access. Mail order pornography added to the demands for literacy and wealth a number of skills not commonly available. Most people did not use the mail to conduct the business of living. Working-class accounts were paid in cash (or in credit), rather than with checks, money orders, and stamps. The development of installment plans allowed workers to afford big purchases, but dealers of pornography did not work on installments. The working classes seldom mailed letters before the exigencies of World War I forced them to do so, let alone correspond overseas for business transactions. Furthermore, postal confiscations, pornographers' frequent moves, and the lack of assurance that letters would reach distributors meant that the purchased goods might never arrive. Any money spent on pornography needed to be money that could be easily written off as a loss.

The working and lower-middle classes probably lost ground when it came to learning about works of pornography. It became harder to search out pornography even if one had the resources and tenacity. Pornographers did not post notices in public places, did not hand out notices to passersby in London, and did not advertise in working-class newspapers. Instead they handed out catalogues to tourists in the streets of Paris and mailed out catalogues to likely buyers. The pornographers used the social register and the society pages to pick these clients. As the Home Office lamented, "The advertisements in question were addressed to adult persons in the upper ranks of Society, some of them ladies, whose names and addresses had apparently been obtained from Directories."[39] Pornographers also sent catalogues "to officers in the Army and Volunteer force, whose names and addresses are more easily attainable by means of the Army List."[40] Pornographers at the end of the century sent out masses of notices, but with a measure of discrimination; they mailed out notices to those with a degree of wealth and distinction.[41] These catalogues described literary works or, if they offered photographic materials, sent contact sheets like the set of "artist's models" in figure 10 for a small fee. Consumers could specify the image and size, then have the photographs discreetly mailed in a plain brown wrapper to their homes.

Although a number of factors that affected access changed profoundly in the late nineteenth and early twentieth centuries, pornography continued to be a product for the elite. Literacy rates went up, poverty diminished, and consumer goods began to flourish, but these were incremental changes that did not transform the social structure or the economics of class relations.This type of literature remained widely unaffordable before 1914 for the struggling working classes and for the middling classes who labored to differentiate themselves from mere workers. The elite had a very different life. Eric Hobsbawm wrote:

> The main body of the "solid," undoubted middle class was not large: in the early 1900s less than 4 per cent of people dying in the United Kingdom left behind them more than 300 pounds worth of property (including houses, furniture, etc.). Yet even though a more comfortable middle class income—say 700–1000 pounds a year—was perhaps ten times as high as a good working class income, it could not compare with the really rich, let alone the super rich.[42]

Pornography belonged primarily to the upper 4 percent. Pornography was not created equal and it held no pretensions to egalitarianism. Instead, it stood as an artifact for a specific part of society—those with wealth, education, social advantages, and even some form of political power. The people who bought pornography needed to be literate, sometimes not only in English but also in Greek, Latin, or French. They needed to be wealthy. They needed to know how to use the mails and write letters, checks, and money orders. In many ways, the meaning of privilege went beyond these simple skills and into a variety of hidden advantages. Political power and social position separated the truly elite, like the unnamed MP whose order for pornography stopped the policy

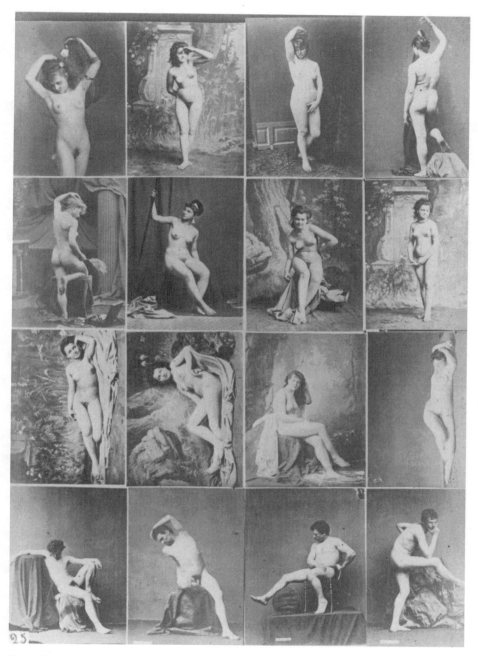

FIGURE 10. Photographs from a catalogue of artist's models. With permission of the Kinsey Institute.

of tracking users, from those who merely had advantages, like Flewelling (the unfortunate man who will only be known for his taste in ballet girls).

The political economy of privilege allowed those in the upper stratum of society access to pornography if they chose. While many in the nineteenth century lived in a world limited by squalid housing, adulterated food, and insecure employment, the few—defined by both wealth and social position—lived in an altogether different world defined by luxury. These factors make Lazenby's accusations against the "piggywiggys" seem more than justified. Only a small proportion of Victorian and Edwardian society met the criteria necessary for either joining moral societies or enjoying immoral practices.

Literary Patterns: The Fiction and The Fetish

The Pearl marks the transition to a new brand of pornography. In spite of the diversity of genres located within its pages—from limericks and nursery rhymes to parodies of the latest news and gossip columns—six serialized novels formed the backbone of *The Pearl*. Each of these novels had a specific fixation; for example, "Sub-Umbra, or Sport Among the She-Noodles" focused on youngsters; "Miss Coote's Confession" centered on flagellation; and "La Rose d'Amour" detailed the search for the most beautiful virgins to deflower. After establishing the main sexual idea, each novel explored permutations on the theme. The serialization of these novels did little to break up their continuity, because the structure of the works relied upon repetition rather than plot or character development. Contemporaries like Ashbee noticed the transformation:

> We cannot fail to perceive that while in the former books [like *Fanny Hill*] the characters, scenes and incidents are natural, and the language not unnecessarily gross, those in the latter are false, while the words and expressions employed are of the most filthy description. CLELAND'S characters—Fanny Hill, the coxcomb, the bawds and debauchees with whom they mix, are taken from human nature, and do only what they could and would have done under the very natural circumstances in which they are placed; whereas the persons in the latter works are the creations of a disordered brain, quite unreal, and what they enact is either improbable or impossible. Thus, the nature of English erotic fiction has been changed.[43]

This later pornography did not necessarily become more violent or explicit. In spite of the diatribes against these works as "creations of a disordered brain," "quite unreal," and "improbable and impossible," late nineteenth-century pornography introduced a number of important transitions toward the development of modern pornography. While Carrington and his mentors continued to reissue older works (particularly because they could avoid paying an author), new works that appeared after the 1880s became more stylized and formulaic.

Pornographic medical tracts, philosophical discussions, and ethnographies dwindled, while descriptive narratives that superficially followed the rough form of the novel flourished. Often these narratives started with only a minimal explanation of the characters and a loose justification. Plot, setting, characterization, tension, resolution, and denouement, as characteristics of the novel, became less important and sometimes vanished altogether as descriptions of sex scenes emerged as the basis of the works. By stripping away literary features of the novel, the authors created room to explore sexuality in ever greater detail. These texts emphasized the consumption of desire for its own sake, rather than in the quest for "liberty" or the "scientific" truth about sexuality. The new emphasis allowed pornography to focus on the world as a locus of sexuality while ignoring the social repercussions of that sexuality. In essence, it recreated the world to fit into newly imagined possibilities for sex, transforming both the narrative process and the subject matter.

While critics have documented this change, they generally explain it as the emergence of "bad" pornography. To use the example of *The Romance of Lust* (1879), Ashbee believed that "it contains scenes not surpassed by the most libidinous chapters of *Justine*. The episodes, however, are frequently improbable, sometimes impossible, and are as a rule too filthy and crapulous."[44] Henry Miles derided *The Romance of Lust* by writing that "the construction of the book, however, is so poor that attempted 'psychological interpretations' may well be stumbling over bad grammar" and that "it takes a special sort of genius to create such a ludicrous situation in such a manner, though a number of Victorian novelists writing in the public domain were able to do so."[45] Finally, Steven Marcus felt that *The Romance of Lust* demonstrated that "inside of every pornographer there is an infant screaming for the breast from which he has been torn."[46] Rather than stumbling over its grammar, its improbability, and its infantile desires, we can examine how *The Romance of Lust* and works like it redirected the process of telling stories about sexuality. Perhaps the apparent weaknesses of *The Romance of Lust* as a novel increased its efficacy as a work of pornography.

The Romance of Lust chronicles a child's growth to adulthood through his sexual awakening and activities. That description, however brief, fully describes the plot, character motivation, and drama of the work. Written as a series of loosely tied vignettes, *The Romance of Lust* mainly concerns itself with penetration. The following example is taken from the middle of the book:

> She took her mouth from off my prick, and paused a moment; then again applied her finger to my fundament, and made it gently penetrate as far as it would go. The previous pause had evidently been for the purpose of moistening her finger with saliva that it might slip in easily. I was delighted to find that she had come to this, but pretending ignorance, I stopped my proceedings to ask her what she was doing to my bottom, which could give me such exquisite delight.
>
> "It is my finger, my dear Charles, my late husband was always delighted with my doing this, and used also to add greatly to my pleasure by doing the same."
>
> "Shall I do so to you, dear mamma?"
>
> "Oh, yes, my darling boy; moisten your finger first and then do it in my bottom-hole, as you have been doing it in my cunt."
>
> "But I think I can do both at the same time, they are so close together."
>
> "You are a delightful darling; do so, and it will be double pleasure to me."
>
> So I immediately commenced to postillion her to her and my extreme gratification. We soon spent with the utmost delight, and both swallowed all we could get, continuing our suctions until the passions of both were again excited. I now declared that I must fuck her again in the kneeling position.[47]

In spite of the reference to "mamma," Charles is not the woman's son. Instead, the incestuous nickname serves to heighten the appeal of penetration by framing the May-December union with an additional piquancy. The passage explains, expands, and reinforces the meanings of the same act that has been described in the first three-hundred-odd pages. Each of the hundreds of vignettes explains that lubrication assists in insertion, the insertor should move gently to let the hole adjust, both women and men can penetrate and be penetrated, and tongues, fingers, clitorises, and penises can penetrate anuses, mouths, and vaginas. Penetration has become the essence of sexual activity. New characters offer new opportunities for penetration, and as each character follows the rules laid out in the text, each finds fulfillment.

The book details the act of penetration for five hundred pages. Aunts, uncles, boys, girls, parents, sisters, friends, and governesses penetrate and are penetrated. The most homey of acts, walking on the beach, going to school, making new friends, talking with family, all lead to penetration. And all penetration is equally good. As this passage describes, oral, anal, and genital stimulation give an interchangeable pleasure with little distinction between them; pleasure can only be doubled, or tripled, with multiple acts. The continued concentration on penetration heightens its importance and creates a formula for its meaning. Through sheer repetition, penetration dominates the sexual world. Each vignette is composed of introduction and culmination, and in each case the process builds only to repeat itself. By focusing on a particular sexual act, the work endows it with extraordinary power. *The Romance of Lust* and similar texts gave organs, individuals, social relationships, and locations meaning in terms of their relationship with the act.

The Pearl's Christmas Annual (three pounds, six colored plates) further abbreviated characterization, setting, and plot. The following monologue opens chapter 1:

> Past four o'clock in the afternoon, and I have only just gotten out of bed; how I have slept since that little devil of a Fuckatilla left me at 7 a.m.! Well, I must dress and make up as if just arrived so as to deceive the old mother, it won't do for her to find out I've slept with the pretty Susan all night. Ha, what a clever little schemer she is to suggest that she would sleep in my bed to air it against the morrow, when I was to return to town, and then let me know so I could let myself in after the old woman was gone to bed. By Jove! I think it is well aired now, we've been fucking in it like steam, spending the old year out and the new year in; I believe our first fuck ended in a delightful spend on both sides just as Big Ben struck twelve. Now I'll make haste then ring for Mrs. Childings, and order supper; what a happy thought that of mine, promising to send her down to my aunt's at Richmond, as soon as I got back, she will stay there all night, and Fuckatilla will fetch her cousin to help, the same as on Christmas Eve, that ever to be remembered Christmas Eve, it beats all the fun I've ever had, but my name's not Priapus Bigcock if we don't top it tonight.[48]

As Henry Miles pointed out, the punctuation (or lack of it) makes ambiguous who did what to whom. The anecdote, "ringing in the New Year," seems forced if not physically impossible. The names of the characters, Fuckatilla and Priapus Bigcock, are satires. However, each of these flaws also sketches out the main point of the matter, "fucking like steam." The brief passage introduces the major components of the work, including fucking with many women, in many places, in ever growing numbers. This work has no pretensions to the form of the novel. Instead, it clearly marks its intention by putting aside all unnecessary details that would interfere with the continual narration of the heterosexual fuck.

Penetration was not the only focus in these works; writers applied the same pattern of formulaic descriptions to a wide range of subject matters. For instance, *Amorous Adventures of a Japanese Gentleman* fixated on Asian sexuality, while *Flossie, a Venus of Fifteen* focused on young girls. *The Birchen Bouquet* and *With Rod and Bum, or Sport in the West End of London* (the latter by the pseudonymous Ophelia Cox) explored flagellation. *Stays and Gloves. Figure-Training and Deportment by means of the discipline of Tight Corsets, narrow High-heeled Boots, clinging Kid Gloves, Combinations, etc., etc.* is self-explanatory, as is *Big Bellied Nelly.*[49] "Negresses," slaves, daughters, and boys; penetration, flagellation, dominance, and torture; shoes and corsets, big breasts and white skin— all became subjects fit for extended discussion. Regardless of the focus, each work used a similar process to build intensity and saturate the subject with importance. The curtailing of the narrative form in favor of the elaboration of the subject allowed for a growing focus on the specific desire.

The subjects of these permutations ranged from routine sex acts like penetration to supposedly more perverse fantasies. *Frank and I* (1902) offered a neat solution to the compounded problem of homosexual, pederast, and flagellant desires. Published shortly after the Oscar Wilde trials, it circumvented the conflicts around male-male desire by displacing the penchant for boys onto girls and by incorporating sadism into the more socially acceptable practice of discipline. By having "Frances" introduced as "Frank," an orphaned boy who has misbehaved and needs to be punished, the text uses the classic ruse of mistaken identity to dodge the complications of desire. Of course, once Charles, the narrator, discovers Frances's identity, she dons outfits befitting her sex. And, of course, she continues to misbehave, allowing the narrative to focus on flagellation—the sexual predilection that ultimately dominates the text. While the text begins with complicated, overlapping desires, it soon submerges these complexities into the act of flagellation. The narrative develops a multipart, highly detailed model for flagellation that involves having Charles undress the flagellant, lay her across his lap, and apply his hand or birch, with intercourse as the denouement.

> I turned up her pretty, blue satin skirt all round, as high as I could get it, rumpling and creasing it a great deal: then, to lengthen out the pleasure, I slowly rolled up, one after the other, her lavender-scented,

lace-flounced, snowy petticoats, and her delicate silk chemise. Then I stopped, and gazed at the rounded contour of her bottom, which was only hidden by her dainty lace-frilled drawers of the finest linen; and owing to the curved position in which she was lying across my knees, the thin garment clung closely to the hemispheres of plump flesh, and I thought I could see a pink tinge showing through the filmy material. Unfastening the drawers, I pulled them entirely off her legs, and looked with glistening eyes and intense admiration, at her broad, deep, lovely milk-white bottom, displayed in all its naked beauty upon my lap. I also glanced with pleasure at her plump, well-rounded thighs, and her beautifully formed legs which were looking most charming in the tightly-fitting pearl-grey silk stockings she was wearing. Her garters were of dark blue satin, and her little feet were encased in high-heeled shoes of maroon-coloured morocco leather.

The description of Fanny's attire slows down the action and concentrates the focus on the upcoming scene of flagellation. The text continues to explain the preparations for several paragraphs before describing the act itself:

I spanked her very slowly, and she winced at the hot slaps, every one of which printed a five-petaled red flower on the lily-white field; and as her bottom grew redder the smart increased and she began to wriggle in pain, quite in the old style. But I experienced a more exquisite sensation of sensual pleasure than I had ever before; because on this occasion, her cool, soft, naked belly was rubbing against the uncovered tip of my upstanding prick.[50]

The scene ends in intercourse, but in this narrative intercourse became subsumed to flagellation through cursory, rather than detailed, description. The detailing of flagellation—from the type of shoes worn to the type of marks left on the woman's posterior—framed this sexual act. Rather than deadening the narrative, the formulaic pattern deepened the intensity and meaning of the narrative's fetish. The bared buttocks, the naked legs, and the averted face became symbolic of sexual desire.

In another Edwardian narrative, the focus shifted to incest. The issues of age, blood, and social class that dominated more respectable literature offered fertile ground for transgression in *Sweet Seventeen: the True Story of a Daughter's Awful Whipping and its Delightful if Direful Consequences* (1910). When Mr. Sandcross realizes his daughter's budding sexuality, he finds an excuse to whip her:

an act that culminates in sexual intercourse, beginning a long-term sexual relationship. On discovering it, the mother dies of shock, leaving the two alone to carry on. Oddly, the endplate illustrates the two lovers gazing at each other over an enlarged skull, presumably that of the deceased mother.

This work uses a series of oppositions to heighten the implications of the incestuous acts. By overemphasizing her purity, youth, and submission and his deviance, advanced age, and domination, these binaries amplify the differences between daughter and father. As they enter into an overtly sexual relationship, she becomes younger and more babyish, and he becomes older and more fatherly. Even the descriptions of her deflowerment emphasize these differences: "One fierce lunge and [her hymen] gave way, as Sandcross felt every inch of his huge fatherly organ nipped by the sore, excoriated lips of his daughter's virgin cleft."[51] By enhancing the "fatherly" state of his huge organ and the "daughterly" state of her virgin cleft, the text establishes and reinforces their oppositions. After intercourse, he tucks her into bed as if she were "his tiny little baby girlie," and she returns to a state of apparent purity: "As her nervous system gradually reverted to its normal state of quietude, so the babyish look returned to her violet eyes, and her face was as full of innocence as heretofore."[52] Through this pattern of infraction and reconstitution, the text heightens the difference between father and daughter and creates a ceremony of incest that it continues to play and replay.

The system of references in this text built upon a structural tension within the culture—the taboo of incest—which it accentuated to create excitement. Social institutions like family, which had long provided a structural framework for sexuality in daily life, offered an opportunity for sexual titillation in pornographic texts. Playing with social barriers and taboos allowed the transgression of social hierarchies without the reordering of society. Likewise, in images like "The Negro's Revenge. Young wife violated by Negro in revenge for cruelties by master" and in catalogue pages like "The Bijoux 118" (figure 11), pornographers offered customers images that temporarily inverted social barriers but ultimately reinforced the symbolic importance of race. Whereas mid-century pornographic works explored the "realities" of biology and nature, these later works wholeheartedly reimagined reality. (Brothers and sisters posed for pornographic photographs. All middle-class paragons secretly longed for vice. A father and daughter could assume a marriage-like relationship after killing the mother.) The stripped-down narrative process allowed for the intense fixation on a specific aspect of sexuality, whether apparently "normal" or seemingly more "perverse."

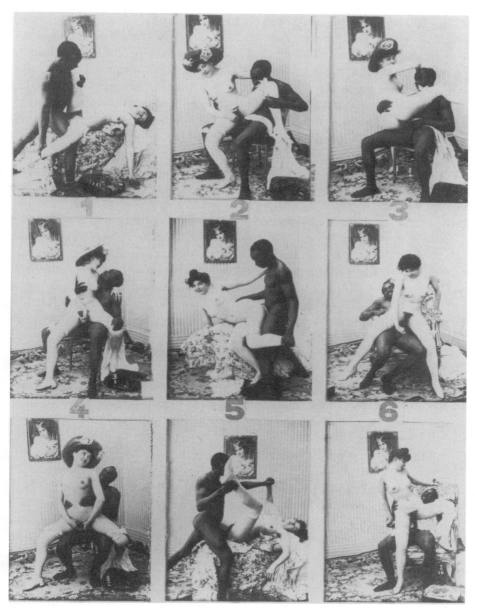

FIGURE 11. Photographic catalogue: "Bijoux 118." With permission
of the Kinsey Institute.

The overemphasis on a specific in pornography echoed the emerging Freudian conceptualization of sexual fetishism.[53] In Freud's work, fetishism was defined by the qualities of exclusivity and fixation. According to Freud, "a certain degree of fetishism is thus habitually present in normal love."[54] But while everyone focused on certain qualities, fetishists inappropriately fixated on normally nonsexualized objects like shoes and hair. "There are some cases which are quite specially remarkable—those in which the normal sexual object is replaced by another which bears some relation to it, but is entirely unsuited to serve the normal sexual aim."[55] In Freudian theory, boys focused on inappropriate sexual objects to avoid the real object of their sexual desires, the mother's genitals. The fixation became repressed during childhood and emerged in adulthood as a fetish for the object.[56] According to Freud, the fixation became a perversion "in its relation to the normal. If a perversion, instead of merely appearing alongside the normal sexual aim and object, and only when circumstances are unfavorable to them and favorable to it—, if, instead of this, it ousts them completely and takes their place in all circumstances—if, in short, a perversion has the characters of exclusiveness and fixation—then we shall usually be justified in regarding it as a pathological symptom."[57] Freud separated normal sexual development from perverted sexual development by the qualities of exclusivity and fixation.

However, if normal is not "natural" but the result of social conditioning, then the insistence on a certain type of sexuality could itself be a fetish—"a perversion that has the characters of exclusiveness and fixation." Descriptions of "normal" women in late nineteenth-century British pornography begin to sound quite perverse when read in succession:

> But what perfection of form; firm bust; tiny waist; swelling hips; massive spherical posteriors; wee feet and hands; satin, fair skin; masses of auburn hair; a tip-tilted, thoroughly Anglo-Saxon nose; with rose leaf nostrils palpitating at the least emotion; a small mouth with pulpy red lips, and her father's perfect dentition.[58]

> Lucia was just a little above the middle height for girls. She had a most lovely figure, vith [sic] beautiful arms, hands, and feet. The lines of her bosom were singularly beautiful, she was full there without being too plump, and her breasts seemed things of life. She had a waist naturally small but not in the least waspish, and from this her hips gradually and gracefully expanded to a most exquisite fulness [sic]. Her head was small, and beautifully poised on a throne of snow. But her face was too exquisite.[59]

Miss Rosa Redquim was indeed a sprightly beauty of the Venus height, well proportioned in leg and limb, full swelling bosom, with a graceful Grecian type of face, rosy cheeks, large grey eyes, and golden auburn hair, lips as red as cherries, and teeth like pearls, frequently exhibited by a succession of winning smiles, which never seemed to leave her face.[60]

The insistence on a cultural type of beauty—medium height, well proportioned, postpubescent, ethnically Anglo-Saxon, with good teeth and small hands and feet—catered to a very specific desire. Photographs of such normative "beauties" showed them as physically matching the literary descriptions: medium-breasted, firm-bellied, round-hipped (figure 12). Soft-focus photography erased dimpling, stretch marks, and blemishes to create an image of purity and to make the women's bodies more luminous. In some photos, the light skin bleeds into the background, creating a bodily halo. Poses reinforced

FIGURE 12. Photograph: Reclining woman. With permission of the Kinsey Institute.

FIGURE 13. Photograph: Woman with garland.

the symbols of classicism, as did props such as garlands, grapes, urns, baths, or togas (figure 13). Both soft-focus photography and classical props deepened the normative implication of such images.[61]

Similarly, the obsessive interest in varieties of heterosexual intercourse appears quite exhaustive (if not exhausting). *The Horn Book* lists over sixty-two positions in part 1 alone that are appropriate for a man and woman. These include, to name the first twenty, the ordinary, the inseparables, ordinary legs up, the baker, the St. George, the ordinary reversed, the back view, the stork, the view of the low-countries, speared sideways, a woman's prayer, a man's prayer, a woman's resignation, the elastic cunt, winnowing on the belly, winnowing on the back, the wheelbarrow, the wheelbarrow reversed, the trot, and impalement backwards.[62] Innumerable photographs (such as figure 14, in which a former owner retouched the man's lower hand) illustrated standard and more exotic positions. The intense focus on these "normal" sex acts allowed for the heavy scripting of heterosexual intercourse at the same time that it expanded the importance of the act.

FIGURE 14. Photograph:
Woman (in bonnet) and man.
With permission of the Kinsey
Institute.

Sexologists like Freud developed minute definitions for sexual pathologies that demarcated and fragmented sexuality into its components.[63] In part,
they developed these models of pathology from pornographers like Sacher-
Masoch.[64] (The term *sadomasochism* memorializes him and de Sade.) And the
converse appears true as well: Pornographers incorporated the taxonomical
model back into their works and into their catalogues. In one catalogue that
reads like a list of pathologies by Krafft-Ebing, Carrington promised illumi-
nation on the topics of "nympho-maniacs, onanists, exhibitionists, fetishists,
necrophilists, practicers of bestiality, Sadists, Masochists and erotic maniacs in
general; both male and female."[65]

Pornographers not only adopted the pathologizing terms of sexologists
but also marketed texts to meet the newly defined desires of their clients.

Carrington suggests in his extended advertisement for *Records of Personal Chastisement* that "there exist male 'flagellomaniacs' who crave 'intensely for the flogging of women'; and there are 'debauchees from whom poor girls earn a few pounds by submitting to a flogging.' If such people exist they have no doubt been eager buyers of this curious volume, for they can find therein everything necessary to arouse their peculiar propensity." [66] If the title did not whet the flagellator's interest, the description surely did. Pornographers used such descriptions to sell works, sight unseen, to their clientele. Normal and perverse desires were defined against each other and marketed the same way.

Photographic pornography followed suit. Begun in the 1840s, it featured a wide variety of naked women from the raw-boned to the delicate, from the sensual to the sad. However, early technical processes limited the extent of the trade; daguerreotypes, for example, were based on a process that gave only one image per exposure. By the 1880s, technical developments allowed multiple images to be printed from the same negative. As a result, photographic pornography gained momentum. These later photographs displayed a wide variety of sexual acts, as catalogues can testify. Photographic pornographers offered images using descriptions that ranged from the casual "The gipsey girls" and "Lesbian Love" to the more prosaic "Fanciful Orgies in Paris. Two Evas and one Adam" and "Pleasure and Plays at the Antique Olympia—man and youth kiss and embrace—fellatio—and then youth presents his hinder for sodomy." [67] Customers ordering "Two Evas and one Adam" could buy black and white photographs or hand-colored photos like the following one in figure 15. In this image, the pornographer added touches of color like the red to the vaginal lips and blue to the stockings to privilege certain aspects of the representation. Red vaginal lips enhanced key ideas and emphasized the penetrative penis.

In many of these images, photographers arranged models at revealing angles to emphasize the curves that two-dimensional representations tended to flatten. Pelvises were thrust forward to emphasize the genitals. Furthermore, by carefully framing the shots so that genitals were situated roughly at the middle of the image, photographers made them the focal point. The same technique worked whether featuring sodomy and masturbation (figure 16) or fellatio (figure 17). Pornographers placed the models in the artificial light and against the artificial backdrops in studios to accentuate the shadows and details of the body. In figure 17, the photographer placed the two men before a screen of the seaside to reinforce the Mediterranean feel evoked by a title like "Antique Olympia." Customers who wanted less contextualized images

FIGURE 15. Photograph: Ménage, two women and one man. With permission of the Kinsey Institute.

could order the "full moon," which excluded all unnecessary "props" like torsos and limbs.

The range of images from the period testifies to the breadth of sexual tastes. Photographs and catalogues allowed consumers to define their inclinations in ever greater specificity, often according to the latest taxonomical models developed by sexologists: "Full Moons. Pregnant Women. Young Children. The Sins of the Priest. Newest and rarest for pederasts. The Sexual Act in Every

FIGURE 16. Photograph:
Ménage, two men and one
woman. With permission of the
Kinsey Institute.

Manner showing smart boots, fine underwear, and elegant petticoats."[68] Images such as these broke sexuality and the body into their component parts
and offered consumers the opportunity to focus intensely on the objects of
their desires.

In the process, pornographers and sexologists removed sexuality from
its political and social context.[69] This transformation may account for the "improbable" and "impossible" labels applied to pornography by contemporary
and later critics. The impulse to represent reality had waned in writings about
sexuality with the demise of scientific pornography, leaving instead a world
full of symbols waiting to be sexualized. In another catalogue, the description
intensified the meanings of race by using signs of a racial system that no longer
existed:

FIGURE 17. Photograph:
Seaside fellatio. With permission
of the Kinsey Institute.

Slaves. Negresses. A Young planter orders one of them to take off all
her clothes. He then seats himself on horseback upon her, chastifying
[*sic*] her violently with a whip, and when the climax of his sensual evo-
lutions has been reached, she has to pump his penus [*sic*] with her big
lips whereby she finally receives as her reward a full avalance [sic] of
her master's sperm in her mouth. $6.25 for 20 cabinet portraits.[70]

In the eighteenth century, a consumer could buy a female slave—could in fact
buy a Negress. However, by 1903, at the time of the catalogue's publication,
slavery had been effectively outlawed. Nonetheless, the description puts the

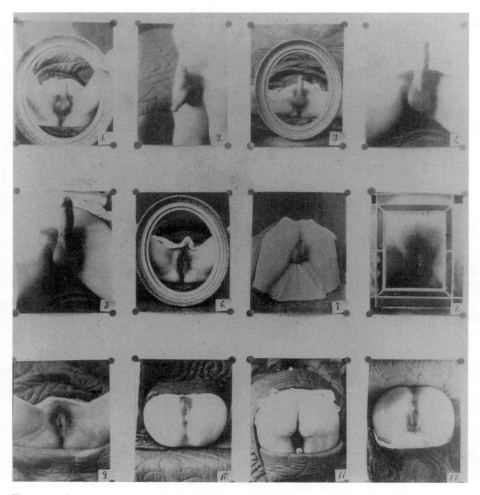

FIGURE 18. Catalogue: "La Lune à 1 mètre." [The moon at 1 meter] With permission of the Kinsey Institute.

idea of slavery onto the flesh of the individual woman whose picture had been taken. The description encouraged a transference of imagined qualities like blackness, whiteness, bondage, domination, luxury, and pain onto the image. The catalogue built upon all of these meanings and gave them precedence over contemporary social relationships. Other vendors' cursory descriptions still advertised their works according to specific fancies. The catalogues cast women's bodies into types like young girls aged eight to twelve, "girl dressed as domino seduced," and "in a Spanish Bordel featuring fleshy legs and national costumes."[71] Perhaps the image featured women photographed in a Spanish bordello, but probably not. It did not really matter as long as the consumers who bought them subscribed to the reality of them.

Marx described this process as commodity fetishism, a perversity arising out of the marketplace. For Marx, an inappropriate devotion to commodities concealed the economic processes that went into their production. Marx stated that commodity fetishism occurred when the signification of the commodities mattered more than either the labor that went into their production or their use-value; the overemphasis on the social meaning of an object sheared the object from its source and its purpose.[72] According to Marx, the process of commodity fetishism allowed people to value goods as if they were objects of devout significance on their own, rather than signifying something larger—labor and use. Applying Marx's commodity fetishism to pornography would mean that the pornography itself obscured the social relations that produced it, and, indeed, the obfuscation of real social relations in the representations went hand-in-hand with an obfuscation of the fictional nature of these works. Rather than recognizing the artistry of the authors, publishers pitched these works as "true"; as they portrayed ever less probable scenarios, they grew ever more insistent that they represented reality. The subtitle of *Sweet Seventeen* reads "The True Story of a Daughter's Awful Whipping." An advertisement for *Frank and I* states that "everything set forth reads as if perfectly true, and there is no doubt in our mind but what the pleasant and amorous incidents recounted in these pages did really take place."[73] Passing fictions off as facts was a component of commodity fetishism but not the whole of it. The process of commodity fetishism rested both on the obfuscation of the relationship between producers and artifacts and the process by which artifacts gained a life and a meaning of their own.

As Michael Taussig explains commodity fetishism:

> Fetishism denotes the attribution of life, autonomy, power, and even dominance to otherwise inanimate objects and presupposes the draining of qualities from the human actors who bestow the attribution. Thus, in the case of commodity fetishism, social relations are dismembered and appear to dissolve into relationships between mere things—the products of labor exchanged on the market—so that the sociology of exploitation masquerades as a natural relationship between systematic artifacts.[74]

In fetishistic pornography, a variety of people, particularly women, but also children, the poor, and the foreign, became recreated objects that gained lives and meanings of their own. Black flesh, stout flesh, transvestite, and Spanish flesh had all been represented in a process that obscured the real actors involved in the production of photographs in favor of the imagined characters. With commodity fetishism of the flesh, the artificial became more important than the real, because the artificial flesh had assumed more meaning as an object than the real. In order to be fully understood, the labors of the woman and the photographer need to be reclaimed from the advertisement for "Slaves. Negresses" and the subsequent purchase of that imagined social and sexual relationship.

Thomas Richards has suggested that had Freud considered advertising, he might have found it shaping desires, doing the "dream work" of consumer society.[75] If so, then Freud's consideration of pornographic advertising might have provided a description of the dream work of sexuality and consumerism and the manner in which they reinforced one another. In these representations, the two meanings of fetishism converged. These representations fixated on an aspect of sexuality—a sexual fetish. Simultaneously, the marketplace emptied them of value and meaning, repackaged them, and sold them according to new signs—a commodity fetish. Like the black woman who became enslaved, the representations became unmoored from the real situations that the images purported to represent. Overlapping, reinforcing fetishisms thereby transformed pornography. Edwardian pornography did not attempt to reflect the natural world but tried instead to reorder the world to meet emerging desires. Through the commodification of sexual fetishism, pornography had entered into the marketplace of signification. Fetishism became a bazaar where pornographers advertised their wares according to an exclusive sexual fixation, whether upon a singular act, actor, or locale: "Lesbian Love," "Genital parts of girls, 15–25," "Monstrosities. Gibbous man and monstrous women," "Tommy Atkins at Transvaal and Cafir maid," and "stout women amusing themselves with candles" and bottles (figure 19).[76] As consumers purchased such photographs, the advertised meanings in the objects camouflaged the processes that went into their production. The dual fetishisms gave publishers a niche in the market and allowed them to contribute to the proliferation of seemingly individualized luxury goods.

Overlapping fetishisms appeared in the pornography not only as a process but also as subjects of desire. "La Rose d'Amour" from *The Pearl* followed the narrative patterns of other works, eliminating plot and character development in favor of a focus on sexual conquest embodied in a profusion of young virginal women. The story begins with an explanation of the narrator's circumstances. Suffering from severe ennui at seventeen, Louis throws off his

FIGURE 19. Photograph: Two women with bottle. With permission of the Kinsey Institute.

studies when his father departs for St. Petersburg, leaving him in the care of his uncle and wild young cousins (all of this is explained on page 1). The remainder of part 1 details the loss of his virginity. By part 2, he and his cousins have explored country pleasures and left for Paris; part 3 takes place at an orgy, and in part 4 Louis sets out for Vienna but he somehow arrives in St. Petersburg. In part 5, young Louis acquires a château with fifty beds and states, "I intended to travel till I had procured fifty of the handsomest women in the world to lay in them."[77] The remainder of the novel details the search for the fifty women and the narrator's sexual conquests of them.

From one very detailed description of intercourse in part 1, the explanations become briefer as the number of virgins deflowered at the head of his "virgin-destroyer" reach gargantuan proportions. As the conquests accrue, the descriptions of them become interspersed with orgies of consumption. The descriptive excess that was reserved for sexual acts at the beginning of the story begins to be applied to material objects: "The floor was covered with a carpet of purple velvet, stuffed with down. The rarest productions of the old masters adorned the walls, mirrors, framed in gold, depending from the beaks of birds wrought in silver, hung between the paintings. In each corner of the room stood a statue of one of the graces, in the bodies of which were set music boxes, made to discourse the sweetest music." And so on.[78]

The focus on articles for consumption and the focus on the conquest of women merge when Louis purchases a vessel to sail to Constantinople so that he can buy his own harem. Women become the ultimate commodity purchase. He buys them two at one time, ten at another, spending (and spending) in a binge of sexualized consumption. In the search for La Rose d'Amour, the Turk disappears (except as a purveyor), international politics give way to the international marketplace, and women and objects become interchangeable as items of fixation. As "La Rose d'Amour" grows more specified in orientation and more ritualized in narrative, it becomes increasingly commodity-oriented in subject. Sexuality and consumerism wrap around each other in a frenzy of desire.

Moreover, "La Rose d'Amour" is emblematic of the relationship between commodities and sexuality. Not only does the text merge sex and objects, but the work, itself, as part of material culture, fundamentally rested upon the intertwining of sex and objects through the marketplace of pornography. The growing emphasis on consumption resituated commodities in society. Objects amused, instructed, and educated; they filled shops, rooms, and lives. The opulence and luxury of Victorian and Edwardian life was expressed in material objects. The world of consumption created the idea that the individual could and should buy things to fulfill individual needs and desires. Just as Louis interchangeably bought objets d'art and women in "La Rose d'Amour" as luxury goods, so the readership could buy exactly what fit their fantasies. Pornography increasingly became about consuming pleasures, rather than mediating, changing, or documenting sexual tastes.

In *The Story of Seven Maidens,* the pleasures of owning magnify the object-status of those imagined. The title page falsely states that the narrative came from the unpublished papers of an eighteenth-century Spanish gentleman. The foreword continues the fiction: "We venture to put into press the following pages, as a document of real life and slavery as it was."[79] Having fictionalized the origin of the work, the editor (and perhaps author) can simultaneously rue and relish the sexual torture of women: "In those [these?] days of feminine claims and of 'Suffragettes,' it sounds strange listening to tales, no: true stories, a woman given away to the cruelty and lust of despotic owners."[80] The foreword places the narrative a hundred years in the past and onto Spanish (not English) society; the work can thus imagine the treatment of slaves in the West Indies without having to confront the social structure of slavery, the realities of the West Indies, or the meanings of slavery to England. The work creates a Fantasyland of sexual possibilities.

This imaginary world reverses the political changes of the nineteenth century. The abolition of slavery, the expansion of democracy, and the establishment of limited rights for women—all major developments in society—are overturned in the narrative. In an attempt to right the "natural" course of the world, the work returns to the world prior to the French Revolution: "For, truly, we live in a strange time. Every authority is shaken down, every thing is scoffed at, if respectable. Every day, we hear fearful news for peaceful citizens. New-England rebels against its mother country. French philosophers write very bad books, forerunners, I am afraid, of a bloody and savage revolt."[81] The narrator "foretells" the coming of the revolution, which he blames on the artificial laxity of owners toward slaves, particularly slave women. In this perspective, slave women are the cause of the social decay of the nineteenth century, since "Women are bold propagators of the poisonous crave for liberty."[82] Free men have an obligation to end these "uncivilized" tendencies in society by first beating and then fucking their slaves:

> Owners of servile flesh are badly in error when they think they must spare their brown lovers from the rod. They simply spoil them and degrade themselves. When you want to play the amorous game with a servant, you are perfectly entitled to it. But you must remain the master, and accordingly, the girl must come into your arms only after having had a good taste of the birch. I request my friend [*sic*] to try this method, if they do not use it already. Whipping a woman is always the easy road to her best love. A whipped girl will willingly do anything her master will care for. I mean a girl thoroughly whipped with good and biting lashes, and not for the fun of the thing.[83]

Without overt and repeated discipline to establish mastery, free men would become enslaved to slaves. The narrator explains that free men need to torture slave women to keep social relationships stable, because without torture these women overtake the souls of men. Torture forces women to accept their natural status as objects. Any act of empathy would be turned against the man—and give the woman the power to objectify. "Without being suspected, their soft mouths speak words of hate and revolt, their pretty hands give over plenty of tracts and libels of the worst kind alluded to before. And my friends laugh at that: they are only women, they said, women babbling of petticoats, gowns, jewels and so and so. A pretty bird, singing and dancing, what harm can they do? Moreover, they are true lovers of white men. You cannot believe a word of such a statement. Coloured women are simply our foes, even from childhood. Love is no more than perfidy, kisses and caresses are nothing than foul play."[84] Because of this perfidy, women need to be whipped before sex and made to kiss the rod afterward, so that both parties will remember who is object and who is owner. The author describes various appropriate physical and psychological torture; including burning the breasts and buttocks, placing nettles in the vulva and anus, whipping, raping daughters in front of mothers, and giving light-skinned women to dark-skinned men. The narrator tells separate stories of the seven maidenheads he plucked, and all describe corporeal and psychological torture.

This example takes pornographic consumerism to a logical extreme; this consumerism implied the unlimited ability to buy goods to meet desires, irrespective of the politics or morality of those desires. By recreating women as objects rather than actors, even when they were described as animate beings, the fetishistic process became an act of mastery. Of course, the extent of this mastery remained textual; consumers did not actually gain mastery over slaves through reading. But they did gain the perception of mastery and an imagined experience through the purchase of the book. While not all works explored torture, the extreme example of torture helps to highlight the crucial relationship between consumerism and sexuality at the end of the nineteenth century. The mutually reinforcing "dream work" of consumerism and sexuality encouraged the forging of identity based upon the desire for objects at the same time that it promised to liberate that identity from all constraints. As Thomas Richards has stated, "The experience of consumption had become all-encompassing, inseparable from the knowledge of self."[85]

This sense of self forged in the marketplace raised dismay, particularly when that market sold sexuality. The major sexual scandals of the period exacerbated fears about the extent of consumer culture. W. T. Stead, writing for the *Pall Mall Gazette*, exposed the sale of girls' virginity in London brothels in the series entitled "The Maiden Tribute of Modern Babylon."[86] According to Stead, these girls were thrown to London's rich to feed their insatiable appetites as surely as the youths of Athens had been thrown to the Minotaur. Stead raised anxieties about procurers and seducers, the London underworld, and a class of men—jaded, dissolute, and dissipated—who needed sacrificial virgins to rouse them from their sexual stupor. He also focused anxieties about the commodity culture in which the price of that virgin started at three pounds and ascended based upon the quality of the girl and her procurer. Stead's exposé mobilized feminist and socialist concerns about sexuality, helped raise the age of consent from thirteen to sixteen, and made homosexuality illegal in private as well as public. It also betrayed an underlying fear of rampant consumerism.

Other major scandals, like Oscar Wilde's trials in 1895 and the Cleveland Street Affair of 1889–1890, had a cross-class character that made the personal associations of those involved particularly suspect and further compounded the problems of "inverted" desire. Although Wilde's troubles began when he sued Lord Queensbury for libel, his trials quickly devolved into an examination of the morality of his art and then into the "gross indecency" of his relationships with younger, working-class men. Charles Parker, Alfred Woods, Edward Shelly, and Fredrick Atkins testified that Wilde served them elegant dinners, provided hotel rooms at the Savoy for trysts, and gave them expensive presents. Similarly, the Cleveland Street Affair involved messenger boys and postal clerks who prostituted themselves to rich men. These cross-class liaisons heightened tensions about the extent of consumer sexuality.[87] The overlap of sexuality and signs of wealth, like the champagne dinners and silver cigarette cases that Wilde gave to his working-class lovers, seemed indicative of a developing consumer culture of sexuality in which the sexual consumer could find all kinds of articles and individuals to meet his tastes (as feminists and socialists quite rightly pointed out). The contrast between the rich and the poor—Wilde's boys, the postal clerks in the Cleveland Street scandal, and Stead's orphaned girls—and the commodities that passed between them created an explosive situation that played out politically as well as sexually. This rift took place where physical desires merged with consumer longings.

Against this backdrop, the forging of sexual identity seemed particularly fraught with tensions and inequalities. One could not be an unmediated sexual subject any more than one could avoid the consumer economy. *Teleny, or Reverse of the Medal,* one of the first pornographic novels to explore homosexuality as an identity rather than a practice, confronted the convoluted relationship between sexuality and economics.[88] The narrator, Camille Des Grieux, understands himself as a homosexual. His sexual desire for men is innate, rather than situational, and his attempts to fight "his nature" end in embarrassment and tragedy. As he explains, "Thinking it over, however, I afterwards came to the conclusion that I had felt the first faint stimulus of love already long before, but as it had always been with my own sex, I was unconscious that this was love." In further explicating his desires, he elaborates the differences between physical desire and romantic love: "Withal, I never understood I loved men and not women. What I felt was that convulsion of the brain that kindles the eyes with a fire full of madness, an eager bestial delight, a fierce sensual desire. Love I thought was a quiet chafty [sic] drawing-room flirtation, something soft, maudlin and aesthetic, quite different than the passion full of rage and hatred which was burning within me. In a word, much more of a sedative than an aphrodisiac."[89] Even after he identifies his desires and finds a lover to explore them, a series of deaths points toward the impossibility of finding fulfilment in this world of moral constraints and economic plenty.

The novel paints equally dismal pictures of heterosexual and homosexual options, since both forms of sexual intercourse are tainted by economics. First, during his introduction to the Quartier Latin, Des Grieux watches as an old woman has a brain aneurism during an orgy: "Before we could understand what was the matter, the body of the tough old prostitute was bathed in blood. The cadaverous wretch had in a fit of lubricity broken a blood vessel, and she was dying—dying, dead! 'Ah! la sale bougre!' said the ghoul-like woman with the bloodless face. 'It's all over with the slut now, and she owes me.'"[90] The sound of the prostitute's death rattle vies with another whore's orgasmic shouts, while the old woman complains about money. The cacophonous combination of sex, death, and money sets the tone for later sexual encounters. During a second orgy, the "inverts" of Paris enjoy the splendors of Briancourt's house; the description rivals the excesses of "La Rose d'Amour," in which luxuries complemented sexual privileges. Against this backdrop of plenty, a second death occurs: A Syrian called only "The Spahi" is sodomized with a bottle smeared with pâté de foie gras. When the bottle breaks, the Spahi is internally injured. Rather than face scorn at the hospital, he settles his affairs and commits suicide.

In a final tragic encounter, Des Grieux's lover, Teleny, prostitutes himself to Des Grieux's mother to meet his debts. After Des Grieux discovers them in flagrante delicto, Teleny commits suicide. The resulting condemnation of Teleny is the final injustice, as Des Grieux makes clear:

> For if Society does not ask you to be intrinsically good, it asks you to make a goodly show of morality, and, above all, to avoid scandals. Therefore a famous clergyman—a saintly man—preached at that time an edifying sermon, which began with the following text: "His remembrance shall perish from the earth, and he shall have no name in the street."[91]

The conflicts among moralism, passion, and economics result not only in death but also in the erasure of Teleny's name. The inability to forge an alternative sexual identity in the face of such moralism conflicted with the promise of consumerism, which guaranteed so much. Conventional morality threatened to derail the self forged in the consumer workshop, while consumption threatened to undo the rigid moral codes of society.

The association of Wilde's name with *Teleny* makes the tragedy in the novel seem, in retrospect, a bit keener. The author's awareness of a misshapen love triangle in which desire, money, and morality replace conventional human actors foreshadows Wilde's own eventual denouncement. And while Wilde's name became synonymous with a queer identity after his trials, the arrival of a name, rather than its erasure, would offer little solace.[92] However, Wilde and his own lover, Lord Alfred Douglas, were not early activists fighting for gay rights but individuals muddling through; both used the whip-hand of money to their own advantage when necessary (and Douglas used the whip itself on an unfaithful Arab lover).[93] The desire to escape conventional morality did not provide an instantaneous escape from the straitjacket of conventional social dynamics.[94]

The simultaneous arrival of a gay identity—defined in part by sexologists—and a full-fledged consumer culture, if anything, magnified those dynamics. On one hand, sexual identity and the desire to create a sense of self unmediated by strict moral limitations warred with the proliferation of possibilities embodied by consumer goods. Pornography furthered the dissonance between emerging desire and contemporary morality by justifying the consumer's urges. On the other hand, consumerism often channeled sexually subversive tendencies into socially conservative arrangements. These took on geographical connotations as northern Europeans flocked to the shores of the Mediterranean to find a local culture more conducive to their passions. John Pemble notes that "it was easy for rich and educated Englishmen to make and maintain contact with young fishermen, gondoliers, *facchini, cocchieri,* urchins, sailors, and boulevard boys."[95] Men could enjoy cross-class associations with far less stigma than at home. However, the sexual tourist culture had hidden costs. In a final example that blurred fiction and fact, Wilhelm von Gloeden, a contemporary photographer, made his home in the Sicilian village of Taormina from the 1890s until the 1930s and turned the impoverished village into a site for his dream of a Grecian past and a homoerotic present. Von Gloeden played benefactor to the town, transforming it from a fishing village to a latter-day Greek polis. As his photographic studies demanded, the young men of Taormina portrayed of the gods and appeared dressed in togas or undressed. Upon visiting von Gloeden's home, tourists like Wilde, King Edward VII, Krupp, Vanderbilt, and Morgan could purchase "Illustrations of Theocritus and Homer"—his homoerotic images of these Sicilian youths. As von Gloeden became impoverished, he offered his studies to the European market via catalogues (using the marketing techniques developed by pornographers) as art and ethnographic studies. Regardless of von Gloeden's close and continued attachment to Taormina, his idylls entered the consumer marketplace, and the boys of the island became permanent icons of a fictional Mediterranean sexuality. His photography and his patronage transformed an obscure town and the rough peasant boys who peopled it into objects for sale in the marketplace.[96]

No matter how sexually subversive, the social dynamics of such arrangements—in which the rich could transform the poor to meet emerging sexual desires—remained conservative. Furthermore, the distinction between real life and fiction became tenuous when poverty encouraged individuals to play the roles assigned to them. In fictional portrayals like *The Story of Seven Maidens* and *Sweet Seventeen,* in photographic catalogues promising "Green Girls" and "Tommy Atkins at Transvaal and Cafir maid," and in real social arrangements like Wilde's and von Gloeden's, impulses that transgressed the boundaries of family, age, race, and class became reinstitutionalized in ways that eroticized inequality. While sexologists defined individuals according to their perversions, and authorities pursued them, pornographers offered solace in exchange for further sales. The sexual dream work of the marketplace offered up others to be consumed in the making of the self. The disenfranchised functioned as models for the desires of the wealthy, but these people could rarely see, let alone reinterpret, the goods—based upon them—that circulated in the marketplace. Just a few years later, however, such models apparently sprang to life with the emergence of a new mass market pornography. Women, people of color, the poor, and children began to access pornography, rather than simply act as the canvases for such projections. And with this, the problems implicit in the relationship between morality and consumerism became even more pronounced.

Chapter 4

Filth in the Wrong People's Hands

POSTCARDS AND THE EXPANSION OF PORNOGRAPHY

OFFICIAL WARNING

The Postmaster-General finds that during the past year there has been a large increase in the number of post-cards, principally of foreign manufacture, sent by post bearing pictorial designs of an objectionable and in some cases indecent character.[1]

The postmaster's warning came at the height of outbursts of "cartomania" and "cartophilia," as the love of postcards was then pathologized.[2] As the official warning makes clear, many of these postcards were objectionable, indecent, and obscene. Although generally overlooked by scholars interested in the more weighty matters of erotic literature and cinema, the simple postcard revolutionized pornography.

Pictures of "naked ladies" have become the staple of pornography in the twentieth-century world, but, before this outbreak of "cartomania," words—not images—dominated communication about sexuality, as shown in the three preceding chapters. During the 1890s, however, the situation reversed itself. Visual images, in the form of cheap ephemera, outstripped older forms of pornography. The emergence of a primarily visual pornography revised the medium of expression, although the content of pornography stayed remarkably similar. Visual pornography continued to focus on women as the objects of desire; ephemera deepened, rather than inaugurated, the imperial gaze; scatological humor, social commentary, and an undifferentiated sexuality returned to pornography after a brief hiatus with the end of radical pornographers. The continuity in themes, however, should not overwhelm the importance of changes in the medium.

The new medium transformed pornography by developing visual cues, by deepening an examination of corporeality, and by establishing the single image as synecdoche for sexuality. The transformation from literary to visual pornography also expanded the audience. The new widespread availability of pornography allowed the working classes, women, children, and people of color to be more than objects of representation: They became consumers of them as well. Although the new visual pornography built on the themes developed in older class-restricted pornography, the expanded dissemination of these ideas transformed their meanings by radically resituating them in society.

Concerned authorities, like the National Vigilance Association, the police, the Home Office, and the postal service, believed that the expanded audience for pornography and its social repositioning fundamentally disrupted an intrinsic moral order. They responded with increased vigilance in policing working-class space. However, the expanded audience appeared to believe that the consumption of pornography remained consistent with that same moral and social order. They apparently saw nothing wrong with images of "themselves." This rift in perceptions between the authorities and the audience highlights the hidden relationship between representation and social control at the end of the nineteenth century.

The Rise of the Pornographic Postcard and the Expansion of Access

Before the advent of ephemeral pornographyin the 1880s, high prices, low literacy rates, class-specific cultural referents, unequal patterns of state repression, and production and distribution patterns restricted the dispersal of pornography in British society. This meant that women, the poor, children, and people of color could only seldom use pornographic representations even though they were often the subjects of them. The class, gender, and racial bases for control of ideas of sexuality and for consumption of commodities stood as an accepted aspect of privilege. By the 1890s, however, these patterns of exclusion began to break down as the working classes gained access to pornography. Working-class pornography differed in format from older forms. The new forms included stereoscopes, mutoscopes, transparencies, and particularly postcards.

Postcards could be viewed at a single glance, rather than requiring time, the skills of literacy, the cultural referents of art and literature, or the languages of Greek, Latin, and French. Pornographic postcards required little financial sacrifice, even for the poor. Mutoscopes, stereoscopes, and transparencies contributed to the rise of the new form of pornography, but postcards quickly dominated. Postcards needed no viewing apparatus (unlike stereoscopes), no previous knowledge of what to look for or how to view an image (as some transparencies did), and as few or as many cultural references as a viewer brought. They also communicated both visually and through their ability to carry written messages, making the postcard uniquely important. The skills of literacy and the finances to travel would have limited the spread of the postcard, even during the emergence of a working-class leisure, if it had been meant only for written communication. But postcards, whether sexual or not, also functioned as a form of visual communication, a pleasure in themselves, worthy of collecting as well as mailing.[3] They were cheap, bright, multipurpose, and pervasive.

The postcard as a form of communication began sans images when "company" postal cards that functioned as business reminders and government-sponsored postal cards developed in the 1860s. By the 1870s, the postcard gained its emblematic visual form when tourist locations began to imprint their images on cards. Tourists bought, kept, and sent cards of their experiences. The images also worked on their own as pleasurable or informative representations when they were sold in packets and singles outside the locality they represented. The popularity of these vistas encouraged the proliferation of images; everything from the latest technological innovation to the most recent exposition became imprinted on postcards. Governments in Europe and across the Atlantic world aided the dispersal of postcards when they approved postcards bearing images as a form of mail. In 1886, postcards gained the full authorization of the Congress of the Universal Postal Union and could be sent internationally; slightly later, in 1894, Great Britain approved these rights.[4] While postcards were not entirely new in the 1890s, widespread postal approval during that time enormously expanded the mass-market culture based in communication.

Sexualized postcards were integrated with other types of postcards and with working-class life more generally. Vendors sold postcards in corner stores, in markets, in tobacconists' and in newsagents' shops, and on the street.[5] Both sexual and nonsexual postcards were bought and sold in the same places, often by the same people. One vendor, Mr. P. J. Huardel of High Holborn, had in his possession 27,550 postcards when the police raided his shop in 1903. Of his stock, 386 postcards were obscene; in this case, sexual postcards formed a small and relatively unimportant part of his stock. But of another vendor's stock of about 6,000 cards, the police found 2,287 problematic ones.[6] James H. McCann, a newsagent, had 70 obscene cards.[7] Other vendors dealt only in indecent wares. A traveling showman added a gimmick to his sales by vending cards through machines.[8] Obscene postcards mingled with other types of postcards in the shops and streets of working-class neighborhoods. Men, women, boys and girls, the native and the foreign, all sold—and were caught selling—indecent picture postcards. Postcards by the 1890s were ubiquitous, and bawdy postcards formed an important part of that commodity culture. Huardel defended himself by saying that he did not sell anything not found in other shops.[9] Indeed, these cards could be found throughout the British Isles and across the Atlantic world in Belfast, Liverpool, London, Manchester, Bristol, Glasgow, Montreal, Yarmouth, Dublin, and Paris. By 1908, the police, told to crack down on the trade of sexualized postcards, labeled the phenomenon "the picture postcard craze."[10]

Pornographic postcards became popular because they were inexpensive to produce, sell, and buy.[11] The invention of photolithography made cards easy to manufacture and lowered their prices. They could be bought "seven of the cards for sixpence," at twopence apiece, and for threepence a card.[12] At those prices, even the poorest could afford an occasional "peep" at such images. They were easy to market and more durable than other ephemera, as they were printed on heavier paper. Postcards appeared in everyday places because they were part of the everyday world rather than segregated by money, access, special places, or special occasions.

Postcards were both locally and internationally produced. While the Continent dominated the production and distribution of literary pornography and high-end photographs, postcards had more diverse origins. They were made and sold throughout Britain and Europe and had captions and publishing information in as many as four languages. By one estimate, Great Britain produced roughly fourteen million postcards, Germany roughly eighty-eight million, and France eight million in 1899. These figures seem paltry when compared with the number of postcards sent internationally a decade later.[13] About 140 billion postcards were sent worldwide between 1894 and 1919, while even more never reached the mails.[14] By 1909, eight hundred million postcards were sent in England alone each year.[15]

Major Themes in Pornographic Postcards

The images in sexual postcards ranged from Greek statues to children urinating, from sexualized images of food to scenes of seduction, from beautiful women to grotesques, from the exotic to the everyday.[16] These images came from a variety of sources and used tropes developed in libertine, scientific, and fetishistic pornography; older ideas were recycled and reformulated in this incipient form of mass communication. Postcards mocked the pretensions of the upper classes, as libertine literature had, and returned the protean body—the pissing, farting, sexualized body—to the gaze of the masses. Postcards of the exotic advertised the oddities of the empire. Postcards naturalized children's uninhibited sexuality. Fetishistic postcards unveiled a diversity of sexual practices to the mass gaze. In short, postcards reproduced preexisting beliefs through which Victorian and Edwardian society ordered people. This social order, which carefully ranked people by social class, gender, race, and age, gave privileges to those with greater status, including the ability to view others as objects. The development of postcards, however, increased access even if the new viewers only saw representations of "themselves." And yet, almost paradoxically, even as the postcards built on these preexisting social divisions, they also exposed these divisions to greater scrutiny and offered the possibility of a more egalitarian system of objectification.

Divisions in Victorian and Edwardian society become apparent in the post's treatment of the cards. Sexual postcards came in two forms: those that could be legally sent through the mails and those that could not. The legal postcards, in which models wore body stockings (figure 20), lingerie, or a great deal of white powder, used many of the same devices and visual elements as the proscribed ones but followed the strict code of covering women's pubic hair, genitals, and nipples. They hinted at what the illegal postcards showed.

Men's genitals were rarely alluded to in these cards, and few cards showed men at all. Illegal postcards could not be sent through the post and had to be placed in an envelope, handed to another person, or kept. However, the same criteria did not apply to postcards picturing "foreign" or "colonial" subjects, particularly people of color.[17] Pubic hair, genitalia, and nipples could pass by the censors if the card portrayed a colonial or foreign subject. The censors even allowed images of naked men to pass if the subjects were "natives." As a result, the cards both hypersexualized and desexualized the colonial and the foreign.

FIGURE 20. Postcard: Woman
in an indiscreet bodystocking.
With permission of the
Kinsey Institute.

People of color were displayed in a "natural" habitat. "Natives" came
from a variety of colonized and exoticized places over which Europeans and
Americans exerted dominion, including places in Central and South America
and the Caribbean, India, Africa, and Asia. Postcards featuring "natives" displayed them in their habitats by showing harem scenes, landscapes, and huts.
These nature-oriented postcards stood at the intersection of pornography,
science, and tourism and were less censorable because the ideas implicit in
them had been completely normalized in late nineteenth- and early twentieth-
century Britain, thanks in part to the early work of the Cannibal Club. They
popularized anthropological beliefs about nonwhite sexuality and offered vi-

L'EUNUQUE

FIGURE 21. Postcard: "L'Eunuque." [The Eunuch] With permission of the Victoria and Albert Museum.

sual access to the wonders of empire.[18] For example, through the "mosaic-style" card, everyone could finally meet "The Eunuch" (figure 21), whose face, at first glance, seems unexceptional despite an exotic headdress. At second glance, however, the naked, writhing women that compose his features become apparent.[19] The card popularized prevailing notions about the eunuch's dilemma; in spite of his obsession with sexuality and women, he could never satisfy his desires.

Postcards played up the exoticism of foreign sexuality with references to harems and oases, peopled by girls (and occasionally boys) who lived in a world of nubile unrestraint. Advertisements for postcards, like advertisements for earlier photographs, juxtaposed popular and geographically dissimilar ideas of the "Orient" with abandon, fulfilling Western preconceptions.

Dear Sir!

Please find the enclosed leaflet of our assortment of artistic photographs of the Orient. The characteristic beauty of the Oriental races,
as well as the landscape with its fertile oasis of Djerid, its quiet palm
groves watered by brooks and ponds, in which slender palm-trees are
reflected, are illustrated by exceedingly beautiful reproductions. We
wish to specially recommend our interesting post-card photos, representing naked, sunlit bodies of racy girls, and piquant types and scenes
of the harem-life, photographed in most graceful, unconstrained positions. These cards are sent postage free to the buyer in one or several
discreetly closed envelopes. State the cards you desire, enclose payment in banknotes of your country and we shall forward them to your
address.[20]

Eroticized "natives" in the cards appeared naked or partially naked, but
their nakedness was staged for perusal by a Western audience. The nakedness
in these cards needs to be thought about on several levels: "native" people's
culture and beliefs about nakedness; the act of taking the picture; the card as a
consumer item; the shipping of the card as a form of communication; and the
meaning of the card in the European context. At each of these levels, postcards
created an "exoticized" sexuality.

In some of the locales, nakedness was clearly a creation of the photographer. Algerian women in public always appeared fully dressed and often
veiled.[21] Postcard photographers, however, portrayed Algerian women as
half-naked, veiled but naked, or fully naked with head coverings. In short, the
photographers used clothes to highlight the women's nakedness—to make the
women appear more naked, rather than less (figure 22). Photographers sometimes posed the women in undisclosed locales, rather than in studios. Studio
portraits, through artificial lighting, deepened shadows, and simple backdrops, might encourage viewers to differentiate the real woman from the artistic representation of "Woman." In contrast, the photographers of "native
subjects" captured the supposed daily practices of "native women" by photographing them in houses and courtyards with visual signs of exoticism such as
hookahs and water jars (figure 23).

Through the use of articles of exoticism and outdoor photography, photographers reinforced the apparent realism of the "native" by creating a record
of her moving through her daily life. In posing these women, the photographers created the "naturalness" of the naked exotic, rather than documenting

FIGURE 22. Postcard: Woman in
headdress and veil.

a culturally genuine image. The production of nakedness underscored the meaning of the card as a consumer item. By buying representations of the exotic (and artificially portrayed) women, consumers gained an apparent familiarity with the closed, inaccessible culture of distant lands. The purchase of these cards implied that everything, even the most intimate scenes and acts, was available to European money and European documentation. The symbol of female nakedness and privacy in Algerian life, for example, could become a highly viewable, public form of communication.

Another card, sent from Port Elizabeth, Africa, to Portsmouth, England, featured a half-naked reclining woman in "tribal garb" (figure 24). Her naked breasts went unremarked by the sender, who instead asked, "How are you getting on old chap" in a near parody of British salutations, before launching into the more important matters of business and travel. The circulation of such

FIGURE 23. Postcard: Women with jars.

cards popularized notions about the casualness of African dress and sexuality. The image, though, did not feature a woman untouched by Western mores; the card, entitled "The Cigarette Girl," showed the woman smoking. The title wryly contrasted her with white cigarette girls, who—though a bit racy—certainly did not appear naked in public. By accentuating the contrast between types of cigarette girls, the photographer heightened the awareness of the African woman's nudity within British society. When Europeans received such a card, the (artificial but apparently natural) nakedness of "exotics" juxtaposed the clothed-ness of Europeans. Postcards of "exotics" insisted on compelling differences between these societies.

In "a Zulu portrait," an unspecified group of men and women posed against a landscape. Here, the photographer added color to accentuate the primitiveness of the scene. The surrounding trees were retouched bright green. Cloth and feather adornments were painted bright red (with small touches of yellow) to bracket the people's nakedness and to expose their bodies more fully. The painted-on, primary colors suggested a primitive, uninhibited gaudiness. Particularly telling, however, was the contrast between the

FIGURE 24. Postcard:
"The Cigarette Girl."

colored ornamentation around the people and the unretouched gray tones of
the people. The monochromatic rendering of "natives" contrasted with representations of white women, who were routinely photographed or drawn in a
stylized whiteness. This card, sent from Natal to Kent, read, "Waiting for
xmass dinner M.T." M.T. was making a joke about the red and green colors,
the line of people, their nakedness, and the oddity of the idea of Zulus cele-
brating Christmas. The joke demonstrated an awareness of the multiple levels
on which the nudity of "others" was perceived.

Postcards of the exotic thus displaced the ideas of primitive sexuality
onto women, children, men, and families in distant places. The cards created
foreignness and ideas of racialism and then documented them. However, the
bodies that appeared were shown not as individuals but as types. Captions

FIGURE 25. Postcard: "Scènes et types—Femmes Arabes—LL." [Scenes and types—Arab Women]

label those represented as "Arab types," "Moorish types," "Haitian types," "Geisha types," and "Cuban types" (figures 25 and 26). These typologies reflected collective meanings of a foreign sexuality that stood in opposition to a domestic, or white, sexuality. In the process, the individuality of the people photographed disappeared. The overlay of detail (Algerians with face coverings, geishas with wide-sleeved kimonos, Africans in tribal garb) fixed the trope of the exotic against the normative images of European society. Such postcards and such images contributed to a fixation on the exotic.

While colonial and foreign cards naturalized ideas of sexual availability outside of Europe, images of white women also contributed to formulations of a "natural" sexuality. Domestic cards, in both their illegal and legal forms,

FIGURE 26. Postcard:
"Type de jeune Haïtienne"
[Type of Haitian girl].

showed white women as inherently sexual, available, and waiting. These normative images of women as the objects of desire used visual tropes that earlier, more expensive photographs had established. In the cards, the placement of women's breasts and genitals slightly off center as the focal point confirmed women's sexuality as located within this erotic triangle, following the visual standards of early daguerreotypes and photographs.[22] Women were shown as receptive figures, rather than sexual actors. The cards show women in a variety of poses that cemented their place in relation to the viewer: standing with one hand behind the head and elbow lifted to raise the breasts and make the figure accessible, lying down with one shoulder tilted back (to lift the breasts) and one leg tilted forward to highlight the pubic **V**, smiling up at the camera while removing stockings. Women's specific body parts, such as breasts or

FIGURE 27. Postcard:
N. Boulanger, "La Rose"
[The Rose].

buttocks, became pictorial synecdoches for female sexuality.[23] The fixation on body parts allowed them to become tokens of sexuality.

Domestic cards also explicitly tied women to nature by using backdrops of pastoral landscapes and by ornamenting the models with props such as plants, flowers, and fruit. In one series, not only is women's hair adorned with flowers as a sign of fertility, gigantic petals surround women's bodies so that the truncated torsos (with exposed breasts) become the stamens (figure 27). The use of flowers, plants, and fruits as signs of femaleness reinforced the position of women as delicate, waiting, and fertile. Likewise, cards perched women (with and without wings) on branches so that they became part of the

FIGURE 28.   Postcard: Woman on tiger skin, holding mirror.

natural landscape. Another favorite trope displayed women on fur (figure 28). These cards played on the metaphor of women as cats (domesticated and stroke-able) and on the idea of cats as prey (wild and untamed). Women sprawled on the quintessential signs of aggressive masculinity—tiger and leopard skins—functioned as trophies of manhood.

This fixation on the female form allowed the origin of the representation to matter less than the image of female "beauty." Recreations of high art in which photographers replicated paintings and sculptures mingled with pho-tolithographic reproductions. Reproductions of the Venus de Milo, *Leda and the Swan,* and *Bons Amis* (a girl and her horse) appeared in postcard form.

The distinction between high art as transcendent and low art as trans-parent broke down in the reworking of images that emphasized the accessibil-ity of female sexuality. As Linda Nochlin notes, "The topos of the artist in his studio assumes that being an artist has to do with man's free access to naked women. Art-making, the very creation of beauty itself, was equated with the

FIGURE 29. Postcard: Salons de Paris, Jan Styka—*Bons Amis* [The Salons of Paris, *Good Friends*].

representation of the female nude."[24] The artist who used female nakedness as the token of beauty and the pornographer who employed the same token underscores the centrality of women's bodies to the Victorian and Edwardian world. High art unproblematically became low art because the central icon— female nakedness—eclipsed the distinctions between the two realms.[25]

Similar to the way the "colonial" card used the paraphernalia of private life to focus on women as sexualized and accessible, domestic cards built on the depiction of the private lives, private worlds, and private bodies of white women. The cards opened women of all classes to close inspection, even if women of all classes did not pose for these cards. Some cards featured women surrounded by pearls, rich fabrics, and fine wallpaper and furniture to in-

FIGURE 30. Postcard: Bride.

scribe the image with the ideas of wealth. Striped stockings and cheap cots marked the "tart" in other cards. Underwear cards showed women in undergarments "from across the ages" as permanently disheveled, half-dressed, and always "caught" midway between respectability and undress.[26] Honeymoon cards showed women partially unwrapped from elaborate wedding veils and dresses in poses that underscored sexual defloration as imminent (figure 30).[27] Such domestic cards, whether serialized or single, cemented the

FIGURE 31. Postcard: Lesbian undressing, part 1.

gaze and firmly placed sexuality onto the bodies of women. Combining special occasions and everyday life, the worlds of the highborn and the low, these domestic cards reinforced current ideas about sexuality and women's centrality to its configuration.

Other cards, however, featured images that clearly transgressed social proprieties and opened a diversity of sexual practices to a mass gaze. One card, for example, featured a black man in a pink-and-white apron massaging and masturbating a reclining white woman.[28] Such a card exposed a form of interracial sexual desire occasionally broached in other earlier forms of pornography but rarely even alluded to in respectable publications. Urination, and the voyeuristic desire to watch it, received a similar attention in cards that showed women pissing into chamberpots for a male audience.[29] Scenes of two women acknowledged a lesbian sexuality that even sexologists and sympathetic observers seldom confronted. One series, for example, explored a lesbian cross-dressing style that grew increasingly popular in burlesque theaters and cabarets (figures 31 and 32).

The disrobing of a woman for her cross-dressed partner revealed their hidden sexuality, thereby transforming a fairly common bedding into a more

FIGURE 32. Postcard: Lesbian undressing, part 2.

transgressive union. Other postcards, like the example of fellatio in figure 33, used the visual tropes and technical processes developed in fetishistic photography. To emphasize the sexual act, the photographer angled the woman's body so that the viewer could see the close relationship between her lips and his penis. The man's bent head further focused the viewer's gaze on the sexual act—to magnify the elements of voyeurism—so that the cardholder looked at the man watching the woman.

The latent element of voyeurism was more explicitly addressed in keyhole cards, in which a skeleton-keyhole shape bordered the image. Keyhole cards allowed consumers the illusion of spying on an unwary couple as they moved from dressed to undressed, distant to intimate. Some images reinforced the idea of voyeurism by showing chambermaids, gentlemen, and others peeping through a keyhole on one side of an image while the unwary have sex on the other side of the closed door. Keyhole cards of both types played with ideas of voyeurism, continuing a tradition that went back to *Fanny Hill* (Fanny spied on two men in the expurgated sodomy scene). These images transgressed social proprieties by exposing a diversity of sexual practices to a mass gaze, exploring nonreproductive sexual practices, and popularizing themes developed in fetishistic publications.

FIGURE 33. Postcard:
Fellatio. With permission of the
Kinsey Institute.

"Comic cards" went even further in their disregard of propriety by ridiculing both the privileged and the low in society. Building on the older, libertine tradition, comic postcards merged sexuality, scatology, and critique in ways that devalued bourgeois seriousness. The most common comic postcard showed sexuality appearing in unlikely places. Cards that displayed pants dropping in inappropriate places, dresses flying up from the wind, and seams splitting from movement illustrated a world on the edge of comic disaster. Exposure threatened everyone, regardless of the way people covered themselves in social proprieties. These cards worked on the principle of double meanings as men, trying to look inconspicuous, knocked at doors numbered 69. The cards mocked the social markers, like clothes and dignity, that spared some people from the perusal of others. In doing so, they inserted disorder in sexuality by using humor as a form of social leveling.

FIGURE 34. Postcard:
Dulio Raineri, "The Hunt." With
permission of the Victoria and
Albert Museum.

By poking fun at the bodies or habits of the powerful, comic cards could attack social proprieties and conventions without accountability or retribution. Specific, class-based symbols took the place of individuals as the object of attack. The fox hunt in England allowed fertile ground for criticism and ribaldry.[30] A postcard from 1905 features a view of the back of a woman in a riding coat and hat (figure 34).[31] However, the woman's buttocks are replaced with a horse's hindquarters. The dimpling of the haunches and the pinkish color make the transposition of buttocks—the visual replacement of horse for woman—more pronounced. The relaxed tail completes a visual illusion of a woman with huge, exposed buttocks complete with an overly wide and especially hirsute furrow (the tail). The postcard transposes criticism of the hunt in general onto the body of the aristocratic woman as the symbolic site of corruption, making the figure both comic and grotesque.

The mockery of the female figure was intensified by the detachment and distance (in real life) of the aristocratic woman. The unavailable figure became monstrous and undesirable through the transposition of fleshy animal and human parts. The card hinted at the grotesque indulgence of the aristocratic classes, visually labeling them as overendowed, overfed, and overconcerned with animals to the point of bestial preoccupation. Another card, from 1906, shows a young woman seated on a bidet shaped like a horse—apparently washing her genitals in an artifact of the hunt. Again, the combination of animals and women, of hunting symbols and female genitals, mocked the sanctity of the hunt as a social form of privilege and connected it to dirt and excrement.[32] Similarly, a postcard depicting lavishly coiffed aristocratic women and their dogs, and another one in which farm dogs fellate peasants, exploit bestiality to attack identifiable groups of people.[33] But bestiality, while a potent symbol, was not the only type of symbolic attack these cards launched.

A 1909 card labeled "He who goes hunting, loses his place" made the hunter into a cuckold, rather than a returning warrior. The man in hunting gear returns to find his woman lying naked in bed while another man dresses in the corner. Thus, the hunter's preoccupation with masculine pursuits left him open to much deeper attacks upon his masculinity as another man appropriated his sexual property.

While women's insatiability remained a central feature of comic cards (hinting at the persistence of an older conception of female sexuality), this insatiability also reflected on aristocratic men's lack of virility. "La Luxure" (figure 35), mistranslated on the card as "Luxury" rather than "Lust," featured a black man and white woman in bed. The appointments—the satin comforter, the draped bed, and the wealth of paintings in the background—placed the union in the homes of the rich, making the mistranslation seem apropos. The bust of a white man's bald head looking at the lovers hinted that the union was not only interracial but also clandestine and adulterous. The wordplay (both accidental and purposeful) implied that such lusts were among rich women's many luxuries. Here again, exposure mocked aristocratic women's lusts and made aristocratic men into cuckolds.

In other images, a gentleman is identified by his elaborate dress—walking stick, coat, high hat—allowing for a form of class-based ridicule, rather than a gender-based attack on masculinity. The class-based items of attire offered visual cues that the gentleman was not like other men and his sexuality

FIGURE 35. Postcard: Xavier Sager, "La Luxure/ Luxury." *Luxure* is mistranslated on the card. It actually means "lust." With permission of the Victoria and Albert Museum.

was suspect. In comic cards, the gentleman appeared overly licentious but unable to satisfy: At the zenith of society, he was unable to act appropriately for his station and emjoy its sexual privileges.

Cards took a topical approach to political critique and launched broad attacks on the basis of social class. One postcard memorialized the Japanese capture of Port Arthur in China (figure 36). In it, the heads of Japanese soldiers were drawn as bared buttocks; they offered flatulence rather than oratory at the raising of the Japanese flag. The dismembered body parts in the image insisted that viewers understood the Japanese victory as grotesque. In a similar postcard, Japanese soldiers, again illustrated as buttocks, receive enemas from their compatriots.[34] These two cards contributed to the racial politics that emerged during the Russo-Japanese War. Another card lampooned the ubiquitous peace conferences of the early twentieth century. The card featured a door with the number 69, a sign reading PEACE CONFERENCE, and a military officer's cap and sword. The caption reads: "Conference for disarmament or disarmed for the conference."[35] The card underscored the dubious results of international diplomacy in which only the diplomats were seen as benefiting from the deliberations.

Some cards combined scatology and social commentary to poke fun at privilege by associating specific groups with unregulated habits. A series of

FIGURE 36. Postcard: "Prise de Port Arthur." [The capture of Port Arthur]

postcards illustrating a nun's furtive preoccupation with sausages destabilized the distinctions between bodies and other matter while attacking the privileges of the church. These cards added to older, libertine attacks on corrupt social privilege new attacks on unregulated and undifferentiated sexual habits. They restored the sanctified and excluded bodies of social superiors to the gaze of the masses. In the tradition of political scatology, the bathroom habits of monarchs warranted close attention. A card showing Kaiser Wilhelm reading on the toilet contributed to more serious efforts of propaganda during World War I. Another card displayed King Edward being administered an enema on the throne as his subjects bowed before him (figure 37).[36] The throne, in this image, became a mere toilet and the ministers mere dung-collectors. Picturing loyal subjects bow before a defecating monarch both emphasized the monarch's disdain for the people and returned that sentiment by playing up the "foulness" of his person. Such social commentaries poked fun at the habits, bodies, and pretensions of specific groups of socially privileged people, like kings and princes, aristocratic women, the clergy, and bourgeois men. The bitter edge to these comic cards explicated their often covert politics.

Scatological themes, as the previous examples illustrate, destabilized the symbolic order of sexuality by placing human sexuality in close contact with

FIGURE 37. Postcard: "Romanzo d' Appendice." "Romance of the Appendix" is the literal translation; it connotes a popular serial. With permission of the Victoria and Albert Museum.

other activities from which it had been carefully separated. Defecation, urination, and flatulence had been removed from the purified, hygienic, sexual body in the course of the nineteenth century. Bourgeois reforms differentiated human bodies from animal bodies and animal pleasures. Postcards mocking these divisions showed beautiful, well-dressed women passing enough wind to put out candles, children and dogs urinating in the milk together, animals eating little girls' excrement, and women defecating to the glow of the rising moon. The cards showed urine mistaken for rainwater, springwater, and tea; flatulence compared with "the odor of love"; and feces served in decorated pots. Scatological cards returned the purified body to the realm of animal pleasures.[37] Like animals (and sometimes with animals), humans in these cards made little distinction between food and feces, between sweet odors and foul, and among the varieties of bodily orifices.

These cards returned socially distinguished people like gentlemen, ladies, and clergy to their own origins, as bodies that smell, act, and leak as do all bodies. However, they also placed all other bodies in the same position. Peasants and gentlemen, girls and boys, the lofty and the low, all live in and from the muck of bodies. These cards mocked the divisions of hygiene instituted by middle-class reforms, ridiculed the pretensions of mind over body, and derided the newly invented insistence on privacy for body functions. All pleasures in these cards were equal; release, regardless of its type, was comic and pleasurable, as were the cards themselves: comic in the display of what people sought to conceal, and pleasurable in the representation of release. Children in these cards functioned as the central actors able to enjoy the pleasures of elimination and the pleasures of sexuality uninhibited by the distinctions of society. Thus, a picture of a boy and girl each on separate chamberpots, holding hands across the spatial divide, showed love and elimination as made of the same stuff. To increase the shock value of such a display, cards also transposed adult heads to children's bodies seated on a chamberpot (figure 38).

 Youth and gristle, sex and filth complemented each other in the creation of these grotesques. Comic cards of all types returned humor to sexual-

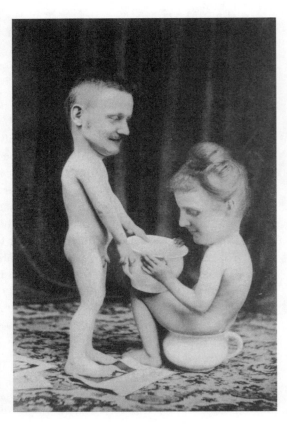

FIGURE 38. Postcard: Grotesques with chamberpots. With permission of the Victoria and Albert Museum.

ity, countering the nineteenth-century tendency to make sexuality a serious business. Comic postcards attacked the idea that sexuality stood apart from other aspects of the body and that human sexuality remained isolated from the rest of nature. Scatology not only attacked specific class-based symbols but also undermined the divisions of a bourgeois conception of a distinctive human sexuality.

Colonial, domestic, and comic cards each portrayed distinct ways of understanding and representing sexuality, and each built on formulations worked out earlier in the century. Domestic cards offered apparently aristocratic women to perusal, finally fulfilling the republican agenda. Comic cards opened socially sensitive situations to derisive humor. Colonial cards continued to typologize natives and popularized ideas that had been circulating in more rarified anthropological venues. A focus on "underwear from across the ages" built on fetishistic ideas, developed and sold in both literary and more expensive photographic form. Some ideas appeared in all types of cards; comic cards often used the symbol of women to critique issues of social class (as in representations of the hunt), while domestic cards reinforced constructions of femininity as essentially passive through images of women (as in pictures of brides.) The terrain of the body as socially inscribed with meaning could attack the social order or could present the benefits of social order.

Because the symbols used in postcards built upon older signs and social meanings, they continued older, often politically conservative themes; both domestic and colonial postcards naturalized certain types of people by fixing their place as naked, waiting, and sexualized. These cards reinforced the social hierarchy by making women into objects for men's perusal and by baring "colonial" subjects to the imperial gaze. The cards objectified women; they fetishized exoticism; and they naturalized children's uninhibited sexuality. Even comic cards that mocked the upper classes (giving them a subversive potential) did not often offer a vision of sexuality outside of the process of social ordering based on class, race, gender, and age. Instead, they primarily used images of the powerless in the upper classes, like women and children, to criticize the existing social hierarchy. Postcards did not offer sexual liberation.

Postcards did revolutionize pornography, however. Cheap, mass-produced representations transformed dirty words into dirty pictures. Sexual ideas now relied on visual, rather than literary, cues. While visual description was not new, the heavy reliance on it and the refinement of visual cues were. The cues themselves imparted a wealth of information that called forth a variety of responses. The signs of exoticism, like primary colors and huts, called into play the meaning of foreignness, the relation between life in the "home" country and experience in a distant one, and the availability of nubile unrestraint, just as cues of social class like the hunt brought a wealth of meaning by questioning the meaning of wealth. These visual cues of a lifted breast or a split blouse became the medium for conveying information, rather than a mere illustration for the more crucial ideas available in the text.

The cards revitalized older notions, like the comic and dislocated aspects of sexuality, which had found expression in libertine literature, bawdy songs, and burlesque theater. While the cards did not invent scatology or comic renderings of sexuality, they successfully formalized these ideas into a permanent article, rather than the experiential form of oral culture. The cards captured jokes, rather than telling them. And the jokes they captured were visually located as permanent punch lines. The freezing of images, whether comic or not, implied imminence rather than closure. A joke was always in the process of narration just as a woman was always waiting. The fixity of images helped perpetuate the idea of exotics as unchanging, of women as forever disrobing, and of the penis as always erect. The continuous imminence of stills—as a facet of the medium—became a central part of the message of pornography.

The cards also hinted at the alternative future of pornography: motion. Card series that showed the unfolding of a scene prefigured film and began to predicate meaning onto action. The narrativity of successive poses in the cards reinforced the idea that sexuality has certain ritually prescribed actions. The serialized path of sexuality cemented the order of sexual activities like the embrace, the disrobing, and breast fondling (figures 39–42). The incomplete,

FIGURE 39. Postcard:
Wedding night embrace, part 1.

FIGURE 40. Postcard:
Wedding night embrace, part 2.

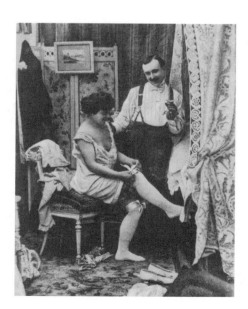

FIGURE 41. Postcard:
Wedding night embrace, part 3.

FIGURE 42. Postcard:
Wedding night embrace, part 4.

imminent images of singular postcards and the culminating, moving images of serialized postcards set the stage for the two futures of modern pornographic representation.

The Social Impact of an Expanded Audience

Perhaps most important, postcards, along with stereoscopes and mutoscopes, made images of sexuality available to a broad public and thus publicized the often implicit politics of sexuality. Witnesses from London, Dublin, and Manchester testified about the picture postcard craze and remarked that women, children, and the working classes made up the new customers for this type of sexual culture. Men and women, boys and girls, publicly began to consume sexualized material artifacts in ways that the authorities found unprecedented and insupportable.[38] The new consumers gave every indication that they condoned the increased availability of a sexualized commodity culture; complaints came not from the working classes but from the police, members of the National Vigilance Association, and women's social purity groups.[39] As one policeman testified:

I may mention that upon one occasion I myself visited the exhibition that was prosecuted on a Sunday night at the Elephant and Castle, and at the least estimate the number of persons, boys and girls, there was over 300. They were indulging in all sorts of indecent acts among themselves, and two were looking round picking out the different machines that bore the most seductive titles and which they thought contained the worst pictures—a boy and a girl each spying on the payment of 1/2 d. in the same machine, touching one another in an indecent manner, and making use of indecent language.[40]

The legal, religious, and reforming communities believed that the multitudes could only be corrupted, not edified, by pornography and that access had to be limited through the eradication of objects like postcards and mutoscopes.

The expansion of access thus helped focus debates over social purity. State agencies and private organizations viewed pornography as a cause of other "social evils."

The trade in obscenity has so easily attained the formidable proportions which disturb consciences and seriously menace morals. This is undoubtedly the place to strike: of all methods used in the corruption of youth this is certainly one of the most serious and may be truly said to be the source of all others, and were it only possible to get the better of this evil it would greatly enable the special legislations in each country to combat the other evils.[41]

They believed that youths, once pulled into the web of vice by naughty images, became innately more corrupt and corruptible. Pornography could lead to lewdness, debauchery, and prostitution. These groups worked in international and national policy spheres to save youths and others unable to control their sexuality and therefore vulnerable to pornography's influence.[42]

Officials and social purists believed they needed to save the working classes from their own folly, for the working classes did not respond with proper outrage at the corruption of their wives, children, and mates. A tobacconist, when charged for exhibiting indecent postcards, was asked:

Would you like me to show to your wife or daughter a card like this?

Defendant: I wouldn't have any objection, sir.

Mr. Noddings: Then you are a strange man.[43]

Another defendant, Mr. Devenny, seemed accused as much for having his "daughter, a girl of 16," work at the shop as for selling postcards. Here again, the defendant stated that he did not see the cards as obscene. "I have never had a complaint before. I can't see they are filthy." The judge stated in response, "If you can't see it, and think they are fit for a girl to sell over the counter, of course, one forms one's own opinion about you."[44] The condemnatory stance taken by officials because the vendors continued to "see" the images as appropriate demonstrates both a rift in perceptions and a form of social discipline. Officials attempted to shame vendors into realizing the inappropriateness of their perceptions. Vendors, even those casually caught up in the business, continued to argue the importance of their own standards. A Mr. Varley of Bloomsbury assisted his niece with sales when the proprietor went to Paris.[45] When called to trial, Varley argued that "the cards were sold by millions all over the world." The magistrate responded:

That is not the point. The question is whether they are indecent.

The Defendant: Who is to decide what is decent?

The Magistrate: I have to decide in the first place.[46]

The authorities insisted that the working classes needed to conform to official standards of public morality.

Vendors contended that they *were* maintaining these public standards. One young lady testified on her own behalf: "For the defense the young lady said that the wholesale vendor assured her that the cards in question had been the subject of seizure that had failed, and that therefore were 'saleable.' She bought them as 'comic,' while others were reproductions of pictures from public galleries. Mr. Chapman said that it was a question of common sense. The cards were indecent."[47] The young lady knew that sexualized postcards had come under legal scrutiny of late, and she justified their sale by arguing that the representations could be found in high art and in public galleries. She explicitly tried to link her postcards with other, more middle-class standards of public viewing.

While many cards did carry reproductions of high art, those images, when put onto postcards and sold on the streets, lost their legitimate status. The new popular context of images took precedence over the origin of the representation. The image of the naked woman, essential to both artistic and pornographic representation, transcended the division that officials tried to maintain. Repeatedly, vendors argued that the origins of the representation should matter and that postcards could not be judged indecent or obscene if they came from "works of art."[48] The authorities disagreed. When asked whether a photograph of the Venus de Medici [sic] equaled other nude representations, the chief constable of Manchester replied, "No, but I suggest that all the circumstances should be taken into consideration; the photograph of nude women under certain circumstances may be all right, but if it is placed in the windows and sold to youths and sold on the streets, then I say it is not for the good of the community, and you should take all the circumstances into consideration when you decide."[49] The issue of the individual viewer's place in society defined the meaning of the object being viewed. Sexual explicitness by itself did not define an object as indecent, obscene, or pornographic. These definitions occurred in the conjunction of people and ideas and in the socially determined relationship of viewer to viewed.

The expansion of access to sexual representations radically undermined the socially prescribed relation of people to ideas. Women seeing nakedness could in itself be dangerous, even though women's nakedness was central to aesthetic objectification. Until 1893, female students could not participate in life drawing classes at the Royal Academy, and after women's admittance, models remained partially draped.[50] Being able to view representations of bodies, rather than be represented as bodies, transformed the meaning of these images and undermined the basis of social control that remained implicit in them. The appropriation of aesthetic objectification and subsequent reaction to it demonstrated that the restrictive "moral standards" of Victorian and Edwardian society rested on "categories of being" rather than egalitarian principles. Women, children, the working classes, and people of color violated their "categories of being" as objects when they laid claim to the same prerogatives of aesthetic objectification as had their social betters.

As women, children, and the working classes began to consume images of a sexualized social order, these artifacts became subversive, and pornography began to take on threatening connotations. Women, children, and the working classes had been sexualized in older forms of high-priced, written pornography. *Flossie: A Venus of Fifteen, Sweet Seventeen: the True Story of a Daughter's Awful Whipping and its Delightful if Direful Consequence,* and *A Pretty Girl's Companion* all sexualized girls but were not accessible to them. A crisis came when those who had been sexualized, like girls, began to consume sexual culture, even in a purified form.[51] When as many as thirty girls and young men used twenty-seven penny-in-the-slot machines labeled FOR GENTLEMEN ONLY, Scotland Yard shut down the premises. The magistrate presiding over the case stated: "If you had found such things in a private house perhaps they would not be regarded as obscene. But [at] an exhibition for boys and girls they clearly are."[52] The cheap machines of the poor established a new and dangerous social context. The danger came not from sexualizing girls but from girls seeing representations of such sexuality.

The dangers implicit in exposure applied not only to girls and the poor but also to people of color. In a case of pornographic importation to South Africa, *The Vigilance Record* reported that "the same logic applies to the 'Black Peril,' and while we must punish the men guilty of these crimes, more effective steps should be taken to bring to justice those white men, who induce the natives to purchase indecent pictures and obscene articles, by which means they poison the minds and stimulate the baser passions of some of these semi-savages."[53] A normative image, like an image of a white woman representing "Beauty," when placed in the hands of a black man became a deviant reality. The image of the naked or partially naked white woman as an item of consumption reinforced the social order only when consumed by white men. When consumed by black men, the same item became dangerous. The idea of black men with white wives could be enjoyed as long as only white men controlled the ideas—as they had in *The Memoirs of Madge Bufford,* an expensive, limited-edition, fetishistic text, and "My Grandmother's Tale," a feature in *The Pearl.* When circumscribed by race, class, and gendered systems of access and ownership, representations such as these allowed wealthy white men to imagine the construction of deviance. When the representations leaked to those who had previously been objects, however, the imagined peoples became potentially dangerous actors. Women, children, blacks, and the poor could act in ways that mocked fantasies of control and undercut fantasies as fantasies.

Apparent dangers arose when pornographic images fell into the hands of women, children, and blacks, at least in the minds of judges called to decide these cases. The leap from symbolic pleasure to real danger in the judges' minds happened effortlessly because the ownership of sexual ideas formed a type of social control. Thus the change in ownership undermined the social order.

> There are indications that an extensive trade is being carried on in immoral productions. Recent outrages indicate that natives who have committed outrages on white women were brought into contact with such baneful influences. The importer of the consignment which has been seized admitted that the contents were for sale to kaffirs. Such disclosures must cause grave anxiety, and we trust the facts revealed

will lead to watchfulness on the part of householders and to action on the part of the police.[54]

Changing the ownership of the imaginary was seen as an act of restructuring the world. When blacks in South Africa looked at pornographic images of the European world, they reconstructed their social situation. The authorities believed that their consumption of pornography had real social implications; pornography could "cause" violence, miscegenation, and sexual lawlessness that would affect the English rather than "kaffirs." Thus, the act of imagining could turn the world upside down, as objects became actors.

Representations of "natives" and "foreigners" had long been a staple in European pornography. The British had been viewing sexualized images and reading sexualized representations of those they conquered for decades, as part of the right of conquest. Pornographers like the Cannibal Club had used a scientific model to justify representations of the colonized sexuality. Pornographers had infused a colonial hierarchy with new meanings for the purpose of titillation in fetishistic representations. They had played up racialized sexuality and reconstituted slavery—long after slavery had ceased—to enjoy explorations of domination, submission, and torture. They had alternately ogled the Turk, buggered the Turk, and impersonated the Turk. But they had not given these representations to the Turk and others they believed were like the Turk. By selling obscene images to the colonized, Louis Hendleman broke the law, but he also encouraged a disruption of prerogative of ownership. He brought the act of imagining to the natives.

> You have committed a grave breach of the law. What makes it still worse is this: you sold and showed these most filthy photos to the natives. What the effect on their minds will be I do not know. For you, a white man, to make a living out of the sale of things like this stamps you as a person of no character. I feel bound to make these remarks because I think it is the duty of every white man to endeavour, so far as lies in his power, to instill into the minds of the natives a respect for white men and white women. If you show and sell to natives this sort of thing, how can you expect the natives to show proper respect towards us?[55]

The ability to reconstruct a people's sexuality was a fundamental part of social control. The direction of ideas—who could imagine whom and therefore who could recreate whom for the purpose of pleasure—remained central to the preservation of the social order that governed both imperial and domestic relations. The social implications of "filth" in the wrong people's hands did more than expose hypocrisy; it exposed sexuality as a method of social control.

Objects, Subjects, and Social Control

When women, children, the poor, and people of color began to consume pornography, they purchased hegemonic constructions of sexuality. They bought and examined images in which ideas of gender, race, class, and maturity reflected the dominant culture's view of the world. The development of a new form of cultural representation like picture postcards did not create a revolutionary new form of working-class expression. It did, however, resituate ideas that had enormous significance, such as women's "natural" sexuality, children's undifferentiated and uninhibited sexuality, and the availability of "colonial" pleasures. Merely shifting the location of those ideas could be dangerous enough because it called attention to how sexual representation constituted a facet of social control. The shift in the placement of ideas complicated a picture of cultural hegemony. For as surely as the widened distribution of pornography contributed to an acceptance of hegemonic formulations of sexuality, it also exposed the fundamental ambiguities in subordination, as the "subject matter" in older formulations of pornography became subjects in their own right. This exposure called for an increased policing of the boundaries of race, class, and gender.

Louis Hendelman received one and a half years' imprisonment and a fine of three hundred pounds, while the "natives" received swift and drastic punishment for accosting white women, actions supposedly "instigated" by pornography. Louis Hendelman made a serious error in judgment in misusing his proprietary rights to objectify subordinates when he sold pornography to black men; however, the "natives" violated a "category of being" that precluded any right to representations at all. The recondite relationship between representation and social control had been clarified; the government resorted to overt forms of policing to reinforce "categories of being" that defined the prerogatives of ownership.

Women, children, the working classes, and people of color belonged to subordinated "categories of being" and therefore could not handle the burdens of aesthetic objectification without disrupting the process of social ordering as essential to social control. While pornographic postcards did not open a path to sexual liberation, they did offer something at once more mundane and more insidious: Erotic ephemera at the turn of the twentieth century let the subordinated gaze upon themselves, with all the pleasures and dangers that this form of objectification entailed.

Conclusion

Sexuality Re-imagined

In the introduction, I explained that my definition of pornography has been informed by the definitions of pornography in nineteenth-century Britain. The pornography that I examine in this study was printed, published, sold, and collected or, alternately, repressed, burned, and archived, as a distinct and distinguishable entity. Though publishers and police, and collectors and members of the Society for the Suppression of Vice, viewed this body of representations quite differently, all seemed to reach a rough accord on the definitions of illicit materials, and all approached the materials with a recognition that these works constituted a special type. Moral authorities, archivists, publishers, and collectors cordoned off certain types of representations to create a distinction between pornography and other forms of expression.

In many ways, pornography continues to be sequestered as a category of representation. Social critics like Andrea Dworkin and Catherine MacKinnon and policy makers in the British and American governments have constructed a definition of pornography that rests on it being fundamentally different from other types of cultural artifacts, although they admit that its influence can spread to other forms of low culture.[1] Even though the definition of pornography remains contested, most people believe that pornography can be defined in and of itself. In contrast, I see the act of separation as an important, socially contingent process that has as much to do with evaluating people as it has to do with evaluating texts.

To make this move, I have taken Foucault's injunctions to heart: "The object, in short, is to define the regime of power-knowledge-pleasure that sustains the discourse on human sexuality in our part of the world. The central issue . . . [is] to account for the fact that it is spoken about, to discover who does the speaking, the positions and viewpoints from which they speak, the institutions which prompt people to speak about it and which store and distribute the things which are said."[2] By following the regime of power, I have explored the ways that pornography became defined as pornographic through the process of sequestering. High art that could be viewed in museums by the bourgeoisie became pornographic when reproduced and sold on the streets to the poor. Pictures of people of color could be scientific, comic, educational, or erotic, but when people of color viewed pictures of naked whites, nakedness became pornographic and constituted a social danger. The construction of pornography as pornography relied upon a model that assessed objects in conjunction with people.

Acknowledging this process of social contingency makes the implications of shifts in access more apparent. With the expansion of access, the process of imagining came to be turned on its head. As the powerless began to view representations—as well as being viewed in them—at the end of the nineteenth century, legal, moral, and cultural authorities created a sex panic. Sex panics seem to imply that access to pornography would provide for some form of social and sexual transformation, but this claim does not hold up under scrutiny. Panics have occurred whether the representations were liberationist or conservative. In some sense, pornography cannot fully provide for sexual and social liberation because it remains defined by the culture. Instead, the issue of access forms the crux of the problem. Who could and who could not handle representations of sexuality? Who would be corrupted? What would be the social repercussions of that corruption? These seem to be the underlying questions. During the sex panic over pornography at the end of the nineteenth century, the social contingency of definitions became highlighted and further reinforced. Moral authorities, who saw themselves as objective, believed that the women and children who viewed pornography grew corrupted. According to the authorities, the very act of viewing hurt women and children by making them easy prey for sexual predators. Access to pornography needed to be restricted to protect women and children. Limiting access, however, only limited the supply of pornography to those already socially subordinated, like women, children, the poor, and the foreign, while those in positions of dominance, like wealthy white men, could still gain access to pornography. Protection from the sources did not guarantee protection from the implications of the sources. Instead, restricting access continued the inequalities in the cultural economy by masking the relationship of signification and social ordering. It formed its own pattern of social control.

This model of defining pornography in relation to specific types of people continues. Implicitly and explicitly, our current debates over pornography are shaped by our perceptions and beliefs about types of people. We divvy up our society into those who victimize and those who are victimized, the violent versus the vulnerable. Laura Kipnis aptly summarizes our fears about the former: "The fantasy pornography consumer is a walking projection of upper-class fears about lower-class men: brutish, animal-like, sexually voracious."[3] On the flip side, we emphasize women as victims and align them with the most vulnerable members of our society, children. When children are drawn into the equation, our rhetoric becomes particularly urgent. I suggest that we deescalate the rhetoric and look behind it. Frankly, not all consumers are (or have been) lower-class men, and not all women are (or have been) victimized by pornography. As Carole Vance has made clear, the overemphasis on women's victimization does a disservice to feminist desires for sexual freedom.[4] Perhaps the rhetoric about villains and victims masks other fears about society relating to commercialization, violence, lack of control, anomie, and race, which all emerge sexualized in pornography. However, pornography is not the cause of these problems. Pornography, as I have tried to show, is itself a cultural artifact that responds to change like any other.

As a cultural product, pornography offers only a culturally contingent picture of utopian possibilities; that is, pornography itself both says and silences. Nineteenth-century British pornography explored the sexual possibilities of exoticism but limited the exploration of male homosexual activities. It emphasized penile/vaginal intercourse but limited buggery. While it changed over the course of the century to include new types of representation, new meanings, and new narratives, the process of change rested not only upon the growth of utopian possibilities but also upon exclusion and condemnation. The British fascination with Indian sexuality grew over the course of the nineteenth century, even while discussions of Indian sexuality condemned the practice of biting. This odd relationship to biting demonstrates that in the nineteenth century, pornography did not tell all equally. The meanings in pornography have been influenced by the developing patterns of normative sexuality and have been limited by the same patterns. As pornography told, retold, and silenced acts and ideas of sexuality, it articulated a range of possibilities.

Pornography does not hold up as a disconnected category of cultural representation, even though it has been set apart as a cultural object. The changes it underwent during the nineteenth century were not explosions of utopian or dystopian possibilities but results of the slower processes of redefinition and refinement. As a cultural artifact, pornography reflected both mainstream and radical cultural and social shifts. The British grew ever more fascinated with the sexuality of the colonized over the course of the nineteenth century. The meanings in pornography were influenced by the developing patterns of radicalism, empire, science, and consumerism and were limited by the same patterns. Racial ideologies, scientific beliefs, and desires for plenty existed in pornography much as they existed in other artifacts of culture. Pornography reflected, refined, and refracted these cultural constructs. The shifts in pornography responded to the developments within the culture more broadly.

The changing patterns of what was told and not told in pornography suggest that a variety of processes went into the transformation of pornography. Some changes, like the development of visual pornography, happened within a few decades of the development of cheap reproductions and point toward change tied to technological innovation. Others, like the transformation of women from subjects of pornography to objects in pornography, took place over the entire period and point toward a more complex process of change. The representation of women as subjects in libertine pornography constructed women's ability to act as politically subversive agents. However, the positioning of women as subversive tied women's sexuality to social transformation and made ideas of women's compliance central to the process of social change. The insistence on women's compliance helped to transform them into objects, which later became categorized, defined, and delineated in scientific pornography of the 1860s and 1870s. Objectification of women deepened in fetishistic pornography when it became possible to buy representations informed by specific cultural meanings but not moored to the implications of those meanings. The multiple processes in the objectification of women point toward a long-term social change related to the shifting position of women in the social structure, the economy, and the culture. No one factor caused change in representations of women. Instead, women's place in the world of sexuality stood much contested and involved in many dialogues. No single process can account for the myriad shifts in form, content, and meaning in nineteenth-century pornography.

Just as there was no single cause of change, there was no linear pattern to change, as pornography's convoluted relationship with politics demonstrates.

Dugdale and other revolutionary pornographers tied a libertine agenda to republican rights. When the state repeatedly sentenced Dugdale to prison for the corruption of Her Majesty's subjects and when Parliament passed Lord Campbell's Act, these were political acts aimed at controlling the passions of the populace. When Monckton Milnes received pornography smuggled in the diplomatic pouch, that too was a political act that distinguished between those above the law and those accountable to it. At a more subtle level, politics continued to play a significant role in the relationship between pornography and society. Pornography at the beginning of the nineteenth century had a politically subversive agenda tied to republican rights that made sexually conservative claims; libertine pornography attempted to destabilize society, but it did so by stressing heterosexual intercourse. Although pornography excluded the overt discussion of politics from sexuality by the 1850s, the segregation of politics from sexuality hid the political implications in pornography, rather than canceling them. The Cannibal Club's turn toward science created a form of sexual solidarity that remained politically conservative. While individual members could exchange bon mots about sexually transgressive acts like flagellation and queer desires, their ability to do so rested upon their separation from the rest of society and their dominance over the rabble at home and abroad.

In the next generation of pornographers, the sexual agenda in pornography remained subversive and the politics implicit in pornography conservative. Fetishism, for example, moved from discussions of politics into discussions of pleasure. The exclusion of overt political statements in late nineteenth-century pornography contributed to claims about sexuality as politically neutral, rather than embedded with a latent politics. Even when pornography became a mass item, revolutionary, scientific, and fetishistic ideas were transformed into articles easily accessible to a wide array of peoples. With this transformation came the implicit political formulations in each permutation; a chain of associations and implicit political relationships trailed after each piece of pornography. The widespread availability of exotic postcards, for example, created a conservative political alignment between consumerism and sexuality that displaced yearnings for a freer sexuality onto the empire. Politics and pornography affected each other across the many levels of society and need to be assessed within a political framework, even if the political engagement remained covert.

Given these complicated political alignments, it would be hard to argue that pornography became worse or better, even though it became more available. This holds true even considering how social and political inequalities in the Victorian world were magnified through erotic longings. In some cases, this magnification—like Hankey's request for a skin taken from a living woman—seems to speak of a straightforward process of domination and subjugation. But the clarity in that case was rare. More often, this magnification took on a more ambiguous form. Though the working classes, women, children, and the colonized gained access with mass production, the articles they bought remained mired in older formulations of sexuality. Any straightforward subordination would be filtered through a more dispersed process of hegemony that could allow for alternative readings of the images.

Instead of looking for a linear path or single definition, we need to accept that pornography was not universally defined and that it offered only refractions of the broader society. By placing pornography in a historical framework, we can get a better sense of how it affected people and how people made sense of it. As I have tried to show, some people legislated about pornography, some people used it, and sometimes they were the same people. Surely, people from such radically different cultural worlds as William Dugdale and the "young member of Parliament" did not see pornography the same way, and in the preceding pages I have tried to show how their worlds might influence their readings by emphasizing the contingency of meaning.

The problem of contingency did not end with World War I, however. I will offer one more reading to demonstrate the relevancy of these issues to the contemporary world. To do so, I would like to return for a moment to figure 34, the postcard transposing a horse's rump onto a woman, which can be read in any number of ways. It can certainly be seen as degrading to women. It mocked their bodies and their habits (both riding and sexual), and it subordinated their bodily privacy to the public gaze. It can also be read as a class-based attack on aristocratic privilege through which the elite were held up to the masses for cheap amusement. As such, it provided the poorer in society an opportunity to lampoon their social betters. The reading of this card depends on the reader. I have no doubt that an aristocratic woman would see it as attack on her "sex," but I also think that, in the hands of workers, it would function as a political document.

These divergent readings seem particularly relevant right now given the stalemate between free-speech scholars and antipornography feminists. Those on the First Amendment side of the pornography wars would say that the political reading provides the most relevant claims and that it is easy to see that pornography is of fundamental relevance to other forms of political freedom. (Dugdale's ghost haunts this debate.) If, however, we define pornography as only a feminist issue, then it is equally apparent that it often objectifies, demeans, and mocks women. Both readings are equally wrong and equally right; pornography is not only a feminist issue, and it is not only a legal issue. These positions have been formulated and are maintained based on decontextualized readings that avoid the issues of social class, race, colonialism, age, agency, and economics. To make our way out of this stalemate, we need to return these issues to pornography by returning pornography to its context. Pornography used sexuality to speak about all of these aspects of society, and to privilege only one reading would do an injustice to the others.

Setting pornography apart by making it either causal, utopian, or dystopian does more harm than good by denying the structural factors that inform pornography. Pornography is easy to vilify and even easier to mock because it captures all the frailties of human sexuality; what could be more fragile than elaborate fantasies spun from the muck of our bodies? But if pornography becomes the bogeyman, then we cannot do anything about it, we cannot even really understand it. If, however, we accept that it reflects other long-term changes, we can make sense of it in meaningful ways. Changes in pornography can be historically located, tied to cultural movements, placed within the context of social formation, and positioned within the global economy. For example, the development of scientific pornography in the mid-nineteenth century can be tied to the ascendance of objectivity as a means of evaluation, placed within the construction of a bourgeois, professionalizing science, and positioned within Britain's imperial aspirations. The study of pornography can and should incorporate the complexities of the developing world in order to assess its impact.

Areas for further study cross disciplinary boundaries and fields of expertise. I have primarily established certain metanarratives of nineteenth-century British pornography, and even there my work can use further elaboration. Specific motifs in nineteenth-century pornography deserve closer study. The implications of a growing fascination with incest in nineteenth-century pornographic representations demand serious attention. Did this fascination extend to people's lives? If so, what does it say about the development of the Victorian family? Did the development of the private family bring with it the development of familial sexuality? As well, I have only touched on the remarkable formulations of race in these works. Nineteenth-century pornographers became fascinated by racialism, and long accounts of whiteness, blackness, and their myriad relationships appear across the works and deserve a focused study of their own. Descriptions of bestiality raise a variety of important questions about the meaning of human sexuality as part of the "great chain of being" and about later Darwinian beliefs about species. The monkeys and apes that pop up in pornography, like the monkeys and apes that appear in H. Rider Haggard novels, seem to encode animals with racial taboos. Making sense of British pornography could take up the lifetime of more than one scholar and could fill any number of dissertations. Furthermore, British pornography has been better documented than that of most other regions and nations; American pornography has been barely touched, and scholars of French and German pornography concentrate on the eighteenth and twentieth centuries respectively. The history of pornographic film in all these regions needs serious attention.

To branch off from a European perspective, colonialism in pornographic representation needs to be further linked to the lives of the people subordinated. The placement of people in the sexual imaginaries has more to do with economic, political, and social relationships between groups than with the imagined group's innate sexuality. However, the creation of signifiers could have real implications in people's lives. Sexual signification helped transform the social order by drawing women, children, and the poor into a system that used them as its rough matter, whether or not they were directly involved in the making of pornography; not all places or all people have existed equally in consumer culture or in representation. Historians of Africa might want to disentangle the ways that European projections about African sexuality contributed to the process of colonialism. Cuban and Mexican pornography (made for the American market) in the early twentieth century deserves close study. Exploring the colonization of sexual possibilities in pornography could offer an important counterweight to the imperial vision of sexuality. Furthermore, the violence of revolutionary movements in Algeria and Cuba seems quite striking when placed in relationship with the hypersexualized roles that these colonies played in European and American pornography. Perhaps, as Frantz Fanon suggests in *Black Skin, White Masks,* the process of decolonization had more to do with ideas of gender and sexuality than we currently acknowledge.

There remains much work to do because pornography continues to be undervalued as a source and politically suspect as a topic. However, it is the suspect nature of pornography that makes this work important. People can make blanket statements about pornography getting worse as long as there is no historical record. They can raise sex panics as long as there remains a dearth of scholarship. They can bring up bogeymen for us to fear as long as we don't look under the bed. I suggest that under the bed, and more appropriately on it, is exactly the place to look right now.

Notes

INTRODUCTION: SEXUAL IMAGININGS

1. *The Pearl* (1879; reprint, New York: Grove Press, 1968), 463.

2. W. T. Stead, "The Maiden Tribute of Modern Babylon," *Pall Mall Gazette* 42, no. 6336 (July 6, 1885), 2.

3. Judith Walkowitz, *Prostitution and Victorian Society: Women, Class, and the State* (Cambridge: Cambridge University Press, 1980) and *City of Dreadful Delight: Narratives of Sexual Danger in Late Victorian London* (Chicago: University of Chicago Press, 1992); Françoise Barret-Ducrocq, *Love in The Time of Victoria: Sexuality and Desire among Working-Class Men and Women in Nineteenth-Century London,* tr. John Howe (New York: Penguin, 1992); Jeffrey Weeks, *Sexuality and Its Discontents* (London: Routledge & Kegan Paul, 1985) and *Sex, Politics, and Society: The Regulation of Sexuality since 1800* (London: Longman Group, 1981); Michael Mason, *The Making of Victorian Sexuality* (Oxford, U.K.: Oxford University Press, 1994).

4. John Tomlinson, *Cultural Imperialism: A Critical Introduction* (Baltimore: Johns Hopkins University Press, 1991), 157, emphasis in original. Tomlinson discusses the "social imaginary" in reference to the works of Cornelius Castoriadis. Both Tomlinson and Castoriadis use the term to critique "modernization" and "development" as cultural constructs that nonetheless have important intellectual, economic, political, and cultural consequences.

5. Roger Chartier, "Intellectual History or Sociocultural History," in *Modern European Intellectual History,* ed. Dominick LaCapra and Steven L. Kaplan (Ithaca, N.Y.: Cornell University Press, 1982), 41–42.

6. Walter Kendrick, *The Secret Museum: Pornography in Modern Culture* (New York: Viking Penguin, 1987), 57.

7. Lesley Hall finds a similar pattern; sexually oriented medical advice literature became obscene if sold cheaply to the general public. Lesley A. Hall, *Hidden Anxieties: Male Sexuality, 1900–1950* (Cambridge, U.K.: Polity Press, 1991), 56.

8. "Report from the Joint Select Committee on Lotteries and Indecent Advertisements, together with the proceedings of the Committee, minutes of evidence, and appendices" (London: HMSO, 1908), 80–81, NVA, Box 107, Fawcett Library.

9. Mary Douglas, *Purity and Danger: An Analysis of the Concepts of Pollution and Taboo* (London and New York: Ark Paperbacks, 1989).

10. Andrea Dworkin, *Pornography: Men Possessing Women* (New York: Putnam, 1981); Susan Griffin, *Pornography and Silence: Culture's Revenge against Nature* (New York: Harper

& Row, 1981); Catherine MacKinnon, *Feminism Unmodified: Discourses on Life and Law* (Cambridge, Mass.: Harvard University Press, 1987) and *Only Words* (Cambridge, Mass.: Harvard University Press, 1993); Lauren Robel, "Pornography and the Existing Law," in *For Adult Users Only: The Dilemma of Violent Pornography,* ed. Susan Gubar and Joan Hoff (Bloomington: Indiana University Press, 1989).

11. Vern L. Bullough, *Prostitution: An Illustrated History* (New York: Crown, 1978) and *Sex, Society, and History* (New York: Science History Publications, 1976); Richard H. Kuh, *Foolish Figleaves? Pornography in and out of Court* (New York: Macmillan, 1967); Ralph Ginzburg, *An Unhurried View of Erotica* (New York: Helmsman Press, 1958).

12. See David Copp and Susan Wendell, eds., *Pornography and Censorship* (Buffalo, N.Y.: Prometheus Books, 1983); Ronald J. Berger, Patricia Searles, and Charles E. Cottle, *Feminism and Pornography* (New York: Praeger, 1991); Joseph F. Kobylka, *The Politics of Obscenity: Group Litigation in a Time of Legal Change* (New York: Greenwood Press, 1991).

13. A number of feminist scholars argue that Dworkin and MacKinnon's model does an injustice to women's experiences and feminist scholarship. See, for example, Laura Kipnis, *Bound and Gagged: Pornography and the Politics of Fantasy in America* (New York: Grove Press, 1996); Carole S. Vance, "Pleasure and Danger: Toward a Politics of Sexuality," in *Pleasure and Danger: Exploring Female Sexuality,* ed. Carole S. Vance (Boston: Routledge & Kegan Paul, 1984); Kate Ellis and others, eds., *Caught Looking: Feminism, Pornography, and Censorship* (Seattle: Real Comet Press, 1988).

14. To understand the historical framework of the debates, I recommend Elizabeth Alison Smith, "Charged with Sexuality: Feminism, Liberalism, and Pornography, 1970–1982" (Ph.D. diss., University of Pennsylvania, 1990).

15. Joan Hoff connects the dearth of historical studies with the proliferation of policies against pornography. Hoff points out that while both the Meese Commission (1986) and the Johnson Commission (1970) acknowledged that the historical work needed to be done, neither commission would sponsor the work. Instead, both commissions recommended broad policy changes based on historical projections. Hoff posits that detailed histories of pornography would interfere with the political agenda of social control. Joan Hoff, "Why Is There No History of Pornography?" in *For Adult Users Only: The Dilemma of Violent Pornography,* ed. Susan Guber and Joan Hoff (Bloomington: Indiana University Press, 1989).

16. Henry Spencer Ashbee (Pisanus Fraxi, pseud.), *Index Librorum Prohibitorum* (1877; reprint, New York: Documentary Books, 1962), xxviii-xxix.

17. Ashbee, *Index Librorum Prohibitorum, Centuria Librorum Absconditorum* (1879; reprint, New York: Documentary Books, 1962), and *Catena Librorum Tacendorum* (1885; reprint, New York: Documentary Books, 1962); Peter Mendes, *Clandestine Erotic Fiction in English, 1800–1930: A Bibliographical Study* (London: Scolar Press, 1993). Also indispensable is Patrick Kearney, *The Private Case: An Annotated Bibliography of the Private Case Erotica Collection in the British (Museum) Library* (London: Jay Landesman, 1981).

18. Steven Marcus, *The Other Victorians* (New York: Norton, 1985).

19. For a closer examination of genre, I recommend Peter Wagner, *Eros Revived: Erotica of the Enlightenment in England and America* (London: Secker & Warburg, 1988).

20. Robert Darnton, *The Literary Underground of the Old Regime* (Cambridge: Harvard University Press, 1982), 207–208.

21. Lynn Hunt, ed., *Eroticism and the Body Politic* (Baltimore: Johns Hopkins University Press, 1991); G. S. Rousseau and Roy Porter, eds., *Sexual Underworlds of the Enlightenment* (Chapel Hill: University of North Carolina Press, 1988); Darnton, *The Literary Underground of the Old Regime.*

22. Iain McCalman, *Radical Underworld: Prophets, Revolutionaries, and Pornographers in London, 1795–1840* (Cambridge, U.K.: Cambridge University Press, 1988).

23. John K. Noyes, *The Mastery of Submission: Inventions of Masochism* (Ithaca, N.Y.: Cornell University Press, 1997), 2.

CHAPTER 1: REVOLUTIONARY PORNOGRAPHY

1. E. P. Thompson, *The Making of the English Working Class* (London: Victor Gollancz, 1963), 674.

2. Rousseau and Porter, *Sexual Underworlds of the Enlightenment.*

3. James G. Turner, "The Properties of Libertinism," *Eighteenth-Century Life* 9, no. 3 (1985): 75–87.

4. David Foxon, *Libertine Literature in England, 1660–1745* (New York: University Books, 1965). See also David O. Frantz, *Festum Voluptatis: A Study of Renaissance Erotica* (Columbus: Ohio State University Press, 1989).

5. Tiffany Potter, *Honest Sins: Georgian Libertinism and the Plays and Novels of Henry Fielding* (Montreal and Kingston: McGill-Queen's University Press, 1999), 10–11.

6. Catherine Cusset, "Editor's Preface," *Yale French Studies* 94, Special Issue: *Libertinage and Modernity* (1998), 8–9. See also Philip E. Simmons, "John Cleland's *Memoirs of a Woman of Pleasure:* Literary Voyeurism and the Techniques of Novelistic Transgression" *Eighteenth-Century Fiction* 3, no. 1, (October 1990): 45.

7. See, for example, Anna Clark, *The Struggle for the Breeches: Gender and the Making of the British Working Class* (Berkeley: University of California Press, 1995), 153–155. Although Roy Porter and Lesley Hall see a decisive break between libertine and Enlightenment philosophies and I see a cross-fertilization, our assessments of texts like *Memoirs of a Woman of Pleasure* are quite similar. Thus, I believe that we point toward the same phenomenon. See Roy Porter and Lesley Hall, *The Facts of Life: The Creation of Sexual Knowledge in Britain, 1650–1950* (New Haven, Conn., and London: Yale University Press, 1995), 14–32.

8. Lynn Hunt, ed., *Eroticism and the Body Politic* (Baltimore: Johns Hopkins University Press, 1991) and *The Invention of Pornography: Obscenity and the Origins of Modernity, 1500–1800* (New York: Zone Books, 1993); Robert Darnton, *The Literary Underground of the Old Regime* (Cambridge, Mass.: Harvard University Press, 1982) and "Censorship and Publishing Industry," in *Revolution in Print: The Press in France, 1775–1800,* ed. Robert Darnton and Daniel Roche (Berkeley: University of California Press, 1989), 27–49.

9. Robert Darnton, *The Forbidden Best-Sellers of Pre-Revolutionary France* (New York: Norton, 1995), 21.

10. Lynn Hunt, "Introduction: Obscenity and the Origins of Modernity, 1500–1800," in Hunt, *The Invention of Pornography*, 36–37.

11. John R. Gillis, *For Better, for Worse: British Marriages, 1600 to the Present* (Oxford, U.K.: Oxford University Press, 1985), 190–228.

12. McCalman, *Radical Underworld*, 235.

13. McCalman, *Radical Underworld*, 156.

14. Edward Royle, *Radical Politics, 1790–1900: Religion and Unbelief* (London: Longman Group, 1971), 26–32.

15. Ashbee, *Index Librorum Prohibitorum*, 127.

16. Sexuality offered productive ground for lampoons and fit into a long tradition of crowd-pleasing. An 1816 Cruikshank lampoon of Princess Charlotte's marriage to Prince Leopold entitled "Scene in the R——l Bed-Chamber; or A Slit in the Breeches!!" derided the Prince's masculinity by showing the royal wedding night as a fight for the family "breeches." It also made use of the slang "slit" for vagina. Tamara Lisa Hunt, "To Take for Truth the Test of Ridicule": Public Perceptions, Political Controversy, and English Political Caricature, 1815–1821" (Ph.D. diss., University of Illinois at Urbana-Champaign, 1989), 217.

17. E. A. Smith, *A Queen on Trial: The Affair of Queen Caroline* (Avon: Alan Sutton, 1993).

18. Satires of the popular press and their support for Caroline abounded as well. In one particularly funny example, a pamphlet reports the radicals singing, "Freedom, freedom, plunder and freedom!/ We will have freedom, mischief and bread:/ Freedom, Freedom! shoot 'em and bleed 'em,/ All who won't join us, we'll knock on the head!" Interspersed with parodies of radical intentions were songs about Caroline and her paramour. *The Radical Harmonist; or, A collection of songs and toasts given at the late crown and anchor dinner. To which is subjoined, the goose's apology; a Michaelmas ode* (London: Printed for W. Wright, 1820), 22.

19. McCalman, *Radical Underworld*, 168–170.

20. McCalman, *Radical Underworld*, 192.

21. Marcus (pseud). *Second edition (with an additional preface) of The book of murder! Vademecum for the Commissioners and Guardians of the new Poor Law throughout Great Britain and Ireland, Being an Exact Reprint of The Infamous Essay on the Possibility of Limiting Populousness, by Marcus, one of the Three.* (London: Printed by John Hill, Black Horse Court, Fleet St., And now Re-printed for the Instruction of the Labourer, By William Dugdale, No. 37, Holywell Street, Strand, 1839), 5.

22. McCalman, *Radical Underworld*, 219.

23. "Letter from Mr. Pritchard to Lord Campbell," January 1858, Social Evil Extracts Album, part 1, NVA Papers, Fawcett Library.

24. John "carried on his business as M. Metford, at No. 10 Middle Row and No. 19 Little Queen Street, Holborn (1830); as J. Turner, at No. 50 Holywell Street and as John Duncombe & Co., at No. 17 Holborn Hill." Ashbee, *Index Librorum Prohibitorum*, 137.

25. Ashbee, *Index Librorum Prohibitorum*, 114.

26. "He carried on business at 23, Russell Court, Drury Lane, at 3, Wych Street, at 5, at 16, and at 37, Holywell Street, and at 44 Wych Street." Ashbee, *Index Librorum Prohibitorum,* 127.

27. PRO, King's Bench Records, KB28/602/2 (1853).

28. Social Evils Extracts Album, part 1, item 68c, *The Times* (London: February 1858).

29. "I may safely say that it has not been one case in six brought under the Society's notice in which they have been able to prosecute, chiefly from the heavy expenses attending a prosecution." "Letter from Mr. Pritchard to Lord Campbell," January 1858, Social Evils Extracts Album, part 1.

30. Edward J. Bristow, *Vice and Vigilance: Purity Movements in Britain since 1700* (Dublin: Gill & Macmillan, 1977), 45.

31. Even the successor organization, the National Vigilance Association, formed in the 1880s had problems with court costs and out-of-pocket expenses. PRO, Home Office Papers, Note on payment of NVA for prosecutions, 1890, HO144/478/28111.

32. Colin Manchester, "Lord Campbell's Act: England's First Obscenity Statute," *Journal of Legal History* 9, no. 2 (1988): 223–241.

33. PRO, King's Bench Papers, KB28/602/1, November 9, 1853.

34. PRO, King's Bench Papers, KB28/512/4 (1830); KB28/535/45 (1835); KB28/600/3 (1852).

35. "Letter from Mr. Pritchard to Lord Campbell," January 1858, Social Evil Extracts Album, part 1.

36. Manchester, "Lord Campbell's Act: England's First Obscenity Statute."

37. *Hansard's Parliamentary Debates: Third Series, Commencing with the Accession of William IV,* vol. 146, 2d vol. of session 1857(b) (London: Cornelius Buck, 1857), 330.

38. After the passage of Lord Campbell's Act, the destruction of property subsequent to a prosecution could be significant. For instance, one pornographer in 1858 was caught with "no less than 12,346 prints, 393 books, 351 copper plates, 88 lithographic stones, and 3 and ½ cut of letterpress. And from another in the same year 15,300 prints, 162 books, 1 cut of letterpress, 96 copper plates, 21 lithographic stones and 114 pounds of stereotype." Given that the letterpress and stereotype, plates, and stones had been confiscated, this should have made a dent in production. However, Mr. Pritchard continues by stating that within two years both men had again amassed large stocks. Regardless of whether the means of production were included in the confiscation, it appears that the pornographers continued to function and thrive. "Letter from Mr. Pritchard to Lord Campbell," January 1858, Social Evil Extracts Album, part 1.

39. Mendes, *Clandestine Erotic Fiction,* 346.

40. See Ashbee, *Index Librorum Prohibitorum,* 397–400.

41. "Letter from Mr. Pritchard to Lord Campbell," January 1858, Social Evil Extracts Album, part 1.

42. Thirty-three percent of men could not sign their names to the marriage register in 1840. Gillian Sutherland, "Education," in *The Cambridge Social History of Britain 1750–*

1950, vol. 3, ed. F.M.L. Thompson (Cambridge, U.K.: Cambridge University Press, 1990), 122.

43. Roy Porter, *English Society in the Eighteenth Century* (London: Penguin Books, 1990), 167.

44. Of course, not all workers were illiterate or unlearned. For discussions of working-class reading, see R. K. Webb, *The British Working-Class Reader, 1790–1848* (London: George Allen & Unwin, 1955), and Patrick Craig Scott and Pauline Fletcher, eds., *Culture and Education in Victorian England* (Cranberry, N. J.: Associated University Presses, 1990).

45. Ashbee, *Index Librorum Prohibitorum,* 135.

46. *The Frisky Songster, Being a Select Choice of such Songs, as are distinguished for their Jolity, High Taste and Humor, and above two hundred toasts and Sentiments of the most delicious order.* Ninth London Edition (London, 1802), frontisplate, 91.

47. Ashbee, *Index Librorum Prohibitorum,* 133–137, 22–23.

48. Society for the Suppression of Vice, *A Few Plain Reasons, Shewing Why the Society for the Suppression of Vice Has Directed Its Attention to Those Criminal Offenses which Are Chiefly Committed by the Lower Orders of the Community* (London: Printed for the Author, By Gilbert and Reed, 1803?), 6.

49. Quoted in Manchester, "Lord Campbell's Act: England's First Obscenity Statute," 226.

50. *Hansard's Parliamentary Debates,* July 3, 1857, 865.

51. Richard Carlile, *Every Woman's Book: or, What is Love?* 4th ed. (London: R. Carlile, 1826), 8 (Microfilm, Woodbridge, Conn.: Research Publications, 1981).

52. Carlile, *Every Woman's Book,* 17, 14.

53. For a history of *Fanny Hill,* see Foxon, *Libertine Literature in England, 1660–1745;* William H. Epstein, *John Cleland: Images of a Life* (New York: Columbia University Press, 1974); and Patrick J. Kearney, *A History of Erotic Literature* (Hong Kong: Dorset Press, 1993).

54. See Ashbee, *Cantena Librorum Tacendorum,* 60–91. Ashbee lists editions of the work from 1749, 1777, 1781, 1784, 1784, an undated eighteenth-century illustrated edition, 1829, 1831, another very similar edition, a Dugdale edition of 1832, the same edition undated, another Dugdale from 1850, two more very similar undated reprints, another Dugdale from 1841, three undated editions, a 1830 Dugdale edition, a New York edition from 1845. There are also at least fourteen French editions, at least two Italian, and one German translation.

55. Peter Sabor, "The Censor Censured: Expurgating *Memoirs of a Woman of Pleasure,*" *Eighteenth-Century Life* 9, No. 3 (May 1985): 192–201.

56. John Cleland, *Memoirs of a Woman of Pleasure,* ed. and introduced by Peter Sabor (1748–1749; reprint, Oxford, U. K.: Oxford University Press, 1999), 2.

57. Cleland, *Memoirs of a Woman of Pleasure,* 24.

58. Cleland, *Memoirs of a Woman of Pleasure,* 43.

59. Cleland, *Memoirs of a Woman of Pleasure,* 67.

60. Cleland, *Memoirs of a Woman of Pleasure,* 84.

61. Cleland, *Memoirs of a Woman of Pleasure,* 92.

62. Cleland, *Memoirs of a Woman of Pleasure*, 129.

63. For a discussion of this incident in the context of eighteenth-century body politics, see Tassie Gwilliam, "Female Fraud: Counterfeit Maidenheads in the Eighteenth Century," *Journal of the History of Sexuality* 6, no. 4 (1996): 518–548.

64. Cleland, *Memoirs of a Woman of Pleasure*, 175.

65. Leonore Davidoff and Catherine Hall provide a classic exploration of the relationship between respectability and radicalism in their discussion of the Queen Caroline affair. Leonore Davidoff and Catherine Hall, *Family Fortunes: Men and Women of the English Middle Class, 1780–1850* (Chicago: University of Chicago Press, 1991), 149–192.

66. Julia Epstein, "Fanny's Fanny: Epistolarity, Eroticism, and the Transsexual Text," in *Writing the Female Voice: Essays on Epistolary Literature*, ed. Elizabeth C. Goldsmith (Boston: Northeastern University Press, 1989), 149. Other scholars see this fictionalizing of female sexuality as more problematic. Philip E. Simmons believes it undermined women's sexual voices and concealed an aristocratic libertine agenda. As he explains, "Cleland covers women's pain with the mask of pleasure, and affects to recover libertine vice with bourgeois virtue." However, the conflation of women's pain with men's pleasure and aristocratic values with vice ignores the important work that Cleland did to create space for a new form of sexual liberty. It misses Cleland's own creation, the rational pleasurist—the epitome of a new form of the libertine as rational, freethinking, and bourgeois. While it would be wrongheaded to insist that *Fanny Hill* or other such libertine works spoke from an authentic female voice, not all libertine works that assumed a fictive female perspective had the same political consequences. See Simmons, "John Cleland's *Memoirs of a Woman of Pleasure*," 45.

67. Lynn Hunt, *Eroticism and the Body Politic*, 2.

68. *A Man of Pleasure at Paris; or, An Account of the Pleasures of that Capital* (Paris: N.p., 1808), 7.

69. *A Man of Pleasure at Paris*, 37–38.

70. Thomas Rowlandson, *Pretty Little Games for Young Ladies and Gentlemen*. With Pictures of Good Old English Sports and Pastimes ([London]: A few copies only for the Artist's Friends [J. C. Hotten], 1845 [1872]). See Ashbee, *Centuria Librorum Absconditorum*, 346–398, for a discussion of Rowlandson.

71. *The Crimes of the Clergy, or the Pillars of Priest-Craft Exposed* (London: Benbow, Printer and Publisher, 1823). See Ashbee, *Centuria Librorum Absconditorum*, 44–50, for the complete list of their "crimes."

72. James Maidment, *Ane Pleasant Garland of Sweet Scented Flowers* ([Edinburgh]: N.p., 1835), 17.

73. Thomas Hamilton, *Select Poems on Several Occasions*. By the Right Hon. the Earl of H*******n. To which are added the Duke of Argyll's Levee and some Ballads. By the Late Lord Binning (London: N.p., 1824), 144–149.

74. Maidment, *Ane Pleasant Garland of Sweet Scented Flowers*, 8.

75. Robert Darnton, *The Great Cat Massacre* (New York: Vintage Books, 1985), 83.

76. Natalie Zemon Davis stresses the carnival's potential for transforming society. "The carnival does not, however, reinforce the serious institutions and rhythms of society as

in other functional theories just mentioned; it helps change them. In Rabelais' day, says Bakhtin, it provided the people with an actual experience of life without hierarchy as against fixed categories of 'official' medieval culture." Natalie Zemon Davis, *Society and Culture in Early Modern France* (Stanford, Calif.: Stanford University Press, 1975), 103. In contrast, E. P. Thompson sees "rough music," mumming, and other forms of carnivalesque behavior as reinforcing the status quo of the people, and thus they are "only as nice and tolerant as the prejudices and norms of the folks allow." E. P. Thompson, *Customs in Common* (New York: New Press, 1991), 530.

77. Robert Storch, introduction to *Popular Culture and Custom in Nineteenth-Century England*, ed. Storch (New York: St. Martin's Press, 1982), 2, 5 (quoted).

78. Robert Storch, "'Please to Remember the Fifth of November': Conflict, Solidarity, and Public Order in Southern England, 1815–1900," in *Popular Culture and Custom*, 71–99; Douglas A. Reid, "Interpreting the Festival Calender: Wakes and Fairs as Carnivals," ibid., 125–153.

79. This focus on the harem emerged as part of the Enlightenment project on sexuality. See G. S. Rousseau and Roy Porter, eds., *Exoticism in the Enlightenment* (Manchester and New York: Manchester University Press, 1990).

80. *The Seducing Cardinal's Amours with Isabella Peto and Others; to which is added The Art of Keeping the Eleventh Commandment, 'Thou Shalt not be Found Out,' being an account of the private Intrigues of a virtuous Wife* (London: Published as the Act directs by madame Le Duck, Mortimer Street; and to be had of all respectable Booksellers, 1830), 45–46.

81. *The Lustful Turk* (1828; reprint, New York: Carroll & Graf, 1983), 106.

82. *The Lustful Turk*, 62–63.

83. *The Lustful Turk*, 190.

84. Edward Said, *Culture and Imperialism* (New York: Vintage Books, 1994), 75.

85. The distinctions between buggery and lesbian sexual intercourse existed in the legal and social realms. See Rictor Norton, *Mother Clap's Molly House* (London: GMP, 1992).

86. *The Exquisite: A Collection of Tales, Histories and Essays, funny, fanciful and facetious, interspersed with Anecdotes, original and select, amorous Adventures, piquant Jests and spicy Savyings, Illustrated with numerous Engravings* ([London]: Printed and Published by H. Smith [William Dugdale], [1842–1844]), 2:75, 112. See Ashbee, *Catena Librorum Tacendorum*, 339–343, for a discussion of *The Exquisite* and for publishing information.

87. See Ashbee, *Catena Librorum Tacendorum*, 99–102, for publication information. Although Ashbee does not specify, *The Authentic Memoirs* seems to be an English work about France rather than a French work translated into English.

88. See Kay Wilkins, "Andréa de Nerciat and the Libertine Tradition in Eighteenth-Century France," *Studies on Voltaire and the Eighteenth Century* 256 (1988): 225–235; *The Exquisite* 2:(78), 139.

CHAPTER 2: SEXUALITY RAW AND COOKED

1. Fawn Brodie, *The Devil Drives: A Life of Sir Richard Burton* (New York: Penguin Books, 1971), 196.

2. James Pope-Hennessy, *Monckton Milnes: The Flight of Youth, 1851–1885* (London: Constable, 1951), 119.

3. Quoted in Pope-Hennessy, *Monckton Milnes*, 119.

4. Quoted in Brodie, *The Devil Drives*, 196.

5. Mendes, *Clandestine Erotic Fiction*, 7–12.

6. Two works that have been particularly helpful in thinking through these issues are Catherine A. Lutz and Jane L. Collins, *Reading National Geographic* (Chicago: University of Chicago Press, 1993), and Anne McClintock, *Imperial Leather: Race, Gender, and Sexuality in the Colonial Context* (New York: Routledge, 1995).

7. "Letter from Richard F. Burton to Dr. R. S. Charnock," February 17, 1873, in *Anthropologia*, vol. 1, 1873–1875 (London: Published for the London Anthropological Society, Ballière, Tindall & Cox, 1875), 2.

8. *Memoirs Read before the Anthropological Society of London*, vol. 2, 1865–1866 (London: Trubner, 1866); *Memoirs Read before the Anthropological Society of London*, vol. 3, 1867–1869 (London: Longman, Green, 1870). The organization was renamed and reformed but continued its diverse interests. *Anthropologia*, vol. 1 1873–1875 (London: Published for the London Anthropological Society, Baillière, Tindall & Cox, 1875).

9. For an overview of the Anthropological Society, and in particular the racist character of the organization, see George W. Stocking, *Victorian Anthropology* (New York: Free Press, 1987), 186–237.

10. David Keith van Keuren, "Human Science in Victorian Britain: Anthropology in Institutional and Disciplinary Formation, 1863–1908" (Ph.D. Diss., University of Pennsylvania, 1982; Ann Arbor, Mich.: University Microfilms, 1982).

11. For a discussion of divorce reform and Lord Penzance's role in it, see A. James Hammerton, *Cruelty and Companionship: Conflict in Nineteenth-Century Married Life* (London: Routledge, 1992).

12. Letter to Swinburne from E. Villine, 1871. Tipped into *The Cannibal Catechism* (London: Printed for private circulation only, 1913). Copy held at Deering Library, Northwestern University.

13. Publisher's note, Algernon Charles Swinburne, *The Cannibal Catechism*, c. 1863 (London: Printed for private circulation only, 1913), 12.

14. Swinburne, *The Cannibal Catechism*, 7, 11.

15. Ian Gibson, *The English Vice: Beating, Sex and Shame in Victorian England and After*, 3d ed. (London: Duckworth, 1992), ch. 6.

16. Frank Fane [Swinburne] to Richard Monckton Milnes, Wallington, Newcastle-on-Tyne, December 27, [1862], *The Swinburne Letters*, ed. Cecil Y. Lang (New Haven, Conn.: Yale University Press, 1959–1962) 1:41.

17. Simeon Solomon to Swinburne, Saracen's Head, Beddgelert, Carnavonshire, 310A, *The Swinburne Letters* 2:34–35, emphasis in original.

18. Swinburne to Richard Monckton Milnes, Fontmel Lodge, Bournemouth, Poole, January 21, 1863, *The Swinburne Letters* 1:70.

19. The importance of the camaraderie around sexual exchanges of these kinds comes through in Swinburne's letter to George Powell: "My Dear Powell, Many thanks for the photo: you sent me of Burton—this one was new to me and it is very characteristic, and I shall keep it and remain obliged to you. This day (Saturday) week some of us go to town—I don't know if I shall—for the 'sacred season,' with an eye to Galilean orgies. Shall you be in town? I suppose not. If I went it would be with antichristian views. Good Friday and Easter Sunday commemorated after the fashion of the Marquis might be made amusing." A. C. Swinburne to George Powell, Holywood, March 13 [1869], *The Swinburne Letters* 2:7.

20. A. C. Swinburne to J. Frederick Collingwood, January 31 [1868?], *The Swinburne Letters* 1:250, 288, emphasis in original.

21. Hotten was part of the literary culture of London, and when he died, the London booksellers gave him a tombstone. Ashbee, *Index Librorum Prohibitorum,* 253. Chattos and Windus bought his store, stock, and publishing rights upon his death and, for a time, referred to him on their publications to legitimize their ventures. As well, the *Dictionary of National Bibliography* recognized his authority as a publisher and writer.

22. Ashbee, *Index Librorum Prohibitorum,* 249–256.

23. While the working classes also read books borrowed from private lending libraries, these libraries did not stock pornography. Only a few of the most select libraries, such as the Bodleian, the Cambridge Library, and the British Library, had collections of pornography. They separated these collections from the rest of their materials through closed stacks under anachronistic call numbers. Even if the vigilant managed to find out about the collections, they could not look at them because of user restrictions. Libraries were not the place for the working classes or women to broaden their sexual literacy. The libraries that currently have collections of pornography began to collect works during the period, but by donation rather than through systematic purchase. The many works that Ashbee amassed were donated to the British Library upon his death in 1900. However, these were not available to the public. Instead, they were kept locked in the Private Case. Duplicate works were sent to the Bodleian or burned.

24. Ashbee, *Index Librorum Prohibitorum,* 280.

25. Quoted in Mendes, *Clandestine Erotic Fiction,* 8. The quote comes from Reddie's letter to Ashbee tipped into the British Library's copy of Martial.

26. Richard Payne Knight, Esq, *A Discourse on the Worship of Priapus, and its connection with the Mystic Theology of the Ancients* (London: [J. C. Hotten], 1865). For prices, information about Payne, and a reproduction of Hotten's advertising circular, see Ashbee, *Index Librorum Prohibitorum,* 5–12.

27. Ashbee, *Index Librorum Prohibitorum,* 229–236, 239–259.

28. For general information about these men, see Sir Leslie Stephan and Sir Sidney Lee, *The Dictionary of National Bibliography* (Oxford, U. K.: Oxford University Press, 1917–).

29. Pope-Hennessy, *Monckton Milnes,* 120.

30. Pope-Hennessy, *Monckton Milnes,* 121.

31. Stephan and Lee, *The Dictionary of National Bibliography* 23, Supplement, 79–80.

32. *The Journal of the Royal Geographic Society* 50 (London: John Murray, 1880), xxix.

33. Brodie, *The Devil Drives,* 295.

34. Algernon Charles Swinburne, "Mr. Whistler's Lecture on Art," ms. facsimile, Bibliophile Society (St. Louis: Private Property by W. K. Bixby, 1913?). For a discussion of the trial, see Kendrick, *The Secret Museum,* 163–167, and Edward de Grazia, *Girls Lean Back Everywhere: The Law of Obscenity and the Assault on Genius* (New York: Random House, 1992), 42. For Vizatelly's defense, see Henry Vizatelly, *Extracts Principally from English Classics: Showing That the Legal Suppression of M. Zola's Novels Would Logically Involve the Bowdlerizing of Some of the Greatest Works in English Literature* (London: Vizatelly, 1888).

35. Quoted in James G. Nelson, "Leonard Smithers and Captain Sir Richard Burton," *Journal of the Eighteen Nineties Society,* 24 (1997): 6.

36. See Frank Mort, *Dangerous Sexualities: Medico-Moral Politics in England since 1830* (London: Routledge & Kegan Paul, 1987), and Walkowitz, *Prostitution and Victorian Society.*

37. The failure to apprehend and prosecute more of the pornographers was much lamented by the SSV. "I may safely say that it has not been one case in six brought under the Society's notice in which they have been able to prosecute, chiefly from the heavy expenses attending a prosecution." "Letter from Mr. Pritchard to Lord Campbell," January 1858, Social Evils Extracts Album, part 1.

38. Sir Edmund Gosse, "An Essay (with Two Notes) on Swinburne," 1917, first published in *The Swinburne Letters,* 6:248.

39. The works of mid-century include the following: two scientific works by John Davenport, *Aphrodisiacs and Anti-aphrodisiacs* (1869) *Curiositates Eroticae Physiologie* (1875), and a recapitulation of his ideas in a third work, *Esoteric Physiology Sexagyma* (1888); a number of works on phallicism, *A Discourse on the Worship of Priapus* (1865), *Phallic Worship* (1886), *The Worship of Priapus,* and *The Masculine Cross;* the three bibliographies by Ashbee and another bibliography, *Bibliotheca Arcana* (1884); a seven-part series on flagellation called *The Library Illustrative of Social Progress,* which includes *Lady Bumtickler's Revels, Madame Birchini's Dance,* and *Exhibition of Female Flagellants* (1860, 1872–1873); other works on flagellation, including *Letters Addressed to Editor of the Englishwoman's Domestic Magazine* (1870), *Indecent Whipping* (1885), [Bertram], *The Merry Order of Saint Bridget* (1865), and *Curiosities of Flagellation* (1875); translations of *The Kama Sutra* (1883), the *Ananga-Ranga* (1885), and *The Perfumed Garden of the Cheikh Nefzaoui* (1888); exotic works such as those by Edward Sellon, including *Annotations on the Sacred Writings of the Hindus* (1865) and *The New Epicurean* (1865); and historical works like the obscene epigrams from Martialis entitled *The Index Expurgatorius* (1868). Other articles on sexuality by the Anthropological Society include Edward Sellon, "On Phallic Worship in India," and W. T. Pritchard, "Notes on Certain Anthropological Matters respecting the South Sea Islanders (the Samoans), in *Memoirs Read before the Anthropological Society of London, 1863–1864* (London: Trubner, 1865); Richard Burton, "Notes on an Hermaphrodite," and Sellon, "Some Remarks on Indian Gnosticism, or Sacti Puja, the Worship of Female Powers," in *Memoirs Read before the Anthropological Society of London, 1865–1866;* C. Staniland Wake, "Sacred Prostitution," and Dr. Charnon, "Facts Relating to Polyandry," *Anthropologia,* vol. 1, 1873–1875.

40. Ashbee, *Index Librorum Prohibitorum,* xxvii continued into note 31.

41. Ashbee discusses the process of ordering his first bibliography on pages liii to lxi of *Index Librorum Prohibitorum*. In it, he gives a justification for alphabetizing his bibliography. In his subsequent works he continues to organize alphabetically by title but also maintains a subject category when he finds it useful; for instance, he uses the classification of American publications on pages 198–237 of *Catena Librorum Tacendorum* and a content category like flagellation on pages 442–470 of *Centuria Librorum Absconditorum*.

42. *Bibliotheca Arcana* (London: George Redway, 1884), ix.

43. Ashbee, *Index Librorum Prohibitorum*, vii.

44. Jeffrey Weeks, *Making Sexual History* (London: Polity Press, 2000), 236–237.

45. Claude Lévi-Strauss, *Myth and Meaning: Cracking the Code of Culture*, foreword by Wendy Doniger (New York: Schocken Books, 1995), 3.

46. Elizabeth Edwards, ed., *Anthropology and Photography, 1860–1920* (New Haven: Yale University Press, 1992). In particular, see Brian Street, "British Popular Anthropology: Exhibiting and Photographing the Other," in that volume.

47. *The Kama Sutra of Vatsyayana* (Cosmopoli: For the Kama Shastra Society of London and Benares and for Private Circulation only, 1883); *Ananga-Ranga or The Hindu Art of Love*, translated from the Sanskrit and annotated by A.F.F. and B.F.R. (Cosmopoli [London]: For the Kama Shastra Society of London and Benares, and for private circulation only, 1885); *The Perfumed Garden of the Cheikh Nefzaoui: A Manual of Arabian Erotology* (Cosmopoli [London]: For the Kama Shastra Society of London and Benares and for Private Circulation only, 1886); *The History of the Sect of Maharajas, or Vallaharcharpas in Western India* (London: Trubner, 60 Paternoster Row, 1865). While I have not had an opportunity to see the last work—Ashbee states that only seventy-five copies were sold in Europe, which makes it doubtful that any remain there—Ashbee offers extensive quotations, and the quotations suggest it belongs with the previous works.

48. Ashbee, *Index Librorum Prohibitorum*, 282.

49. *The Kama Sutra*, 5.

50. *The Kama Sutra*, 5.

51. *The Kama Sutra*, 41.

52. *The Kama Sutra*, 7.

53. Ashbee, *Index Librorum Prohibitorum*, 283.

54. In the preface to the *Ananga-Ranga*, Burton and Arbuthnot again make a similar point. "The originality is everywhere mixed up, it is true, with a peculiar quaintness resulting from the language and from the peculiarities of Hindu thought" (viii).

55. Ashbee, *Catena Librorum Tacedorum*, 465.

56. *The Kama Sutra*, 61.

57. Ashbee, *Catena Librorum Tacedorum*, 465.

58. *The Kama Sutra*, 77.

59. Ashbee, *Catena Librorum Tacedorum*, 467.

60. John Shortt, M.D., F.L.S., M.R.C.P.L, etc., Surgeon General Superintendent of Vaccination, Madras Presidency, "The Bayadère, or, Dancing Girls of Southern India"

Memoirs Read before the Anthropological Society of London, 1867–1869, 182–194, 191–192, 194, italics in original .

61. James Hunt, "On the Negro's Place in Nature" *Memoirs Read before the Anthropological Society of London, 1863–1864,* 51.

62. James Hunt, "On the Negro's Place in Nature," 47.

63. James Hunt, "On the Negro's Place in Nature," 55.

64. John Davenport, *Curiositates Eroticae Physiologaie;* or, Tabooed Subjects Freely Treated (London: Privately Printed, 1875), 2, italics in original.

65. Davenport, *Curiositates Eroticae Physiologaie,* 16, 17.

66. Davenport, *Curiositates Eroticae Physiologaie,* 18.

67. John Davenport, *Aphrodisiacs and Anti-Aphrodisiacs: Three Essays on the Powers of Reproduction* (London: Privately Printed [J. C. Hotten], 1869 [1873]), *22–23.*

68. Davenport, *Curiositates Eroticae Physiologiae,* 164.

69. Richard F. Burton, "Notes on an Hermaphrodite," *Memoirs Read before the Anthropological Society of London, 1865–1866,* 262–263.

70. R.B.N. Walker, F.R.G.S., F.A.S.L., Local Secretary A.S.L., etc., "On the Alleged Sterility of the Union of Women of Savage Races," *Memoirs Read before the Anthropological Society of London, 1865–1866,* 284.

71. *The Masculine Cross* (London: Printed for Private Circulation, 1886), 19.

72. *Phallic Worship* (London: Printed for Private Circulation, 1886), 6–7.

73. Davenport, *Aphrodisiacs and Anti-Aphrodisiacs,* 10–11.

74. *Fashionable Lectures: Composed and Delivered with Birch Discipline, etc.* The Fourth Edition, with Considerable Additions (London: Printed for G. Peacock [J. C. Hotten, 1873]), 43–44, italics in original.

75. *Fashionable Lectures,* 50, 55, 59.

76. *Fashionable Lectures,* 68–69.

77. Ashbee, *Index Librorum Prohibitorum,* 241–242.

78. Ashbee points out this unidirectional arrangement: "further, it is always the woman who wields the rod, and this, to say the least of it, is entirely one sided." Ashbee, *Index Librorum Prohibitorum,* 242.

79. See, for example, Ian Gibson, *The English Vice,* chs. 2 and 3; John Chandos, *Boys Together: English Public Schools, 1800–1864* (New Haven: Yale University Press, 1984); P. J. Rich, *Chains of Empire: English Public Schools, Masonic Cabalism, Historical Causality, and Imperial Clubdom* (London: Regency Press, 1991); and Jonathon Rutherford, *Forever England: Reflections on Race, Masculinity and Empire* (London: Lawrence & Wishart, 1997).

80. *The Role of Flogging in Venereal Affairs* (London: J. C. Hotten, 1872), 41.

81. A. C. Swinburne to George Powell, Grantown, July 8, [1872], *The Swinburne Letters* 2: 179.

82. As feminists interested in the epistemological basis of objectivity have argued, "knowers are detached, neutral spectators, and the objects of knowledge are separate from them; they are inert items in the observational knowledge gathering process." See

Vrinda Dalmiya and Linda Alcoff, "Are 'Old Wives' Tales' Justified?" in *Feminist Epistemologies,* ed. Linda Alcoff and Elizabeth Porter (New York: Routledge, 1993), 217–244; Stephen Jay Gould, *The Mismeasure of Man* (New York: Norton, 1981); and Sandra Harding, *Whose Science? Whose Knowledge?* (Ithaca: Cornell University Press, 1991).

83. The development of an American imperial agenda later in the century brought a similar scientific pornography. By the end of the nineteenth century, America, with a heightened interest in overseas possessions and control, began to focus on issues of the "other" located in the Far East and the Caribbean in a manner similar to the ways British pornography centered on India. See J. E. DeBecker, *Yoshiwara: The Nightless City* (Paris [Chicago?]: Charles Carrington [Targ?], 1907); and *Amorous Adventures of a Japanese Gentleman* (Yokohama [Paris?]: Printed for the Daimo of Satsuma [Charles Carrington or Isadore Liseux], 1897).

CHAPTER 3: *THE PEARL* BEFORE SWINE

1. *The Pearl* (1879; reprint, New York: Grove Press, 1968), 1.

2. Mendes, *Clandestine Erotic Fiction,* 4–7, 200–204.

3. Mendes, *Clandestine Erotic Fiction,* 4.

4. Mendes, *Clandestine Erotic Fiction,* 439. Mendes believes that Lazenby might have blackmailed his clients into helping him flee.

5. Mendes, *Clandestine Erotic Fiction,* 5, 439, 452.

6. Mendes, *Clandestine Erotic Fiction,* 16–18.

7. "His failure was attributable to his inability to recover book debts to a large amount, to his serious illness which deprived the business of his direction, to possession being taken for the debenture-holders, and to the loss of L 4,300 in Stock Exchange speculation." Mendes, *Clandestine Erotic Fiction,* 459.

8. PRO, Criminal Court Papers, "The Information and Complaint of Charles Arrow and the Deposition of the Same Person" against H. S. Nichols, January 10, 1900, Crim60/4/xc6797.

9. In 1908, Nichols emigrated to New York City, supposedly with a copy of *My Secret Life* hidden in the false bottom of a suitcase. In New York he continued to publish. In 1939 he died in Bellevue Mental Hospital.

10. Stanley Weintraub, *Beardsley: A Biography* (New York: George Braziller, 1967), 243–244.

11. The NVA, like the SSV before it, was a voluntary society that relied on donations. The lack of funds, particularly to cover the costs involved in entrapping the pornographers, put them in an importunate relationship with the Home Office. PRO, Home Office Papers, Note on payment of NVA for prosecutions, 1890, HO144/478/28111.

12. "Report from the Joint Select Committee on Lotteries and Indecent Advertisements" (London: HMSO, 1908), NVA Box 107, vi.

13. PRO, Home Office Papers, Prosecution under Post Office Protection Act, Warrant issued to stop obscene circulars, 1891, HO144/238/A52539.

14. "Report from the Joint Select Committee on Lotteries and Indecent Advertisements," 18–19.

15. Pornographers shipping to London included G. Arthur of Switzerland, alias A. de Sailles of Paris; J. Berge of Rotterdam; C. Carrington of Paris and Brussels, alias H. Robert of Paris; Charles Chaillon of Paris, alias Charles Offenstadt; L. Chaubard of Paris; H. Daragon of Paris; Jean Fort of Paris; A. Mazoyer of Lyons, alias L'Economie of Lyons; H. Pouwells of Paris; the Novelty Warehouse of Barcelona; Charles Schraeter of Barcelona; and Señor Zarubaly of Barcelona. PRO, Home Office Papers, HO151/9, Warrant for mails from twelve overseas pornographers, December, 1909, 414–415.

16. The Art Studio, the World Office, and the Head Office of the Tobacco Manufacturing Company were among the "fronts" operating out of Amsterdam in the 1890s for individual vendors like Adolf Estinger, alias Rambo. PRO, Home Office Papers, HO151/5, Letter re: Graphic Toy Company, February, 1891, 30.

17. One client knew that the post office censored the mails when he wrote to Adolf Estinger of Budapest that the materials should be carefully packed because the post people were a "sharp lot." PRO, Home Office Papers, Letter from John Flewelling to Adolf Estinger, 1894, HO144/238/A52539E. For information about Estinger, see PRO, Home Office Papers, "Communication from the Postmaster General to the Under-Secretary of State," 1894, HO144/238/A52539E.

18. "Report from the Joint Select Committee on Lotteries and Indecent Advertisements," 38.

19. "Report from the Joint Select Committee on Lotteries and Indecent Advertisements," 39.

20. Many of the vendors landed in Paris because of France's antipathy to prosecution. France would only prosecute if the traffic took place in France and only if it happened in public. "The French government, however, said that no action could be taken in France unless the traffic was carried on in a public place." PRO, Home Office Papers, "The Stoppage of Letters to or from Dealers in Obscene Matter," 1898, 2, HO45/9752/A59329. Holland and France had legislation in place to prosecute the pornographers, but neither government did so. PRO, Home Office Papers, "Draft for Approval," 1891, 2, HO144/238/A52539B. While some prosecutions took place in the various locations, mostly a vast international shuffling of the problem occurred. For example, one "dealer obtained his supplies from Hungary, Germany, and Italy, and the names of the manufacturers were sent to those countries, and proceedings appear to have been taken in all cases by the respective governments. One dealer fled from Amsterdam to Antwerp to escape punishment. In the following August a number of plates, from which photographs were printed, were seized in Holland. By that time most of the dealers had left the country." PRO, Home Office Papers, "The Stoppage of Letters to or from Dealers in Obscene Matter," 1898, 2, HO45/9752/A59329.

21. See PRO, Home Office Papers, Chart of Warrant Issues, 1898, HO45/9752/A59329.

22. PRO, Home Office Papers, "The Stoppage of Letters to or from Dealers in Obscene Matter," PRO, H045/9752/A59329; Home Office Papers, HO151/6, HO151/7, HO151/8, HO151/9.

23. PRO, Home Office Papers, Letter from John Flewelling to Adolf Estinger, 1894, HO144/238/A52539E.

24. PRO, Home Office Papers, Letter from General Post Office to UnderSecretary of State, 1894, HO144/238/A52539E xc13846.

25. PRO, Home Office Papers, Chart of Warrant Issues, 1898, HO45/9752/A59329 xc13898, no. 18.

26. See, for example, [Charles Carrington], *Forbidden Books: Notes and Gossip on Tabood Literature* (Paris: For the Author and His Friends [Carrington], 1902).

27. Eric Hobsbawm, *Industry and Empire* (London: Penguin Books, 1968), 166.

28. "Catalogue of Rare Curious and Voluptuous Reading" ([Paris], 1896), 12, Bodleian Library.

29. Album 7, item 25, "Catalogue of a Choice Collection of Rare and Curious English Books" (London, 1903).

30. Mendes, *Clandestine Erotic Fiction,* 344.

31. Mendes, *Clandestine Erotic Fiction,* 234–235.

32. Album 7, item 25, "Catalogue of a Choice Collection of Rare and Curious English Books" (London, 1903); "Catalogue of Rare, Curious, and Voluptuous Readings" (1897), in "Prospectuses," British Library.

33. Album 7, item 25, "Catalogue of a Choice Collection of Rare and Curious English Books" (London, 1903). See also Mendes, *Clandestine Erotic Fiction,* 161–166.

34. Roughly 280,000 people in Britain had an income of over 160 pounds in 1860; by 1880 there were 620,000, and by 1914 more than a million. However, as W. Hamish Fraser makes clear, even given these incomes the middle classes had to skimp on food. W. Hamish Fraser, *The Coming of the Mass Market, 1850–1914* (London: Macmillan, 1981), 23, 41, 75.

35. Aquarelles are a type of illustration in which the outlines are first printed and the water colors are manually stenciled in to fill in the outlines. Each stencil has a different color. It is generally thought of as a French process. Album 7, item 21, "Catalogue of Rare, Curious and Voluptuous Reading" (Paris?, 1901).

36. Because Paris became an international distribution center for English-language pornography, prices were often given in dollars as well as pounds. Album 7, item 12, "Strictly Confidential" (Paris, c. 1903).

37. Album 7, item 9, "Erotic Photos" (Paris?, 1902).

38. Photography at this point seemed as close to novelties as to literature. Dealers might sell dildos, preservatives, moving figures, transparent cards, Venus rings, etc., as well as photographs. See Album 7, item 26, untitled (London, c. 1900?), and untitled catalogue (London, 1892), in "Prospectuses," British Library.

39. PRO, Home Office Papers, General Post Office to Home Office concerning overseas pornographers, 1896, 3, HO144/192/A6657D/63.

40. Society for the Suppression of Vice, *Abstract of the Seventy-Sixth Annual Report for 1879* (Lincoln's Inn Fields: Society's Chambers, 1879), 1.

41. Purveyors of birth control sent out catalogues and notices to those who placed birth announcements in newspapers.

42. Eric Hobsbawm, *The Age of Empire, 1875–1914* (New York: Vintage Books, 1989), 181.

43. Ashbee, *Catena Librorum Tacendorum,* xlii–xliii.

44. Ashbee, *Catena Librorum Tacendorum,* 185.

45. Henry Miles, *Forbidden Fruit* (London: Luxor Press, 1973), 48, 49.

46. Marcus, *The Other Victorians,* 274.

47. *The Romance of Lust* (1873; reprint, New York: Grove Press, 1968), 346.

48. *The Pearl, Christmas Annual* (London: Privately Printed, 1881), 5

49. *Amorous Adventures of a Japanese Gentleman* (Yokohama [Paris]: Printed for the Daimo of Satsuma [Charles Carrington or Isadore Liseux], 1897); *Flossie, a Venus of Fifteen, by One who knew this Charming Goddess and Worshipped at her Shrine* (London and New York [Paris]: Printed for the Erotica Biblion Society [Charles Carrington?, c. 1900]); *The Birchen Bouquet; or Curious and Original Anecdotes of Ladies fond of administering the Birch Discipline, and Published for the Amusement as well as the Benefit of those Ladies who have under their Tuition sulky, stupid, wanton, lying or idle young Ladies or Gentlemen* (Birchington-on-Sea [London: Edward Avery?], 1881); *Ophelia Cox, With Rod and Bum, or Sport in the West End of London* (London; New York: Erotica Biblion Society, 1898); *Stays and Gloves. Figure-Training and Deportment by means of the discipline of Tight Corsets, narrow High-heeled Boots, clinging Kid Gloves, Combinations, etc., etc.* (London, 1909); *Big Bellied Nelly, or Confessions of a doctor* (Paris; London: N.p., 19—?).

50. *Frank and I* (1902; reprint, New York: Blue Moon Books, 1987), 132, 133.

51. *Sweet Seventeen: the True Story of a Daughter's Awful Whipping and its Delightful if Direful Consequence* (Paris: [Charles Carrington], 1910), 35.

52. *Sweet Seventeen,* 37.

53. For a discussion of Freud and other early sexologists, see Weeks, *Sexuality and Its Discontents, 68.*

54. Sigmund Freud, *Three Essays on the Theory of Sexuality,* 6th ed., tr. James Strachey (Leipzig and Vienna: Deuticke, 1925; reprint, New York: Basic Books, 1975), 20.

55. Freud, *Three Essays,* 19.

56. Freud, *Three Essays,* 21 note 2.

57. Freud, *Three Essays,* 27.

58. *Sweet Seventeen,* 10.

59. *The Simple Tale of Suzan Aked or Innocence Awakened, Ignorance Dispelled* (London and New York: Printed for the Erotica Biblion Society, 1898), 12–13.

60. *The Pearl* (1968; reprint), 73. See Ashbee, *Cantena Librorum Tacendorum,* 343–347.

61. These early photographs of white women were the predecessors of current centerfolds. "This classical body—a refined, orifice-less, laminated surface—is homologous to the forms of official high culture which legitimated their authority by reference to the

values—the highness of the classical body." Laura Kipnis, "(Male) Desire and (Female) Disgust: Reading *Hustler,*" in *Cultural Studies,* ed. Lawrence Grossberg, Cary Nelson, and Paula Treichler (New York: Routledge, 1992), 376.

62. *The Horn Book: A Girl's Guide to the Knowledge of Good and Evil* (London: Erotica Biblion Society, 1899).

63. Richard von Krafft-Ebing, *Psychopathia Sexualis* (1886; reprint, New York: G. P. Putnam's Sons, 1965); Weeks, *Sexuality and Its Discontents,* 68.

64. Noyes, *The Mastery of Submission,* 50.

65. [Carrington], *Forbidden Books,* 33.

66. [Carrington], *Forbidden Books,* 91.

67. Album 7, item 12, "Strictly Confidential" (Paris, c. 1903).

68. Album 7, item 12, "Strictly Confidential" (Paris, c. 1903).

69. Noyes, *The Mastery of Submission,* 50–79 in particular.

70. Like many catalogues intended for an international audience, this one gave prices in dollars but then provided the exchange rate for the pound. Album 7, item 12, "Strictly Confidential" (Paris, c. 1903).

71. PRO, Home Office Papers, Letter from John Flewelling to Adolf Estinger, 1894, HO144/238/A52539E; Album 7, item 12, "Strictly Confidential" (Paris, c. 1903).

72. Karl Marx, *Capital,* vol. 1 (1887; reprint, New York: International Publishers, 1967), 76–87.

73. Mendes, *Clandestine Erotic Fiction,* 344.

74. Michael T. Taussig, *The Devil and Commodity Fetishism in South America* (Chapel Hill: University of North Carolina Press, 1980), 31–32. See also Sut Jhally, *The Codes of Advertising: Fetishism and the Political Economy of Meaning in the Consumer Society* (New York: Routledge, 1990).

75. Thomas Richards, *The Commodity Culture of Victorian England: Advertising and Spectacle, 1851–1914* (Stanford, Calif.: Stanford University Press, 1990), 210.

76. Album 7, item 9, "Erotic Photos" (Paris?, 1902); untitled catalogue (London, 1892), in "Prospectuses," British Library.

77. *The Pearl,* (1968 reprint), 397.

78. *The Pearl,* (1968 reprint), 396.

79. *The Story of Seven Maidens: Slavery in West India* (Cambridge, U. K. [Paris]: James Andrews [Carrington], 1907), v.

80. *The Story of Seven Maidens,* vi.

81. *The Story of Seven Maidens,* 9–10.

82. *The Story of Seven Maidens,* 12.

83. *The Story of Seven Maidens,* 17–18.

84. *The Story of Seven Maidens,* 12.

85. Richards, *The Commodity Culture of Victorian England,* 7.

86. W. T. Stead, "The Maiden Tribute of Modern Babylon," *Pall Mall Gazette* 42, nos. 6336–6340, (July 6–10, 1885). See Walkowitz, *City of Dreadful Delight,* 81–134.

87. When the police investigated thefts at the Central Post Office in 1899, they discovered that some of the postal clerks and messenger boys worked as prostitutes for middle- and upper-class men at 19 Cleveland Street. See H. Montgomery Hyde, *The Cleveland Street Scandal* (New York: Coward, McCann & Geoghegan, 1976), for a general overview, and Morris B. Kaplan, "Did 'My Lord Gomorrah' Smile?: Homosexuality, Class, and Prostitution in the Cleveland Street Affair," in *Disorder in the Courts: Trials and Sexual Conflict at the Turn of the Century,* ed. George Robb and Nancy Erber (New York: New York University Press, 1999), 78–99.

88. [Oscar Wilde?], *Teleny or Reverse of the Medal,* Traveller's Press Companion Series (1893; reprint, Paris: Olympia Press, n.d.). Original printed by Nichols for Smithers. Mendes details the fascinating publication of this work in *Clandestine Erotic Fiction,* 252–254. *Teleny* was apparently written by a group of authors, of which Oscar Wilde was the most famous. The authors used Charles Hirsh's shop in London as a drop-off site for the manuscript.

89. [Wilde?], *Teleny,* 39–41.

90. [Wilde?], *Teleny,* 53.

91. [Wilde?],*Teleny,* 202–203.

92. Ed Cohen, *Talk on the Wilde Side: Towards a Genealogy of a Discourse on Male Sexualities* (New York and London: Routledge, 1993); Alan Sinfield, *The Wilde Century* (London: Cassell, 1994).

93. Jonathon Dollimore, *Sexual Dissidence: Augustine to Wilde, Freud to Foucault* (New York: Oxford University Press, 1991), 336–339.

94. Even the fictional tragedy of Teleny's death was undermined by the promise of further adventures through a sequel. The vignette form and the promise of future sales took priority over the clear statement on contemporary morality.

95. John Pemble, *The Mediterranean Passion: Victorians and Edwardians in the South* (Oxford, U. K.: Clarendon Press, 1987), 160.

96. Peter Weiermair, *Wilhelm von Gloeden* (Cologne: Taschen, 1996).

CHAPTER 4: FILTH IN THE WRONG PEOPLE'S HANDS

1. *Vigilance Record* (London), January 1905, 8.

2. Paul Hammond, *French Undressing: Naughty Postcards from 1900 to 1920* (London: Bloomsbury Books, 1974), 9.

3. H. L. Lipman's of Philadelphia established the first "company card" in 1861 when it published preprinted reminders for businesses and travelers. Other companies quickly followed suit. Dorothy B. Ryan and George Miller, *Picture Postcards in the United States, 1893–1918* (New York: Clarkson N. Potter, 1982), 1–2. The Austro-Hungarian Empire issued official "state" postal cards in 1869. These company cards and state cards, though, did not have illustrations and instead functioned as inexpensive ways to send information.

4. By the 1890s, governments allowed privately printed postcards the same postal privileges as government-issued cards. Giovanni Fanelli and Ezio Godoli, *Art Nouveau Postcards* (New York: Rizzoli International, 1987), 15, note 7. Postcards could be sent through the mails cheaply both locally and internationally. The link between visuals and the cheap passage of information was tightened. Visual images became a form of mass communication.

5. For corner stores, see "Report from the Joint Select Committee of Lotteries and Indecent Advertisements," 61–62; and *Vigilance Record,* September 1902, 71, and February 1905, 14–15. For markets, see *Vigilance Record,* April 1902, 30. For tobacconists, see *Vigilance Record,* August 1904, 3, and November 1904, 7. For newsagents, see *Vigilance Record,* April 1904, 5, and November 1904, 6. For street vending, see *Vigilance Record,* September 1902, 59; September 1903, 72; May 1904, 7; and August 1905, 68.

6. *Vigilance Record,* December 1904, 4.

7. *Vigilance Record,* April 1904, 4.

8. *Vigilance Record,* November 1904, 7.

9. *Vigilance Record,* November 1903, 82.

10. "Report from the Joint Select Committee on Lotteries and Indecent Advertisements," 58.

11. Hammond, *French Undressing,* 9.

12. *Vigilance Record,* January 1906, 7; March 1906, 23; and March 1910, 24.

13. Hammond, *French Undressing,* 9.

14. Fanelli and Godoli, *Art Nouveau Postcards,* 16.

15. *Vigilance Record,* August 1909, 62.

16. The postcards I analyze come from the Kinsey Institute, the Victoria and Albert Museum, and from private collectors and dealers. I have also haunted ephemera shows and sales for three years to gauge the representativeness of these sample. I have relied most heavily upon the Milford Haven collection of postcards, held at the Victoria and Albert Museum, even though his collection is not as extensive as the collection at the Kinsey Institute. However, the Milford Haven collection has remained intact, while the Kinsey Institute's collection is the result of long-term acquisitions. While this does not mean that the Milford Haven collection offers a representative sample of cards at the beginning of the twentieth century, it does offer a wide range of images developed by an important collector known for the breadth of his tastes. I have supplemented the Milford Haven collection with postcards from private dealers and owners because of the inadequacy of images of "exotics" in comparison to those produced and circulated in the late nineteenth century.

    The Milford Haven collection, catalogued by E. J. Dingwall in 1960, has 631 postcards. Dingwall organized the collection according to fifteen categories such as "nudes," "breasts," "prostitution," etc. I have chosen not to follow this organizational schema in my analysis because I believe that many images—whether "nudes," "breasts," or "prostitutes"—offer similar visual tropes.

17. For a discussion of exoticism, see Said, *Culture and Imperialism;* Mary Louise Pratt, *Imperial Eyes: Travel Writing and Transculturation* (New York: Routledge, 1992); and Edward Said, *Orientalism* (New York: Vintage Books, 1979).

18. For other examples of the popularization of anthropological conceptions of natives, see Brian Street, "British Popular Anthropology: Exhibiting and Photographing the Other," in *Anthropology and Photography,* ed. Elizabeth Edwards (New Haven: Yale University Press, 1992), 122–131; Ben Shephard, "Showbiz Imperialism: The Case of Peter Lobengula," in *Imperialism and Popular Culture,* ed. John M. Mackenzie (Manchester, U.K.: Manchester University Press, 1986), 94–112; Sander L. Gilman, "Black Bodies, White Bodies: Towards an Iconography of Female Sexuality in Late Nineteenth-Century Art, Medicine, and Literature," in *Race, Writing, and Difference,* ed. Henry Louis Gates (Chicago: University of Chicago Press, 1986), 223–261.

19. E. J. Dingwall, "The Milford Haven Collection of Postcards," card 5.

20. Postcard (Germany: W. O. Hochherz, Dresden, Fischhausstrasse 6, n.d.), Kinsey Institute P.O. 1/60.

21. For a more complete discussion of Algerian postcards and the relationship between postcards and culture, see Malek Alloula, *The Colonial Harem* (Minneapolis: University of Minnesota Press, 1986).

22. Dingwall, "The Milford Haven Collection of Postcards," cards 72–121.

23. Dingwall, "The Milford Haven Collection of Postcards," breasts: cards 323–335; buttocks: cards 350–419.

24. Linda Nochlin, *Women, Art, and Power: And Other Essays* (New York: Harper & Row, 1988), 17.

25. Linda Nochlin emphasizes the ways in which unimpeded access to the nude contributed to the conception of artist as creator. "One might add that the passivity implicit to the imagery of the naked woman in Western art is a function not merely of the attitude of the owner-spectator, but that of the artist himself: indeed the myth of Pygmalion, revived in the nineteenth century, admirably embodies the notion of the artist as sexually dominant creator: man—the artist—fashioning from inert matter an ideal erotic object for himself, a woman cut from the very pattern of his desires." Nochlin, *Women, Art, and Power,* 143. In fact, the postcards themselves played up the sexual relationship between artists and models by showing scenes of the model seduced by the artist.

26. Dingwall, "The Milford Haven Collection of Postcards," cards 163–204.

27. For an overview of the symbolic meanings of ritual wedding dress, see Gillis, *For Better, for Worse,* and Pamela R. Frese, "The Union of Nature and Culture: Gender Symbolism in the American Wedding Ritual," in *Transcending Boundaries: Multi-Disciplinary Approaches to the Study of Gender,* ed. Pamela R. Frese and John M. Coggeshall (New York: Bergin & Garvey, 1991), 97–112.

28. Dingwall, "The Milford Haven Collection of Postcards," card 405.

29. Dingwall, "The Milford Haven Collection of Postcards," cards 205 and 206, 209–212, and 496–498, respectively.

30. For a discussion of the hunt and poaching, see Porter, *English Society in the Eighteenth Century.*

31. Dingwall, "The Milford Haven Collection of Postcards," card 354 (Milano: No. 16 U from the house of Dulio Rainero, 1905).

32. Dingwall, "The Milford Haven Collection of Postcards," card 262.

33. Both cards are from a private collection. They appear to be from the 1890s.

34. Dingwall, "The Milford Haven Collection of Postcards," cards 374 and 375.

35. Dingwall, "The Milford Haven Collection of Postcards," card 294.

36. Dingwall, "The Milford Haven Collection of Postcards," cards 439 and 440.

37. Dingwall, "The Milford Haven Collection of Postcards," cards 420–504.

38. The presence of children exacerbated the already problematic situation. When the police observed children viewing such images, the courts heightened fines and gave sentences of hard labor to vendors. One defendant, George Smith, was fined twenty-five pounds in part because Inspector Cheyney "saw children looking in the shop window." *Vigilance Record,* April 1905, 31. Another vendor, Jacob Bloom, had "a crowd of children" standing outside his shop. *Vigilance Record,* September 1905, 74. Likewise, "a number of young boys and girls" stood outside the shop window of John and Margaret Allon. *Vigilance Record,* September 1906, 75.

39. For example, a photographic "peepshow" had run for eight years without complaint before the police arrested the proprietor. *Vigilance Record,* May 1904, 7.

40. "Report from the Joint Select Committee on Lotteries and Indecent Advertisements," 44–45.

41. "Translation Concerning Correspondence Respecting the International Conference on Obscene Publications and the 'White Slave Trade,'" 1912, 4, NVA Papers, Box 107.

42. Eighty-six associations, including "the powerful National Vigilance Association," took part in an international conference aimed at ending the expansion of pornography in 1912. "Translation Concerning Correspondence," 6.

43. *Vigilance Record,* November 1904, 7.

44. *Vigilance Record,* April 1905, 31–32.

45. It appears in this case that the niece, rather than Mr. Varley, was the main culprit. However, the police followed the earlier pattern that went back to Dugdale's daughter of not recognizing female proprietors when a male relative was present.

46. *Vigilance Record,* September 1903, 71.

47. *Vigilance Record,* December 1906, 100.

48. *Vigilance Record,* April 1902, 30; April 1903, 72; and November 1904, 6.

49. "Report from the Joint Select Committee on Lotteries and Indecent Advertisements," 80–81.

50. Nochlin, *Women, Art, and Power,* 159.

51. For a discussion of the "cult of little girls" as sexualized beings, see Wolf von Eckardt, Sander L. Gilman, and J. Edward Chamberlin, *Oscar Wilde's London: A Scrapbook of Vices and Virtues: 1890–1900* (Garden City, N.Y.: Anchor Press, 1987), 238–261; James Kincaid, *Child Loving: The Erotic Child and Victorian Literature* (New York: Routledge, 1994).

52. *Vigilance Record,* May 1902, 39.

53. *Vigilance Record,* July 1911, 54.

54. *Vigilance Record,* July 1911, 54. Reprinted from *The Natal Mercury* (South Africa), (June 5, 1911).

55. *Vigilance Record,* September 1911, 72.

Conclusion: Sexuality Re-imagined

1. Gordon Hawkins and Franklin E. Zimring, *Pornography in a Free Society* (Cambridge, U. K.: Cambridge University Press, 1988).

2. Michel Foucault, *The History of Sexuality: An Introduction,* vol. 1 (New York: Vintage Books, 1980), 11.

3. Kipnis, *Bound and Gagged,* 175.

4. Vance, "Pleasure and Danger," 7.

References

MANUSCRIPT SOURCES

Fawcett Library Papers

National Vigilance Association Papers

NVA Box 107. 1930s. Catalogues of American pornography found in England.

NVA Box 107. "Notice on the Origin of the International Conference on Obscene Publications and the White Slave Trade," 1912.

NVA Box 107. "Indecent Advertisements (Amendment). A Bill Instituted to Amend the Indecent Advertisements Act, 1889." London: Printed by Eyre and Spottiswoode, 1910.

NVA Box 107. "Report from the Joint Select Committee on Lotteries and Indecent Advertisements, together with the proceedings of the Committee, minutes of evidence, and appendices." London: HMSO, 1908.

NVA Box 108. Letter to the National Vigilance Association from Reading, January 1905, concerning Port Said.

The Social Evil Extracts Album, an unpublished album of letters, newspaper articles, and items of interest to the NVA.

Public Records Office

Home Office Papers

HO45/055453 Sessions House Transcripts, 1854.

/9752/A59329	History of Foreign Obscenity Problems.
	Chart of Warrant Issues, 1898.
	"The Stoppage of Letters to or from Dealers in Obscene Matter," 1898.
/9806/B6712	Indecent Advertisements Bill, various drafts.
/9989/x78852	Letter from Constabulary of Hertford, 1900.
HO144/154/A40202E	Opinion re: prosecution of *Pall Mall Gazette*, 1885.
HO144/192/A46657	New Scotland Yard report on Carter alias Harris, 1894.
/A46657	Opinion re: *Funny Times* and *Side Lights*, 1897.

/A46657	Vizatelly prosecution for Zola's works, 1888.
/A46657/64	*Times* article on immoral books, 1889.
/A46657D	Home Office notes concerning obscene books and catalogues sent to Eton, 1890.
/A46657D/38	Methods to suppress indecent photographs and catalogues from abroad, 1890–1899.
/A46657D	Draft for Approval to Undersecretary of State, Foreign Office, 1894.
/A46657D	Information about seizure in Amsterdam, 1895.
/A6657D/6	Letter concerning overseas pornographers listing addresses, 1897.
/A46657D/63	General Post Office to Home Office concerning overseas pornographers, 1896.
/A6657D	Newspaper clipping, 1898.
/A46657E	Trial of Alfred Van Dyck, 1897.
/A46657E	Report of A. Van Dyck's arrest, 1897.
/A46657E	Celebration of Carrington's arrest in Paris, 1899.
/A46657E	Discussion of New Zealand Post Office Protection Acts, 1899.
HO144/238/A52539	Letter to the Assistant Commissioner of the Criminal Investigation Unit, 1891.
	Metropolitan Police Report, 1891.
	Prosecution under Post Office Protection Act, Warrant issued to stop obscene circulars, 1891.
/A52539B	Chart on laws concerning pornography, 1890?.
	Letter from CID concerning Graphic Toy Company, Amsterdam, 1891.
	"Draft for Approval," 1891.
	Letter from Chief Constable, Manchester, 1892.
	Correspondence between Home Office and Foreign Office, 1892.
	Post Office to Under Secretary of State, 1891. Letter and catalogue.
H0144/238/A52539E	Letter from John Flewelling to Adolf Estinger, 1894.
	Additional order from Flewelling to Estinger, 1894.
	Post Office report on Estinger's mail, 1894.
	Further postal report on Estinger.
	Letter from the Headmaster of Winchester College concerning catalogue, 1894.
	Letter from General Post Office to Under Secretary of State, 1894.

	"Communication from the Postmaster General to the Under-Secretary of State," 1894.
	Letter concerning confiscated money, 1895.
HO144/478/28111	Note on payment of NVA for prosecutions, 1890. Letter, 1890.
HO144/543/A54388	"*Times* article on police prosecution of pornographer, 1893.
/A54388	Letter listing items sent through the mail, 1901.
/A54388/10	Scotland Yard Report describing importer's premises, 1901.
/A54388/12	Scotland Yard Report, 1901.
/A54388/13	Letter from Cairo concerning raid on pornographer's shop, 1901.
HO144/9752/A59329	"Confidential Report on the Stoppage of Letters—A Brief History," 1898.
/A59329	Draft of Post Office Protection Act, 1898.
HO144/1043/183473	CID report re: purchase of obscene books from Messrs. Swan, Bloomsbury, 1909.

HO151/2 p. 132 Letter from A. F. O'Liddell concerning indecent publications and police report, 1882.

p. 221 Letter re: prosecution of Villiers, 1882.

p. 443 Letter re: books left in cab, 1882.

HO151/5 p. 30 Letter re: Graphic Toy Company, 1891.

p. 559 M. Cohen catalogues.

p. 606 Letter to U.S. government re: mutual importation of indecent catalogues from Amsterdam, 1895.

HO151/6 p. 2 Letter re: catalogue, 1895.

p. 58 Letter re: Charles Shroeter, 1896.

p. 84–86. Memo re: stopped letters from Barcelona pornographer, 1896.

p. 226 Letter re: ad in Sheffield paper from Italian pornographer, 1898.

p. 245 Letter re: French pornographer, 1898.

HO151/7 p. 116 Warrant for mail from W. A. Heck, Berlin, 1892.

p. 215 Warrant for mail from Van Gotten, Amsterdam, 1894.

p. 269 Warrant for mail from Charles Schroeter, Barcelona, 1896.

p. 297 Warrant for mail from five French dealers, 1897.

p. 300 Warrant for mail from A. Van Dyek, Antwerp, 1897.

p. 382 Warrant for mail from R. Gennert, Paris, 1899.

p. 383 Warrant for mail to and from Le Blanc, Paris, 1899.

HO151/8 p. 10 Request to Spanish government for action against Zarnbaly, 1899.

p. 22 Letter re: D. Pulver sending catalogue to schoolboy, 1899.

p. 281 Request for punishment of R. Masson, Great Holborn St., 1901.

p. 397 Warrant for mail from François Remaud, Paris, 1902.

p. 602 Request for action by German government against W. Parker, 1904.

HO151/9 p. 391 Request for action by Swiss government against G. Arthur, 1909.

p. 414–415 Warrant for mail from twelve overseas pornographers, 1909.

p. 441–442 Warrant for mail from thirteen overseas pornographers, 1909.

p. 488 Warrant for mail from four overseas pornographers, 1910.

p. 916–917 Warrant for mail from ten overseas pornographers, 1913.

Criminal Court Papers

Crim1/60/4 Deposition against H. S. Nichols by arresting officer, 1900.
XC6797 "The Information and Complaint of Charles Arrow and the Deposition of the
Same Person," January 10, 1900.

King's Bench Records

KB28/473/13   (1829) John Duncombe

KB28/509/21   (1829) John Duncombe

KB28/509/22   (1829–1830) Edward Duncombe

KB28/512/4   (1830) William Dugdale

KB28/512/19   (1830) John Benjamin Brookes

KB28/515/13   (1830) George Cannon

KB28/534/14   (1835) Edward Duncombe

KB28/535/45   (1845) William Dugdale

KB28/543/4   (1837) Edward Duncombe

KB28/600/3   (1852) William Dugdale

KB28/602/1   (1853) Edward Duncombe

KB28/602/2   (1853) John Dugdale

KB28/602/3   (1853) Edward Dyer

Private Collections

Uwe Scheid Collection. Daguerreotypes from 1850s. Erotic photographs from 1840s to
present. Uberherrn/Saar, Germany.

Stereoscopic cards. Miscellaneous cards, n.d. French series on paper, 1850s. Italian series
on paper, 1850s. Unknown origin on glass, 1890s. Jonathan Ross, London.

Postcard collection. Assorted nineteenth- and twentieth-century postcards from America, France, Germany, and England. Held in private collection. Pennsylvania.

Michael Goss, Delectus Books Collection. Nineteenth-century French and British literary
pornography and erotic ephemera. London.

Library and Museum Collections

Victoria and Albert Museum

Milford Haven Collection of Postcards. Late nineteenth- and early twentieth-century postcards.

Thomas Rowlandon Prints. Loose prints and illustrations, n.d.

Aubrey Beardsley Illustrations. Loose prints and illustrations, n.d.

Kinsey Institute for Research in Sex, Gender, and Reproduction

Ephemera Collection. Coins, statues, glasses, and other ephemera.

Photograph Collection. Photographs from the 1860s to present.

Erotic Literature Collection.

New York Public Library

*** Collection of erotica. Magazines, pamphlets, and comics.

Photography Collection. Includes stereoscopic cards from 1890s through 1920s.

Rare Books. Ephemera Collection. Twentieth-century magazines.

British Library

Private Case Collection. Literary pornography, including the collections of Ashbee and Dawes.

Prospectuses of the Rund Collection.

Prospectuses and miscellaneous catalogues of erotica.

Bodleian Library

Phi Collection. Literary pornography.

Prospectuses of pornographic publications.

Trinity College at Oxford

Danson Collection. Literary pornography.

Cambridge University Library

PRIMARY SOURCES (NONPORNOGRAPHIC)

Acton, William. *Prostitution.* 1857. Reprint, New York: Frederick A. Praeger, 1969.

Album 7. A collection of ephemeral printed materials and catalogues from the turn of the twentieth century. The first six albums contain contemporary photographs. Held at the British Library.

Anthropologia, vol. 1, *1873–1875.* London: Published for the London Anthropological Society, Ballière, Tindall, & Cox, 1875.

Ashbee, Henry Spencer (Pisanus Fraxi, pseud.). *Catena Liborum Tacendorum,* 1885. Reprint, New York: Documentary Books, 1962.

———. *Centuria Librorum Absconditorum.* 1879. Reprint, New York: Documentary Books, 1962.

———. *Index Librorum Prohibitorium.* 1877. Reprint, New York: Documentary Books, 1962.

Bibliotheca Arcana. London: George Redway, 1884.

Carlile, Richard. *Every Woman's Book: or, What is Love?* 4th ed. London: R. Carlile, 1826. Microfilm, Woodbridge, Conn.: Research Publications, 1981.

[Carrington, Charles.] *Forbidden Books: Notes and Gossip on Tabood Literature.* Paris: For the Author and His Friends [Carrington], 1902.

Gosse, Sir Edmund. "An Essay (with Two Notes) on Swinburne." 1917. First published in *The Swinburne Letters,* vol. 6, ed. Cecil Y. Lang. New Haven: Yale University Press, 1962.

Hansard's Parliamentary Debates: Third Series, Commencing with the Accession of William IV. Vol. 146, 2d vol. of session 1857(b). London: Cornelius Buck, 1857.

The Journal of the Royal Geographic Society, vol. 50. London: John Murray, 1880.

Lang, Cecil Y., ed. *The Swinburne Letters.* 6 vols. New Haven, Conn.: Yale University Press, 1959–1962.

Marcus (pseud.). *Second edition (with an additional preface) of The book of murder! Vademecum for the Commissioners and Guardians of the new Poor Law throughout Great Britain and Ireland, Being an Exact Reprint of The Infamous Essay on the Possibility of Limiting Populousness, by Marcus, one of the Three.* London: Printed by John Hill, Black Horse Court, Fleet St., And now Re-printed for the Instruction of the Labourer, By William Dugdale, No. 37, Holywell Street, Strand, 1839.

Memoirs Read before the Anthropological Society of London, 1863–1864. London: Trubner, 1865.

Memoirs Read before the Anthropological Society of London, vol. 2, *1865–1866.* London: Trubner, 1866.

Memoirs Read before the Anthropological Society of London, vol. 3, *1867–1869.* London: Longman, Green, 1870.

The Pall Mall Gazette 42, nos. 6336–6340 (July 6–10, 1885).

Parliamentary Papers, House of Commons. "Sale of Obscene Books & c. Prevention." 1857 (session 2), 4:503–514.

———. "Correspondence Respecting the International Conferences on Obscene Publications and the 'White Slave Traffic,' Held in Paris, April and May, 1910." 1912–1913, 43:689–733.

The Radical Harmonist; or, A collection of songs and toasts given at the late crown and anchor dinner. To which is subjoined, the goose's apology; a Michaelmas ode. London: Printed for W. Wright, 1820.

Society for the Suppression of Vice. *Abstract of the Seventy-sixth Annual Report for 1879.* Lincoln's Inn Fields: Society's Chambers, 1879.

———. *Annual Report.* London: N.p., 1802.

———. *The Constable's Assistant.* London: N.p., 1808.

———. *A Few Plain Reasons, Shewing Why the Society for the Suppression of Vice Has Directed Its Attention to Those Criminal Offenses which Are Chiefly Committed by the Lower Orders of the Community.* London: Printed for the Author, By Gilbert and Reed, 1803?.

Swinburne, Algernon Charles. *The Cannibal Catechism.* C. 1863. London: Printed for private circulation only, 1913.

———. "Mr. Whistler's Lecture on Art." Ms. facsimile, Bibliophile Society. St. Louis: Private Property by W. K. Bixby, [1913?].

The Vigilance Record: The Organ of the National Vigilance Association, London, 1891–1914.

Vizatelly, Henry. *Extracts Principally from English Classics: Showing That the Legal Suppression of M. Zola's Novels Would Logically Involve the Bowdlerizing of Some of the Greatest Works in English Literature.* London: Vizatelly, 1888.

PRIMARY SOURCES (PORNOGRAPHIC)

Because of the scarcity of the works, I have included locations whenever possible. The edition listed is available at the first location; alternate locations, though not necessarily the same edition, are listed subsequently. Any errors about editions, authors, or publishers are mine. This list should not be thought of as all-inclusive. The abbreviations are as follows: K.I. = Kinsey Institute; Bod. L. = Bodleian Library; T.C. = Trinity College, Oxford; Cam. = Cambridge University Library; B.L. = British Library. I have retained original capitalizations and misspellings.

Aglea: An Idyll: Written by Pallas. Athens: Erotika Biblion Society, 1889. Bod. L., K.I.

The Adventures of Lady Harpur. Her Life of Free Enjoyment and Ecstatic Love Adventures. Glascow [Paris]: William Murray [Charles Carrington], 1894 [1907]. K.I., B.L.

The Adventures of Young Maiden's. Paris [London]: Printed for private circulation, 1904. K.I.

"Album Diabolico." [1890?]. B.L.

The Amatory Adventures of Tilly Touchitt. London: Printed for the Editor at Moss Down Villas, Late Crescent Palace [Edward Avery], n.d. [1890]. Bod. L.

Amatory Episodes in the Life of Sir Clifford Norton and Others, from the diary of a sybarite. [London?: N.p., 1874?]. K.I.

Amorous Adventures of a Japanese Gentleman. Yokohama [Paris]: Printed for the Daimo of Satsuma [Charles Carrington or Isadore Liseux], 1897. K.I.

The Amours of Alibeck and Stanton, The Mysteries of Venus: a Nuptial Interlude. London [Naples?]: Printed for Mary Wilson, 1882. K.I.

Ananga-Ranga or The Hindoo Art of Love. Translated from the Sanskrit and annotated by
    A.F.F. and B.F.R. Cosmopoli [London]: For the Kama Shastra Society of London
    and Benares, and for private circulation only, 1885. Bod. L., K.I., B.L.

Argens, Jean-Baptiste. *Therese Philosophe,* translated as *The Philosophical Theresa or Mem-
    oirs of a Gay Girl.* London: [William Dugdale, c. 1860].

Aristophanes. *Lysistrata.* Translated into English with eight full-page drawings by Aubrey
    Beardsley. London: [Leonard Smithers?], 1896. B.L., K.I., Bod. L.

*The Autobiography of a Flea, told in a Hop, Skip, and Jump, and Recounting all his Experiences
    of Human and Superhuman Kind, both Male and Female; with his curious Connections,
    Backbitings and Tickling Touches; the whole scratched together for the delectation of the
    delicate, and for the Information of the Inquisitive, etc, etc.* Cythera [London]: Pub-
    lished by Authority of the Phlebotomical Society, 1789 [c. 1887]. Numerous edi-
    tions, B.L., K.I.

*The Bagnio Miscellany, containing the adventures of Miss Lais Lovecock written by herself; and
    what happened to her at Miss Twig's Academy, and afterwards. Dialogues between a Jew
    and a Christian, a whimsical entertainment lately performed in Duke's Place. The Force
    of Instinct: a true story, wherein is detailed the curious experiment resorted to by a young
    lady in order to make hair grow on the bottom of her belly, with other droll matters and
    quaint conseits.* London: Printed for the Bibliophilists, 1892. B.L., K.I.

Beranger, Lugi. *Sub Umbra.* London: Royal Press, 1932. Verbatim copy of 1888 manu-
    script. K.I.

[Bertram, James G.]. *The Merry order of Saint Bridget.* Personal recollections of the use of
    the Rod by Margaret Anson. York [London?]: Printed for the Author's Friends [J.C.
    Hotten], 1857 [1868]. Stamped "Sold by E. Avery, London." B.L., K.I., Bod. L.

Big Bellied Nelly, or Confessions of a doctor. By Doctor Mortimer R. Paris and London: N.p.,
    19-?. K.I.

*The Birchen Bouquet; or Curious and Original Anecdotes of Ladies fond of administering the
    Birch Disciple, and Published for the Amusement, as well as the Benefit of those Ladies
    who have under their Tuition sulky, stupid, wanton, lying or idle young Ladies or Gentle-
    men.* Birchington-on-Sea [London]: [Edward Avery?], 1881. B.L., Bod. L.

The Birchen Bouquet, and other Curious Conceits of ye olden Times. London [Paris: Charles
    Carrington], 1895 [1896]. B.L., Bod. L.

[James Francis Bloxam]. *The Priest and the Acolyte.* [London]: Printed for private circula-
    tion, [c. 1902]. K.I., B.L., Bod. L.

Boccaccio. *The Decameron Plates.* N.p., 1893. Bod. L.

Bone, Sir Walter. *Lord Roxboro Series.* London: N.p., 1898. K.I.

The Boudoir: A magazine of Scandal, Facetiae, & c., nos. 1–6. London: H. Smith [Edward
    Avery?], 37 Holywell Street, Printed for the Booksellers, 1860 [1883]. K.I., B.L.

Boy Worship. Oxford: N.p., 1880. Bod.L.

The Bride's Confession. N.p., n.d. Bod. L.

Byron, Lord. *Don Leon; a poem by the late Lord Byron, author of Childe Harold, Don Juan,
    &c., &c. and forming part of the private journal of his lordship, supposed to have been*

entirely destroyed by Thos. Moore. London: Printed for the Booksellers [William Dugdale], 1866. Numerous editions, B.L., K.I., Bod. L.

The Cabinet of Venus including The Voluptuous Night and The Cardinal's Amours. London [Paris]: Printed by the Erotica-Bibliomaniac Society [Charles Carrington], 1896. B.L., K.I., Bod. L.

A Cairene (pseud.). *Sixfold Sensuality or The Sensual Pleasure-giving Exercises of an ingenious acrobatic Family.* London and New York [Paris?]: Erotic Biblion Society, c. 1902. B.L.

Casanova di Seingalt. *The Memoirs of Jacques Casanova, written by himself.* Now for the first time translated into English in Twelve volumes. [London]: Privately Printed [H.S. Nichols], 1894. B.L., K.I.

[Bloxum, John Francis, ed.]. *The Chameleon,* vol. 1., no. 1. London: Gay and Bird, 1894. B.L.

Clara Alcock, Her Initiation in the ways of Love and full enjoyment of its sweets. Related by Lord Ferrars. Glasgow [Paris]: William Murray [Charles Carrington], 1898 [c. 1908]. B.L.

Cleland, John. *Memoirs of a Woman of Pleasure.* London: Printed for G. Fenton in the Strand, 1749. Numerous editions, B.L., K.I.

———. *Memoirs of a Woman of Pleasure.* 1748–1749. Ed. and introduced by Peter Sabor. Reprint, Oxford: Oxford University Press, 1999.

Cluny, Henry de. *Private Memoirs of an Officer of the Dragoons.* London: At the sign of the blue nose, 1898. K.I.

The Cockchafer, A Choice of Selection of Flash, Frisky, and Funny Songs, never before printed and adapted for gentlemen only. London: William West, 1865. B.L.

Coleman, George. *The Rodiad.* London: N.p., 1898. Private collection.

Confessions of Madame Vestris; in a series of familiar Letters to handsome Jack, giving a glowing picture of her early Seductions; her Intrigues with Captain Anstruther; her curious Adventures on the Wedding Night; Parisian Frolics. Including curious and original anecdotes of many eminent Persons, Her early Youth and Times, &c. [London?]: Printed for the new Villon Society and issued only to Subscribers [Edward Avery?], 1891. B.L.

Country Retirement; or How to pass Time pleasantly in a Manor house, Flollowed by a Letter from a Member of the She-Romp's Club. Birchingham-on-Sea: N.p., 1880. Bod. L.

The Court martial on Miss Fanny Hayward, by an ex-infantry captain. Paris: Librairie des Bibliophiles [Charles Carrington], 1899. K.I.

Cox, Ophelia. *With Rod and Bum, or Sport in the West End of London.* London, New York: Erotica Biblion Society, 1898. K.I.

The Cremorne; A Magazine of Wit, Facetiae, Parody, Graphic Tales of Love, etc. Cheyne Walk [London]: Privately Printed [Edward Avery?], 1851 [1882]. B.L., K.I.

The Crimes of the Clergy, or the Pillars of Priest-Craft Exposed. London: Benbow, Printer and Publisher, 1823.

Crissie. A Music-Hall sketch of To-Day. The Alhambra, 1899. B.L., T.C.

Crowley, Aleister (pseud.). *The Scented Garden of Abdullah the Satirist of Shiraz.* London: Privately Printed, 1910. B.L., Cam.

————. *White Stains: The Literary Remains of George Archibald Bishop, a Neuropath of the Second Empire*. London: Leonard Smithers, 1898. B.L., K.I.

The Cuckhold's Nest of Choice, Flash, Smutty and Delicious Songs, with Rummy Toasts. Adapted for Gentlemen Only. London: W. West, c. 1863. B.L.

Curiosities of Flagellation. London: [Charles Carrington?], 1891. K.I.

Cythera's Hymnal; or Flakes from the Foreskin. A Collection of Songs, Poems, Nursery Rhymes, Quiddities, etc., etc. never before published. Oxford: Printed at the University Press, for the Society for Promoting Useful Knowledge, 1870. B.L., Bod. L.

Davenport, John. *Aphrodisiacs and Anti-Aphrodisiacs: Three Essays on the Powers of Reproduction; with some account of the Judicial "Congress" as practiced in France during the seventeenth century*. London: Privately Printed [J.C. Hotten], 1869 [1873]. B.L., Bod. L., Cam.

————. *Aphrodisiacs and Anti-Aphrodisiacs: Three Essays on the Powers of Reproduction; with some account of the Judicial "Congress" as practiced in France during the seventeenth century*. London: Privately Printed [Edward Avery], 1869 [1887]. B.L.

————. *Curiositates Eroticae Physiologiae; or, Tabooed Subjects Freely Treated*. London: Privately Printed, 1875. B.L., Bod. L.

————. *Esoteric Physiology Sexagyma*. [London]: Privately Printed for Subscribers, 1888. B.L.

DeBecker, J. E. *Yoshiwara: The Nightless City*. Paris [Chicago?]: Charles Carrington [Targ?], 1907. K.I., Cam.

Denervillyani, A. *Six Nouvelles Amoureuses*. Translated from the French. Athens [London]: Imprinted by the Erotika Biblion Society for Private Distribution Only [Leonard Smithers], 1891. B.L., K.I., T.C.

Discipline in School and Cloister by Dr. Jacobus X. Paris: Isadore Liseux, 1902. T.C.

Devereux, Captain. *Venus in India, or, Love Adventures in Hindustan*. Paris and London: For Private Circulation Only, 1898. Numerous editions, B.L., K.I.

Dubois, Michael. *A Modern Messaline*. London and Paris [New York]: Royal Press [Miller Brothers?], 1899 [1900?]. Reprint of 1899 edition. K.I.

Du Bouleau, M. le Comte. *Gynococracy: a narrative of adventures and psychological experiences of Julian Robinson (afterwards Viscount Ladywood) under petticoat rule, by himself*. Paris; Rotterdam, 1893). K.I.

————. *The Petticoat Dominant, or, Woman's Revenge*. The Autobiography of a young nobleman, as a pedant to Gynococracy. Paris and New-York: N.p., 1898. B.L., K.I.

————. *The Yellow Room, or, Alice Darvell's subjection, a tale of the birch*. London [Paris?]: Privately printed, 1891. B.L., K.I.

[Dumoulin, Edmund]. *The Callipyges: The whole philosophy and secret mystery of female flagellation*. London: Privately printed for subscribers only [Charles Carrington?], 1903. K.I.

[————]. *The Callipyges: The whole philosophy and secret mystery of female flagellation*. Paris: Pall Mall Press, 1957. Private collection.

The Elements of Tuition, and Modes of Punishment, in Letters from Mdlle Dubouleau, a cele-brated Parisian tutoress, addressed to Miss Smart-Bum, Governess of the Young Ladies School at——with some secrets developed of Mock Tutors, who have taken delight in ad-ministering Birch Discipline. London: Printed for the Booksellers [Edward Avery?, c. 1880]. B.L., K.I.

Evelina, or The amours and adventures of a young lady of fashion. Paris: Printed for private subscription amongst private subscribers, 1904. T.C., Alternate editions K.I.

The Exhibition of Female Flagellants. London: Printed at the Expense of Theresa Berkley for the Benefit of Mary Wilson. [William Dugdale, c.1860]. B.L.

The Exhibition of Female Flagellants in the Modest and Incontinent World. London: Printed for G. Peacock [J.C. Hotten], 1777 [1872]. B.L., T.C., Cam.

Experiences of Flagellation: a series of remarkable instances of whipping inflicted on both sexes, with curious anecdotes of ladies fond of administering birch discipline, compiled by an amateur flagellant. London: Printed for private circulation, 1885. K.I., Alternate editions T.C., B.L.

The Exquisite: A Collection of Tales, Histories and Essays, funny, fanciful and facetious, inter-spersed with Anecdotes, original and select, amorous Adventures, piquant Jests and spicy Sayings. Illustrated with numerous Engravings. Vols. 1, 2, 3. [London]: Printed and Published by H. Smith [William Dugdale], [1842–1844]. B.L.

Family Connections, by Ramrod. London–Paris–New York [Paris]: The International Publishing Office, [c. 1905]. B.L.

Fashionable Lectures: Composed and Delivered with Birch Discipline, etc.. The Fourth Edition, with Considerable Additions. London: Printed for G. Peacock [J.C. Hotten], [1873]. B.L., T.C., Private collection.

Female Lust as Illustrated in the Ridingcocke Papers. Vichy [Paris?]: Now for the First Time Published for Subscribers Only [Charles Carrington?], 1901. B.L.

The Festival of the Passions; or, Voluptuous Miscellany, vol. II. By Philo Cunnus. Glenfucket, foot of Bennard [London]: Printed and Published by Abdul Mustapha [Andrew White], [1863]. B.L.

The Flash Chaunter, a Slashing, Dashing, Friskey and Delicious Collection of Gentleman's Songs, now singing at Offley's, Cider Cellars, Coal Hole, &c., &c. [London: William West, c. 1865]. B.L.

Flossie, a Venus of Fifteen, by One who knew this Charming Goddess and Worshipped at her Shrine. London and New York [Paris]: Printed for the Erotica Biblion Society [Charles Carrington?, c. 1900]. Numerous editions, K.I., B.L., T.C., Cam.

Forbidden Fruit. Luscious and Exciting Story of a Boy seduced by his pretty young Aunt, then his Nursemaid and Chambermaid, and finally in the arms of his beautiful Mother. Lon-don [Paris?]: For Subscribers Only, 1898. B.L.

Forbidden Fruit (More) or Master Percy's Progress in and beyond the domestic Circle. His Ad-ventures at the Cottage with Phoebe, her Sister and the little Girls. To which is added *The Lovely Senorita, a thrilling Tale of the city of Mexico.* Harvard, U.S.A. [Paris?]: Privately Printed for Subscribers Only, 1901. B.L.

France, Hector. *Musk, Hashish, and Blood,* by the translator of *The Chastisement of Mansour.* Paris: Charles Carrington, 1899 [1900?]. K.I.

Frank and I. Paris: [Charles Carrington], 1902.

Frank and I. 1902. Reprint, New York: Blue Moon Books, 1987.

The Frisky Songster, Being a Select Choice of such Songs, as are distinguished for their Jollity, High Taste and Humor, and above two hundred toasts and Sentiments of the most delicious order. Ninth London Edition. London, 1802. K.I.

The Gallant Captain's Merry Mistresses and some other funny tales. London [Paris?]: Privately printed [Charles Carrington?], 1893. K.I.

Genuine and Authentic Memoirs of a Well-known Woman of Intrigue, containing a great variety of curious and interesting anecdotes, which have never yet appeared in print, of several of the first characters in the fashionable world. Written by herself. London: Printed for J. Ridgeway, No. 196, Piccadilly, 1880. Bod. L.

Grant, John Cameron. *The Ethiopian: a narrative of the Society of Human Leopards.* Paris: Charles Carrington, 1900. K.I.

Grassal, Georges. *The Memoirs of Dolly Morton, The story of a Woman's part in the struggle to free the Slaves. An Account of Whippings, Rapes and Violences that preceded the Civil War in America. With Curious Anthropological Observations on the radical Diversities in the conformation of the female Bottom and the way different Women endure chastisement.* Now issued for the first time. Paris: Charles Carrington, 1899. Numerous editions, B.L., K.I.

Hamilton, Thomas. *Select Poems on Several Occasions.* By the Right Hon. the Earl of H*******n. To which are added the Duke of Argyll's Levee and some Ballads. By the Late Lord Binning. London: N.p., 1824. Numerous editions, B.L., T.C.

The History of the Human Heart, or, The Adventures of a Young Gentleman. London: Printed for J. Freeman, near Ludgate, MDCCXLIX [1885]. Bod. L.

Home discipline: a story of flagellation detailing the strange experiences of a country girl in London in the West End mansion of the baronet her uncle, who as a wielder of the birch showed himself a masterful man, and proved once more how love obeys the lash and that in every household 'tis the rod that rules. London: [Carrington?], 1903. K.I.

The Horn Book: A Girl's Guide to Good and Evil. London: Erotica Biblion Society, 1899. Numerous editions. K.I., T.C.

How Women Are Flogged in Russian Prisons, by an English doctor. Paris: Libraire des Bibliophiles [Charles Carrington], 1899. K.I.

Illustrations of Phallicism. Consisting of ten Plates of remains of ancient Art, with Descriptions. A supplement to Hargrave Jenning's *Phallicism.* Presented by the Publisher. N.p., n.d. B.L.

Indecent Whipping. [London: N.p., 1880?]. B.L.

Intrigues and Confessions of a Ballet Girl; Disclosing startling and voluptuous Scenes before & behind the Curtain, enacted by well-known Personages in the Theatrical, Military, Medical, & other Professions; with kisses at Vauxhall, Greenwich, &c., &c. and a full disclosure of the secret and amatory Doings in Dressing Rooms, Under & Upon the Stage, in the Light and Dark, by one who has had her share. London: Rozez & Co., c. 1870. B.L.

The Inutility of Virtue. London: William Dugdale, c. 1860.

The Inutility of Virtue. London: Printed for the Society of Vice [Paris?: N.p., c. 1885]. B.L

[Jacolliot, Louis]. *The Basis of Passional Psychology. A study of the Laws of Love in Man and the lower Animals.* By Doctor Jacobus X***, French Army-Surgeon. Paris: Charles Carrington, 1901. B.L.

The Kama Sutra of Vatsyayana. Cosmopoli: For the Kama Shastra Society of London and Benares and for Private Circulation only, 1883. Bod. L., K.I., Cam., T.C.

Kate Handcock. N.p., n.d. Bod. L.

Kirkwood, John Poole. *Sadopaideia. Being the Experiences of Cecil Prendergast, undergraduate of the University of Oxford, shewing how he was led through the pleasant paths of Masochism, to the supreme joys of Sadism.* Edinburg [Paris]: G. Ashantee & Co., 1907. B.L., Bod. L.

Knight, Richard Payne, Esq. *A Discourse on the Worship of Priapus, and its connection with the Mystic Theology of the Ancients.* London: [J. C. Hotten], 1865. K.I.

Lady Bumtickler's Revels. A comic opera in two acts, as it was performed at Lady Bumtickler's private theatre in Birch Grove, with unbounded Applause. The songs adapted to favorite airs. London: Printed for George Peacock [J.C. Hotten, 1872]. B.L., T.C., Private collection.

Lady Gay Spanker's Tales of Fun and Flagellation, etc. [Paris?]: Privately Printed for Subscribers Only, 1896. B.L., K.I.

Lashed into Lust: the caprice of a flagellator. [Paris?]: [Charles Carrington?], 1899. K.I.

Laura Middleton, Her Brother and her Lover. Brussels: N.p., 1890. B.L.

Letters Addressed to the Editor of the Englishwoman's Domestic Magazine, on Whipping of Girls and the general Corporal Punishment of Children. London: N.p., 1870. B.L.

Letters from a Friend in Paris. London: N.p., 1874. B.L.

Letters from Laura and Eveline giving an account of their Mock-Wedding, Wedding-Trip etc. Published as an appendix to *The Sins of the Cities.* London [Paris?]: N.p., 1903. B.L.

The Libertine Enchantress, or, the adventures of Lucinda Hartley. By the author of *Confessions of a Washington Belle.* New Orleans: N.p., 1863. K.I.

The Life and Amours of the Beautiful, Gay and Dashing Kate Percival, the Belle of Delaware. New Orleans: N.p., 1864.

The Life and Amours of the Beautiful, Gay and Dashing Kate Percival, the Belle of Delaware. Illustrated by Mademoiselle Louver. London; Paris: 1903. K.I.

Life On board a Yacht. London: Privately printed for subscribers only [Charles Carrington?], 1891. K.I.

The Little People. [Paris?]: Printed for the Erotica Biblion Society of London and New-York, [c. 1900]. B.L.

Love and Safety, or, Love and Lasciviousness with Safety and Secrecy. A Lecture delivered with practical Illlustrations by the Empress of Asturia (The Modern Sappho);

assisted by her favorite Lizette and Others. London–New York [Paris]: The Erotica Biblion Society [Charles Carrington?, 1908]. B.L

Lovely Nights of Young Grils, served up and seasoned for amatory Feasts. London and New York [Paris]: Printed for the Erotica Biblion Society, [c. 1895]. B.L.

The Love of Venus: or the Young Wife's Confession. Dublin [London]: Privately Printed for the Irish Land Leaguers [Edward Avery, 1881]. B.L.

The Lustful Memoirs of a Young and Passionate Girl. Written by herself. Paris and London: Printed for Private Circulation, 1904. B.L.

Lustful Stories. London, New York [New York]: Erotica Biblion Society [Miller Brothers], 1901 [19—?]. K.I.

The Lustful Turk. London: N.p., 1828.

The Lustful Turk. 1828. Reprint, New York: Carroll & Graf, 1983.

Madam Birchini's Dance. A Modern Tale. With considerable Additions and original Anecdotes collected in the fashionable Circles. Now first published by Lady Termagant Flaybum. London: Printed for George Peacock [J.C. Hotten, 1872]. B.L., T.C., Private collection.

Maggie, or, The amours of my governess. N.p., [189-?]. K.I.

Maidment, James. *Ane Pleasant Garland of Sweet Scented Flowers.* Edinburgh: Privately printed, 1885. Bod. L.

Maidenhead Stories told by a Set of joyous Students. New York [Paris]: Printed for the Erotica Biblion Society, [1897]. K.I., B.L., Bod. L.

Maillot, Rene. *The Delights of Sex.* N.p., n.d. Bod. L.

A Man of Pleasure at Paris, or An Account of the Pleasures of that Capital. Paris: N.p., 1808. T.C.

Margot the Birching Beauty. Her Whipping Adventures as confided to Rebecca Birch, her friend, late teacher at Mrs. Busby's Young Ladies' Boarding School. London [Paris?]: Printed for the Flogging Club, 1905. B.L., Bod. L.

The Masculine Cross. London: Printed for Private Circulation, 1886. Private collection.

Martialis. *The Index Expurgatorius. . . .* literally translated; comprising all the Epigrams hitherto omitted by English translators. To which is added an original metrical version and copious explanatory notes. London: Printed for Private Circulation, 1868. B.L., K.I.

Maudie. Revelations of Life in London, and an unforeseen denouement. By the author of "Nemesis Hunt." Now for the first time printed. London: Imprinted for members of the "Chatty" Club, 1909. B.L., T.C.

May's Account of Her Introduction to the Art of Love. From an unsophisticated Manuscript, found amongst my Grandmother's papers, after her death, supposed to have been written about A.D. London-Paris: N.p., 1904. B.L.

[May, Sam.]. *Amours, Intrigues, and Adventures of a musical Student.* [London: William Dugdale, 1860]. B.L.

[———]. *The Loves of a musical Student, being the History of the Adventures and amorous Intrigues of a young Rake with many beautiful Women, disclosing a number of volup-*

tuous *Anecdotes never before printed, founded on Facts, and interspersed with remarkable Narratives.* Written by himself. Paris: Societe des bibliophiles etrangers [Charles Carrington], 1897. B.L.

Memoirs of a Russian Princess. Gleaned from her Diary. Compiled, noted and arranged by Katoumbah Pasha. London [Paris?]: Privately Printed (Not to be Sold), 1890. B.L., numerous editions K.I.

The Memoirs of a Voluptuary: The Secret Life of an English Boarding School. London: James Kennedy, 1908. B.L.

The Merry Adventures of a bachelor otherwise known as Count Alexis the Gay. Edited by the ex-Reverend Peter Pry. Madagascar: New York Erotica Biblion Society, [c. 1890]. K.I.

Mirabeau, H.G.R. *The Curtain Drawn Up, or The Education of Laura.* From the French of the Comte Mirabeau. Revised edition. London [Paris]: Putitin, Roger and Co., Nineinch Street, 1818 [c.1900]. B.L.

Mistress and Slave: A Masochist Realistic Love Story. Athens [London]: Imprinted for its members by the Erotika Biblion Society, 1905. T.C.

The Modern Eveline, or The Adventures of a young Lady of Quality who was never found out. . . . Paris: Printed for Distribution amongst Private Subscribers Only [Charles Carrington], 1904. K.I., B.L., T.C.

[Momas, Alphonse?]. *Green Girls.* By Donewell. Translated from the French. London-Paris: N.p., 1899. B.L., T.C.

———. *Miss Gregor.* London-Paris: Privately Printed for the French and English Bibliophiles Society [G. & R. Briffaut?], 1907. B.L.

———. *Miss Mary.* London-Paris: Privately Printed for the French and English Bibliophiles Society [G. & R. Briffaut?], 1906. B.L.

Monnier, Henry. *The Grisette and the Student.* N.p., n.d.. Bod. L.

———. *Rosa's Maidenhead.* [Paris?: N.p., 189-?]. Bod. L.

Moslem Erotism, or adventures of an American Woman in Constantinople. Folowed by the Meditations of Shiek Nefzaoui. [Amsterdam?: N.p., c. 1900]. B.L., Bod. L.

Musset, Alfred de. *Gamiani, or, Two Passionate Nights.* By Baron Alcide de M***. A Literal Translation of the original French Edition. Brussels [London]: N.p., 1833 [1908]. B.L., numerous editions K.I.

My Cousin's Account or the Frigging Countess and the Zaire's Repository. N.p.: Printed for the Voluptuaries of Venus, 1802. Bod. L.

My Secret Life. Amsterdam: Not for Publication [Auguste Brancart?, c. 1890]. Numerous editions, B.L., K.I.

My Secret Life. French language edition. Londres: N.p., 1885. T.C.

The Mysteries of Venus: A Nuptial Interlude and a Preceptor for Ladies and Gentlemen on their Wedding-Eve. London: N.p., 1893. Bod. L.

Nadia. Athens: Erotica Biblion Society, 1895. T.C.

Nash, Thomas. *The Choise of Valentines, or The Merrie Ballad of Nash his Dildo.* Edited by John S. Farmer. London: Privately Printed for Subscribers Only, 1889. K.I., B.L., Cam.

A New Collection of Trials for Adultery: or, General History of modern Gallantry and Divorces . . . from the year 1780 to the present Time . . .Taken in Short Hand, from the Records of the Courts . . . by a Civilian of Doctors' Commons. London: Printed for the Proprietors and sold by J. Gill, 1799, 1802. B.L.

The New Ladies' Tickler; or, The Adventures of Lady Lovesport and the audacious Harry. London: Printed for the Booksellers [William Dugdale], 1866. K.I., B.L.

A Night of Sport. N.p.: Published by a connoisseur, [c. 1895]. K.I.

A Nocturnal Meeting, by Ramrod. London–Paris–New York [Paris]: The International Publishing Office, [c. 1900]. B.L., Private Collection.

Nunnery Tales; or Cruising under false Colours: A Tale of Love and Lust. London [Amsterdam]: Printed for the Booksellers [Auguste Brancart, c. 1890?]. B.L., numerous editions K.I.

The Odalisque, or The History of the Amours of the eunuch Zulphicara. Translated from the Turkish by Voltaire. Constantinople [London]: N.p., 1779–1868 [1868?]. B.L.

On the Uses of Night-Caps, or, Seven Years' Experience on the Practicality of Limiting the Number of the Family, by the best known Methods, including some valuable & novel Information never before published. By a Married Man with six Children! London: J. Turner, 23, Russel Court, Drury Lane [William Dugdale?, c. 1845]. B.L.

Orange Blossoms: The Story of a Beautiful Marchioness under the Second Empire. Paris: Printed Privately, 1903. Bod. L.

The Pearl. A Journal of Facetiae Voluptuous Reading, vols. 1–3. London [Amsterdam]: Printed for the Society of Vice [Brancart], 1879 [c.1890]. B.L., K.I.

The Pearl, 1879. Reprint, New York: Grove Press, 1968.

The Pearl. (Supplement) *Christmas Annual.* London: Privately Printed, 1881. K.I.

The Pearl. (Supplement) *Swivia; or, The Briefless Barrister. The Extra-Special number of The Pearl, containing a variety of complete Tales, with five illustrations, Poetry, Facetiae &c.* [London: Lazenby], Christmas, 1879. B.L.

The Pearl. (Supplement) *The Haunted House, or The Revelations of Theresa Terence . . . Being the Christmas number of "The Pearl."* London: [Lazenby] Privately Printed, 1880. B.L.

The Perfumed Garden of the Cheikh Nefzaoui. A Manuel of Arabian Erotology. Cosmopoli [London]: For the Kama Shastra Society of London and Benares and for Private Circulation only, 1886. Bod. L., T.C.

Perret, Paul. *The Romance of My Alcove.* Athens [London]: Imprinted by the Erotika Biblion Society [Leonard Smithers], 1889. B.L.

———. *Tableaux Vivants.* Completely Translated from the original French by a Member of the Council. Athens [London]: Imprinted by the Erotika Biblion Society for Private Distribution Only [Leonard Smithers], 1888. B.L., K.I., Bod. L.

Phallic Worship. London: Printed for Private Circulation, 1886.

Pleasure Bound "Afloat." The Extraordinary Adventures of a Party of Travellers, et leurs affaires galants. Told by Flood and Field. By the author of "Nemesis Hunt." London: Imprinted for members of the "Chatty" Club, 1908. B.L.

Pleasure Bound "Ashore." Being the further Adventures of our Party of Travellers, et leur affaires galantes. By the author of "Nemesis Hunt" and "Maudie." London: Imprinted for the members of the "Chatty" Club, 1909. B.L.

The Power of Mesmerism. A Highly erotic narrative of voluptuous facts and fancies. Moscow [Amsterdam]: Printed for the Nihilists [Auguste Brancart?], 1891. B.L., K.I.

"A Pretty Girl's Companion and Guide to Loves Sweetest Delights." N.p, n.d. [1900–1910?] K.I.

Priapeia, or The Sportive epigrams of divers poets on Priapus now first completely done into English prose from the original Latin, with Introduction, Notes explanatory and illustrative and Excursus: to which is appended the Latin text. Athens [London]: Imprinted by the Erotika Biblion Society for Private Distribution Only [Leonard Smithers], 1888 [1889]. Numerous editions, B.L., Bod. L., K.I, T.C., Cam.

A Private Interview, between young William & Sweet Lucy. A Poem distinguished. . . . Dedicated to the Votaries of Venus. [London?: N.p., c. 1890]. B.L.

Private Letters from Phyllis to Marie, or the Art of Child-Love, or The Adventures and Experiences of a little Girl. Showing how pretty little Maidens indulge those secret Passions, alone and with others, which but too often lead to their Seduction at an early age. London and Paris, 1898. B.L., K.I.

The Quintessence of Birch Discipline. A Sequence to the *Romance of Chastisement.* London: Privately Printed, 1870. B.L.

The Rambler's Flash Songster. Nothing but Out-and-Outers, adapted for Gentlemen only and now singing at Offley's, Cider Cellers, Coal Hole & c. London: William West, c. 1865.

Randiana; or Excitable Tales; being the Experiences of an erotic Philosopher. New York [London]: [Edward Avery?], 1884. B.L.

Randiana; or Excitable Tales; being the Experiences of an erotic Philosopher. [Paris: Charles Carrington, 1891]. K.I.

Raped on the Railway: a true story of a lady who was first ravished and then chastised on the Scotch express. [Paris?]: Cosmopolitan Bibliophile Society [Charles Carrington?, 1894?]. K.I.

Realistic Pleasures gathered from the Diary of a Sybarite. Alexandria [Paris?]: N.p., 1900–1901. B.L.

Records of the most Ancient and Puissant Order of Beggar's Benison and Merryland, Anstruther. Anstruther [London?]: Printed for Private Distribution Only, 1892. B.L.

[———, supplement] *Notes on "The Records of the Beggar's Benison Society and Merryland of Anstruther, Fife," 1739–1836.* Anstruther [London]: Printed for Private Circulation, 1892. Bod. L.

[———, supplement] *Supplement to the Historical Portion of the "Records of the most Ancient and Puissant Order of the Beggar's Benison and Merryland, Anstruther,"* being an account *of the proceedings at the Meetings of the Society, together with excerpts from Toasts, Recitations, Stories, Bon-Mots, Speeches and Songs delivered thereat.* Anstruther [London?]: Printed for Private Distribution Only, 1892. B.L., National Library of Scotland.

[Reddie, James Campbell]. *The Adventures of a Schoolboy; or, The Freaks of Youthful Passion.* London: Printed for the Booksellers [William Dugdale], 1866. B.L

[———]. *The Amatory Experiences of a Surgeon.* Moscow: Printed for the Nihilists, 1881. B.L., K.I.

Rex, Emodus. *Brotherly Love, or A boy's experiences in passion's paradise.* [Paris?: Privately printed, 1898.] K.I.

———. *Passion's Paradise, or girls will be girls.* [Paris: Privately printed for subscribers, 1898?] K.I.

Rochester's Sodom. Paris: Verlag Von R. Welter, 1904. Cam.

The Role of Flogging in Veneral Affairs. London, J. C. Hotten, 1872.

The Romance of Lust; or Early Experiences. London: N.p., 1873–1876. B.L., K.I.

The Romance of Lust; or Early Experiences. [Rotterdam: Berge, c. 1895]. K.I., B.L.

The Romance of Lust. 1873. Reprint, New York: Grove Press, 1968.

Rosy Tales! Exhibited for the Delectation of All True Lovers of the Birch. London, Whipwell & Co. Bottom Lane: For Private Circulation Only, n.d. Private collection.

Rowlandson, Thomas. *Pretty Little Games for Young Ladies & Gentlemen.* With Pictures of Good Old English Sports and Pastimes. [London]: A few copies only for the Artist's Friends [J. C. Hotten], 1845 [c. 1872]. B.L., T.C.

Sacher-Masoch, Leopold von. *Venus in Furs.* New York: Privately printed for Subscribers only, 1928. Private collection.

Sackville, Charles (pseud.). *Mr. Howard goes Yachting and subjects to his voluptuous caprices with young Ladies captured and imprisoned on board.* London-Paris: Printed for Subscribers only [Charles Carrington?], 1908. B.L.

———. *Two Lascivious Adventures of Mr. Howard: a continuation of Maude Cameron and her guardian.* London: Printed for subscribers only, 1907. K.I.

———. *Whipping as a Fine Art, being an Account of exquisite and refined Chastisement inflicted by Mr. Howard on grown-up Schoolgirls.* London-Paris: [Charles Carrington], 1909. B.L., K.I.

[Sala, George Augustus]. *Harlequin Prince Cherrytop and the Good Fairy Fairfuck, or The Frig, the Fuck and the fairy. New and Gorgeous Pantomime.* Oxford: Oxford University Press, 1879. Numerous editions, K.I., B.L., T.C.

[———]. *The Mysteries of Verbena House, or, Miss Bellasis birched for thieving.* By Etonensis. London: Privately printed, 1882. K.I.

School Life in Paris. [Paris]: Privately Printed [Charles Carrington], 1897. B.L.

School Life in Paris. London-New York: Erotica Biblion Society, 1901. K.I.

The Seducing Cardinal's Amours with Isabella Peto and Others; to which is added The Art of Keeping the Eleventh Commandment, 'Thou Shalt not be Found Out,' being an account of the private Intrigues of a virtuous Wife. London: Published as the Act directs by madame Le Duck, Mortimer Street and to be had of all respectable Booksellers, 1830. B.L.

A Secret History of a Votary of Pleasure. New York: Calvin Blanchard, 1866. K.I.

Selected Poetical Works from the Earls of Rochester, Roscomon and Dorset; including "The Cabinet of Love." London: Edward Avery, 1885. Bod. L.

Sellon, Edward. *Annotations on the Sacred Writings of the Hindüs, being an epitome of some of the most remarkable and leading tenets in the Faith of that people.* London: N.p., 1865. B.L.

———. *The New Epicurean, or The Delights of Sex facetiously and philosophically considered in graphic Letters addressed to young Ladies of Quality.* London: [Lazenby], 1740 [1875]. B.L., K.I.

The Simple Tale of Susan Aked, or Innocence Awakened, Ignorence dispelled. Honni Soit Qui Mal Y Pense. London and New York [Paris]: Printed for the Erotica Biblion Society, 1898 [c.1920?]. K.I., B.L.

The Sins of the City of the Plain, or The Recollections of a Mary-Ann. London: Privately Printed, 1881. Numerous editions, B.L., K.I.

The Spirit of Flagellation or The Memoirs of Mrs. Hinton. London: Printed and Published by Mary Wilson, 1892. Bod. L.

St. Anthony Settled at Last: or, The Powers of Cunt. Oxford: Puzeyite Press, Privately Printed, 1850. Bod. L.

Stays and Gloves. Figure-Training and Deportment by means of the discipline of Tight Corsets, narrow High-heeled Boots, clinging Kid Gloves, Combinations, etc., etc.. London: N.p., 1909. K.I., B.L.

[Stock, St. George H.]. *The Romance of Chastisement; or Revelations of the School and Bedroom,* by an Expert. [London: J.C. Hotten], 1870 [1871]. B.L.

The Story of Seven Maidens: Slavery in West India. Cambridge [Paris]: James Andrews [Carrington], 1907. Cam.

Sublime of Flagellation: In Letters from Lady Termagant Flaybum of Birch-Grove, to Harriet Tickletail of Bumfiddle-Hall. In which are introduced the beautiful tale of La Coquette chatie (here ascribed to the abbé Grécourt), in French and English; and The Boardingschool Bumbrusher, or, the Distress of Laura. London: Printed for George Peacock [John Camden Hotten, 1872]. B.L., Bod. L., T.C.

Sweet Seventeen: the True Story of a Daughter's Awful Whipping and its Delightful if Direful Consequence. Paris: [Charles Carrington], 1910. K.I.

Tales of Villa Brigitte. Translated from the French by M. A. Oxon. London and Melbourne [Paris]: H. J. Vicar & Sons [H.S. Nichols?], 1910. B.L.

Tales Told out of School. London [Paris: Charles Carrington], 1901. B.L.

The 36 Joys of a Woman. N.p. [Paris?], n.d. [189?]. Bod. L.

Tips to Maidens. London–New York: Erotica Biblion Society [Miller Brothers], 1901. K.I.

A Town-Bull or, The Elysian Fields. New Orleans [Amsterdam?: Auguste Brancart, 1893]. B.L. Alternate editions, K.I., B.L.

A Treacherous Plot. The Fate of Isabel Seaton. A Scene in a Boarding School. By James Holmes and Others. Paris: Librarie des Bibliophiles [Charles Carrington?, c. 1900]. B.L.

A Treatise on the Use of Flogging in Venerial Affairs. London: Printed for G. Peacock [J.C. Hotten], 1777 [1872]. T.C., Private collection.

The Trial of Oscar Wilde. From Shorthand Reports. Paris: Privately Printed [Charles Carrington], 1906. B.L., K.I.

Two Girls in a Foreign Land: also, extract of love. N.p., [1895?]. K.I.

Venus School Mistress, or, Birchen Sports. By R. Birch translator of "Manon's Memoirs." London: N.p., 1808–1810. K.I.

Victims of Lust, or, a flagellators paradise. London [Paris?: Charles Carrington?], 1904. K.I.

Villiot, Jean de. *The Magnetism of the Rod, or, the Revelations of Miss Darcy.* London [Brussels?]: Printed for private distribution amongst subscribers only [Charles Carrington], 1901. K.I.

———. *Woman and her Master: adventures of an Englishwoman in the Mahdi's camp.* Paris: Charles Carrington, 1904. K.I., Bod. L.

Vocabularia Amatoria: A French-English Glossary of Words, Phrases, and Allusions. London: Privately Printed for Subscribers, 1896. Bod. L.

The Voluptuarian Museum: or History of Sir Henry Loveall. Paris [London]: Printed for the Proprietors, [1790s?]. T.C.

A Voyage to Lethe. By Captain Samuel Cock. London: Printed for J. Conybeare in Smock-Alley, 1741 [1890s?]. Private collection.

The Way of a Man with a Maid. Parts 1 and 2. Liverpool: H. W. Pickle & Co., 1908. T.C.

The Wedding Night, or The Battle of Venus, a voluptuous disclosure. London: Printed for booksellers, [c. 1841]. K.I.

A Weekend Visit. By the author of "A man with a maid," "Parisian Frolics," etc. London: Printed for private circulation only, [ca. 1900?]. K.I.

When a Child Loves and When She Hates: a Tale of Birch and Bed. By a Gentleman. London?: Privately printed for the author and his friends, [189–?]. K.I.

When a Child Loves and When She Hates: a Tale of Birch and Bed. [Paris?: Charles Carrington?, c.1908].

The Whippingham Papers. A Collection of Contributions in Prose and Verse, chiefly by the author of "The Romance of Chastisement." London: [Edward Avery], 1888 [1887]. B.L., Cam.

[Wilde, Oscar?]. *Teleny, or, The Reverse of the Medal.* A Physiological Romance of Today. In Two Volumes. Cosmopoli [London?]: [Leonard Smithers], 1893. K.I., B.L., T.C.

[———]. *Teleny, or, The Reverse of the Medal.* Cosmopoli [Paris]: N.p., 1906. B.L., K.I.

[———.] *Teleny or Reverse of the Medal,* 1893. Reprint, The Traveler's Press Companion Series, Paris: Olympia Press, n.d..

Wilkes, John. *An Essay on Woman.* Suppressed by Authorities. London: Printed and Published by R. Smith, Drury Lane [William Dugdale?], [c. 1860]. Numerous editions, B.L., K.I., Cam.

————. *An Essay on Woman.* By Pego Borewell. With notes by Roger Cunaeus, Vigerus Mutoniabus, &c., and a Commentary by the Rev. Dr. Warburton. Inscribed to Miss Fanny Murray. [London: George Redway, 1883]. B.L.

Wilmot, John. *The Singular Life, Amatory Adventures, and . . . Intrigues of John Wilmot . . . to which are added the poems of Lord Rochester, carefully collected and revised.* Now first printed from the manuscript in his Lordship's handwriting. [London]: Printed and Published by Henry Smith, 37 Holywell Street [William Dugdale], [c. 1860]. B.L.

The Wolf in the Fold, being the Love Adventures of a French Don Juan including his Account of Sleeping Beauty and the seductive Artifices of the Queen of the Air. Written by Himself. Constantinople [Paris: Charles Carrington], 1897. B.L., Bod. L.

Yvonne, or, The Adventures and Intrigues of a French Governess with her Pupils. A real Tale, translated from the French by Mary Suckit. London and Paris: N.p., 1898. K.I., B.L.

SECONDARY SOURCES

Abelove, Henry. "Some Speculations on the History of Sexual Intercourse during the 'Long Eighteenth Century' in England." In *Nationalisms and Sexualities,* ed. Andrew Parker and others, 335–342. New York: Routledge, 1992.

Alloula, Malek. *The Colonial Harem.* Minneapolis: University of Minnesota Press, 1986.

Appadurai, Arjun, ed. *The Social Life of Things: Commodities in Cultural Perspective.* Cambridge: Cambridge University Press, 1986.

Assiter, Alison. *Pornography, Feminism, and the Individual.* London: Pluto Press, 1989.

Barret-Ducrocq, Françoise. *Love in the Time of Victoria: Sexuality and Desire among Working-Class Men and Women in Nineteenth-Century London.* Tr. John Howe. New York: Penguin, 1992.

Berger, Ronald J., Patricia Searles, and Charles E. Cottle. *Feminism and Pornography.* New York: Praeger, 1991.

"Bodleian Handlist of the Phi Collection." Danson Collection, Trinity College, Oxford.

Bristow, Edward J.. *Vice and Vigilance: Purity Movements in Britain since 1700.* Dublin: Gill & Macmillan, 1977.

Brodie, Fawn. *The Devil Drives: A Life of Sir Richard Burton.* New York: Penguin Books, 1971.

Bullough, Vern L. *Prostitution: An Illustrated History.* New York: Crown, 1978.

————. *Sex, Society, and History.* New York: Science History Publications, 1976.

Callaway, Helen. *Gender, Culture, and Empire.* Urbana: University of Illinois Press, 1987.

Carnes, Mark C., and Clyde Griffen, eds. *Meanings for Manhood: Constructions of Masculinity in Victorian America.* Chicago: University of Chicago Press, 1990.

Chandos, John. *Boys Together: English Public Schools, 1800–1864.* New Haven, Conn.: Yale University Press, 1984.

Chartier, Roger. "Intellectual History or Sociocultural History." In *Modern European Intellectual History,* ed. Dominick LaCapra and Steven L. Kaplan, 13–46. Ithaca, N.Y.: Cornell University Press, 1982.

Clark, Anna. *The Struggle for the Breeches: Gender and the Making of the British Working Class.* Berkeley: University of California Press, 1995.

Code, Lorraine. "Taking Subjectivity into Account." In *Feminist Epistemologies,* ed. Linda Alcoff and Elizabeth Potter, 15–49. New York: Routledge, 1993.

Cohen, Ed. *Talk on the Wilde Side: Towards a Genealogy of a Discourse on Male Sexualities.* New York and London: Routledge, 1993.

Copp, David, and Susan Wendell, eds. *Pornography and Censorship.* Buffalo, N.Y.: Prometheus Books, 1983.

Cornog, Martha, ed. *Libraries, Erotica, Pornography.* Arizona: Oryx Press, 1991.

Cusset, Catherine. "Editor's Preface." *Yale French Studies* 94, Special Issue: *Libertinage and Modernity,* 1998.

Dalmiya, Vrinda, and Linda Alcoff. "Are 'Old Wives' Tales' Justified?" In *Feminist Epistemologies,* ed. Linda Alcoff and Elizabeth Potter, 217–244. New York: Routledge, 1993.

Darnton, Robert. *The Forbidden Best-Sellers of Pre-Revolutionary France.* New York: Norton, 1995.

———. *The Great Cat Massacre.* New York: Vintage Books, 1985.

———. *The Literary Underground of the Old Regime.* Cambridge, Mass.: Harvard University Press, 1982.

———, and Daniel Roche, eds. *Revolution in Print: The Press in France, 1775–1800.* Berkeley: University of California Press, 1989.

Davidoff, Leonore, and Catherine Hall. *Family Fortunes: Men and Women of the English Middle Class, 1780–1850.* Chicago: University of Chicago Press, 1991.

Davis, Natalie Zemon. *Society and Culture in Early Modern France.* Stanford, Calif.: Stanford University Press, 1975.

Dawes, C. R. [Charles Reginald]. "Catalogue of the Erotica Collectioin of C. R. Dawes." Private Case Collectioni, British Library, London.

de Grazia, Edward. *Girls Lean Back Everywhere: The Law of Obscenity and the Assault on Genius.* New York: Random House, 1992.

D'Emilio, John, and Estelle B. Freedman. *Intimate Matters: A History of Sexuality in America.* New York: Harper & Row, 1988.

Dingwall, E. J. "The Milford Haven Collection of Postcards." Catalog, December 1960. Victoria and Albert Museum, London.

Dollimore, Jonathan. *Sexual Dissidence: Augustine to Wilde, Freud to Foucault.* New York: Oxford University Press, 1991.

Donnerstein, Edward I., Daniel Linz, and Steven Penrod. *The Question of Pornography: Research Findings and Policy Implications.* New York: Free Press; London: Collier Macmillan, 1987.

Douglas, Mary. *Purity and Danger: An Analysis of the Concepts of Pollution and Taboo.* London and New York: Ark Paperbacks, 1989.

Dworkin, Andrea. *Pornography: Men Possessing Women.* New York: Putnam, 1981.

Eckardt, Wolf Von, Sander L. Gilman, and J. Edward Chamberlin. *Oscar Wilde's London: A Scrapbook of Vices and Virtues, 1880–1900.* Garden City, N.Y.: Anchor Press, 1987.

Edwards, Elizabeth, ed. *Anthropology and Photography, 1860–1920.* New Haven, Conn.: Yale University Press, 1992.

Ellis, Kate, and others, eds. *Caught Looking: Feminism, Pornography and Censorship.* Seattle: Real Comet Press, 1988.

Epstein, Julia. "Fanny's Fanny: Epistolarity, Eroticism, and the Transsexual Text." In *Writing the Female Voice: Essays on Epistolary Literature,* ed. Elizabeth C. Goldsmith, 135–153. Boston: Northeastern University Press, 1989.

Epstein, William H. *John Cleland: Images of a Life.* New York: Columbia University Press, 1974.

Fanelli, Giovanni, and Ezio Godoli. *Art Nouveau Postcards.* New York: Rizzoli International, 1987.

Farwell, Byron. *Burton: A Biography of Sir Richard Francis Burton.* London: Penguin Books, 1990.

Febvre, Lucien, and Henri-Jean Martin. *The Coming of the Book.* London: NLB, 1976.

Foucault, Michel. *The History of Sexuality: An Introduction,* vol. 1. New York: Vintage Books, 1980.

Foxon, David. *Libertine Literature in England, 1660–1745.* New York: University Books, 1965.

Frantz, David O. *Festum Voluptatis: A Study of Renaissance Erotica.* Columbus: Ohio State University Press, 1989.

Fraser, W. Hamish. *The Coming of the Mass Market, 1850–1914.* London: Macmillan, 1981.

Frese, Pamela R. "The Union of Nature and Culture: Gender Symbolism in the American Wedding Ritual." In *Transcending Boundaries: Multi-Disciplinary Approaches to the Study of Gender,* ed. Pamela R. Frese and John M. Coggeshall, 97–112. New York: Bergin & Garvey, 1991.

Freud, Sigmund. *Three Essays on the Theory of Sexuality.* 6th ed. Tr. James Strachey. Leipzig and Vienna: Deuticke, 1925; reprint, New York: Basic Books, 1975.

Fryer, Peter. *Mrs. Grundy: Studies in English Prudery.* New York: London House & Maxwell, 1963.

Gibson, Ian. *The English Vice: Beating, Sex, and Shame in Victorian England and After.* 3d ed. London: Duckworth Press, 1992.

Gibson, Pamela Church, and Roma Gibson, eds. *Dirty Looks: Women, Pornography, Power.* London: British Film Institute, 1993.

Gilfoyle, Timothy J. *City of Eros: New York City, Prostitution, and the Commercialization of Sex, 1790–1920.* New York: Norton, 1992.

Gillis, John R. *For Better, for Worse: British Marriages, 1600 to the Present.* Oxford, U. K.: Oxford University Press, 1985.

Gilman, Sander L. "Black Bodies, White Bodies: Towards an Iconography of Female Sexuality in Late Nineteenth-Century Art, Medicine, and Literature." In *Race, Writing, and Difference,* ed. Henry Louis Gates, 223–261. Chicago: University of Chicago Press, 1986.

Ginzburg, Ralph. *An Unhurried View of Erotica.* New York: Helmsman Press, 1958.

Gould, Stephen Jay. *The Mismeasure of Man.* New York: W. W. Norton, 1981.

Griffin, Susan. *Pornography and Silence: Culture's Revenge against Nature.* New York: Harper & Row, 1981.

Gwilliam, Tassie. "Female Fraud: Counterfeit Maidenheads in the Eighteenth Century." *Journal of the History of Sexuality* 6, no. 4 (1996): 518–548.

Hall, Lesley A. *Hidden Anxieties: Male Sexuality, 1900–1950.* Cambridge, U.K.: Polity Press, 1991.

Hammerton, A. James. *Cruelty and Companionship: Conflict in Nineteenth-Century Married Life.* London: Routledge, 1992.

Hammond, Paul. *French Undressing: Naughty Postcards from 1900 to 1920.* London: Bloomsbury Books, 1976.

Harding, Sandra. *Whose Science? Whose Knowledge?* Ithaca, N. Y.: Cornell University Press, 1991.

Harris, P. H., ed. *The Library of the British Museum.* Cambridge, U.K.: Cambridge University Press, 1991.

Hawkins, Gordon, and Franklin E. Zimring. *Pornography in a Free Society.* Cambridge, U.K.: Cambridge University Press, 1988.

Hobsbawm, Eric. *The Age of Empire, 1875–1914.* New York: Vintage Books, 1989.

———. *Industry and Empire.* London: Penguin Books, 1968.

Hoff, Joan. "Why Is There No History of Pornography?" In *For Adult Users Only: The Dilemma of Violent Pornography,* ed. Susan Guber and Joan Hoff, 17–46. Bloomington: University of Indiana Press, 1989.

Hunt, Lynn, ed. *Eroticism and the Body Politic.* Baltimore: Johns Hopkins University Press, 1991.

———. *The Invention of Pornography: Obscenity and the Origins of Modernity, 1500–1800.* New York: Zone Books, 1993.

Hunt, Tamara Lisa. "'To Take for Truth the Test of Ridicule': Public Perceptions, Political Controversy, and English Political Caricature, 1815–1821." Ph.D. diss., University of Illinois at Urbana-Champaign, 1989.

Hyde, H. Montgomery. *The Cleveland Street Scandal.* New York: Coward, McCann & Geoghegan, 1976.

Jhally, Sut. *The Codes of Advertising: Fetishism and the Political Economy of Meaning in the Consumer Society.* New York: Routledge, 1990.

Kaplan, Morris B. "Did 'My Lord Gomorrah' Smile?: Homosexuality, Class, and Prostitution in the Cleveland Street Affair." In *Disorder in the Courts: Trials and Sexual Conflict at the Turn of the Century,* ed. George Robb and Nancy Erber, 78–99. New York: New York University Press, 1999.

Kearney, Patrick J. *A History of Erotic Literature.* Hong Kong: Dorset Press, 1993.

———. *The Private Case: An Annotated Bibliography of the Private Case Erotica Collection in the British (Museum) Library.* London: Jay Landesman, Limited 1981.

Kendrick, Walter. *The Secret Museum: Pornography in Modern Culture.* New York: Viking Penguin, 1987.

Kincaid, James. *Child Loving: The Erotic Child and Victorian Culture.* New York: Routledge, 1994.

Kipnis, Laura. *Bound and Gagged: Pornography and the Politics of Fantasy in America.* New York: Grove Press, 1996.

———. "(Male) Desire and (Female) Disgust: Reading *Hustler.*" In *Cultural Studies,* ed. Lawrence Grossberg, Cary Nelson, and Paula Treichler, 373–391. New York: Routledge, 1992.

Kobylka, Joseph F. *The Politics of Obscenity: Group Litigation in a Time of Legal Change.* New York: Greenwood Press, 1991.

Krafft-Ebing, Richard von. *Psychopathia Sexualis.* 1886. Reprint, New York: G. P. Putnam's Sons, 1965.

Kuh, Richard H. *Foolish Figleaves? Pornography in and out of Court.* New York: Macmillan, 1967.

Laqueur, Thomas. *Making Sex: Body and Gender from the Greeks to Freud.* Cambridge, Mass.: Harvard University Press, 1990.

Lévi-Strauss, Claude. *Myth and Meaning: Cracking the Code of Culture.* Foreword by Wendy Doniger. New York: Schocken Books, 1995.

———. *The Raw and the Cooked.* Chicago: University of Chicago Press, 1990.

———. *Structural Anthropology.* New York: Basic Books, 1963.

Lewinski, Jorge. *The Naked and the Nude: A History of Nude Photography.* London: Weidenfeld and Nicolson, 1987.

Lucie-Smith, Edward. *The Invented Eye.* New York: Paddington Press, 1975.

Lutz, Catherine A., and Jane L. Collins. *Reading National Geographic.* Chicago: University of Chicago Press, 1993.

McCalman, Iain. *Radical Underworld: Prophets, Revolutionaries, and Pornographers in London, 1795–1840.* Cambridge, U.K.: Cambridge University Press, 1988.

McClintock, Anne. *Imperial Leather: Race, Gender, and Sexuality in the Colonial Context.* New York: Routledge, 1995.

MacKenzie, John M., ed. *Imperialism and Popular Culture.* Manchester, U.K.: University of Manchester Press, 1986.

———. "The Imperial Pioneer and Hunter and the British Masculine Stereotype in Late Victorian and Eduardian Times." In *Manliness and Morality: Middle-Class Masculinity in Britain and America 1800–1940,* ed. J. A. Mangan and James Walvin, 176–198. New York: St. Martin's Press, 1987.

MacKinnon, Catherine. *Feminism Unmodified: Discourses on Life and Law.* Cambridge, Mass.: Harvard University Press, 1987.

———. *Only Words.* Cambridge, Mass.: Harvard University Press, 1993.

Manchester, Colin. "Lord Campbell's Act: England's First Obscenity Statute." *Journal of Legal History* 9, no. 2 (1988): 223–241.

Marcus, Steven. *The Other Victorians.* New York: Norton, 1985.

Marx, Karl. *Capital,* vol. 1. 1887. Reprint, New York: International Publishers, 1967.

Mason, Michael. *The Making of Victorian Sexuality.* Oxford, U.K.: Oxford University Press, 1994.

Mendes, Peter. *Clandestine Erotic Fiction in English, 1800–1930: A Bibliographical Study.* London: Scolar Press, 1993.

Miles, Henry. *Forbidden Fruit.* London: Luxor Press, 1973.

Mort, Frank. *Dangerous Sexualities: Medico-Moral Politics in England since 1830.* London: Routledge & Kegan Paul, 1987.

Mukerji, Chandra, and Michael Schudson, eds. *Rethinking Popular Culture: Contemporary Perspectives in Cultural Studies.* Berkeley: University of California Press, 1991.

Nelson, James G. "Leonard Smithers and Captain Sir Richard Burton." *Journal of the Eighteen Nineties Society* 24 (1997): 3–12.

Nochlin, Linda. *Women, Art, and Power: And Other Essays.* New York: Harper & Row, 1988.

Norton, Rictor. *Mother Clap's Molly House.* London: GMP, 1992.

Noyes, John K. *The Mastery of Submission: Inventions of Masochism.* Ithaca, N.Y.: Cornell University Press, 1997.

Pemble, John. *The Mediterranean Passion: Victorians and Edwardians in the South.* Oxford, U.K.: Clarendon Press, 1987.

Pope-Hennessy, James. *Monckton Milnes: The Flight of Youth, 1851–1885.* London: Constable, 1951.

Potter, Tiffany. *Honest Sins: Georgian Libertinism and the Plays and Novels of Henry Fielding.* Montreal and Kingston: McGill-Queen's University Press, 1999.

Porter, Roy. *English Society in the Eighteenth Century.* London: Penguin Books, 1990.

———, and Lesley Hall. *The Facts of Life: The Creation of Sexual Knowledge in Britain, 1650–1950.* New Haven, Conn., and London: Yale University Press, 1995.

Pratt, Mary Louise. *Imperial Eyes: Travel Writing and Transculturation.* New York: Routledge, 1992.

Radway, Janice A. *Reading the Romance: Women, Patriarchy, and Popular Literature.* Chapel Hill: University of North Carolina Press, 1984.

Reid, Douglas A. "Interpreting the Festival Calender: Wakes and Fairs as Carnivals." In *Popular Culture and Custom in Nineteenth-Century England,* ed. Robert Storch, 125–153. New York: St. Martin's Press, 1982.

Rich, P. J. *Chains of Empire: English Public Schools, Masonic Cabalism, Historical Causality, and Imperial Clubdom.* London: Regency Press, 1991.

Richards, Thomas. *The Commodity Culture of Victorian England: Advertising and Spectacle, 1851–1914.* Stanford, Calif.: Stanford University Press, 1990.

Robel, Lauren. "Pornography and the Existing Law." In *For Adult Users Only: The Dilemma of Violent Pornography,* ed. Susan Guber and Joan Hoff, 178–197. Bloomington: Indiana University Press, 1989.

Rodgerson, Gillian, and Elizabeth Wilson, eds. *Pornography and Feminism: The Case against Censorship.* London: Lawrence & Wishart, 1991.

Rose, Alfred. *Register of Erotic Books.* 2 vols. New York: Jack Brussel, 1965.

Rousseau, G. S., and Roy Porter, eds. *Exoticism in the Enlightenment.* Manchester and New York: Manchester University Press, 1990.

————. *Sexual Underworlds of the Enlightenment.* Chapel Hill: University of North Carolina Press, 1988.

Royle, Edward. *Radical Politics, 1790–1900: Religion and Unbelief.* London: Longman Group, 1971.

Rutherford, Jonathon. *Forever England: Reflections on Race, Masculinity and Empire.* London: Lawrence & Wishart, 1997.

Ryan, Dorothy B., and George Miller. *Picture Postcards in the United States, 1893–1918.* New York: Clarkson N. Potter, 1982.

Sabor, Peter. "The Censor Censured: Expurgating *Memoirs of a Woman of Pleasure."* *Eighteenth-Century Life* 9, no. 3 (May 1985): 192–201.

Said, Edward. *Culture and Imperialism.* New York: Vintage Books, 1994.

————. *Orientalism.* New York: Vintage Books, 1979.

Scheid, Uwe. *Akademien.* Überherrn, Germany: Privately printed, 1991.

————. *Bilderlust.* Heidelberg: Edition Braus, 1985.

Scott, Patrick Craig, and Pauline Fletcher, eds. *Culture and Education in Victorian England.* Cranbury, N.J.: Associated University Presses, 1990.

Shephard, Ben. "Showbiz Imperialism: The Case of Peter Lobengula." In *Imperialism and Popular Culture,* ed. John M. Mackenzie, 94–112. Manchester: Manchester University Press, 1986.

Simmons, Philip E. "John Cleland's *Memoirs of a Woman of Pleasure:* Literary Voyeurism and the Techniques of Novelistic Transgression." *Eighteenth-Century Fiction* 3, no. 1 (October 1990): 43–63.

Sinfield, Alan. *The Wilde Century.* London: Cassell, 1994.

Smith, E. A. *A Queen on Trial: The Affair of Queen Caroline.* Avon, U. K.: Alan Sutton, 1993.

Smith, Elizabeth Alison. "Charged with Sexuality: Feminism, Liberalism, and Pornography, 1970–1982." Ph.D. diss., University of Pennsylvania, 1990.

Snitow, Ann, and others, eds. *The Powers of Desire: The Politics of Sexuality.* New York: Monthly Review Press, 1983.

Soble, Alan. *Pornography: Marxism, Feminism, and the Future of Sexuality.* New Haven, Conn.: Yale University Press, 1986.

Staff, Frank. *The Picture Postcard and Its Origins.* New York: Praeger, 1966.

Stephan, Sir Leslie, and Sir Sidney Lee. *The Dictionary of National Bibliography.* Oxford, U. K.: Oxford University Press, 1917–.

Stocking, George W. *Victorian Anthropology.* New York: Free Press, 1987.

Storch, Robert. Introduction to *Popular Culture and Custom in Nineteenth-Century England,* ed. Robert Storch, 1–19. New York: St. Martin's Press, 1982.

————. "'Please to Remember the Fifth of November': Conflict, Solidarity, and Public Order in Southern England, 1815–1900." In *Popular Culture and Custom in Nineteenth-Century England,* ed. Robert Storch, 71–99. New York: St. Martin's Press, 1982.

Street, Brian. "British Popular Anthropology: Exhibiting and Photographing the Other." In *Anthropology and Photography,* ed. Elizabeth Edwards, 122–131. New Haven, Conn.: Yale University Press, 1992.

Sutherland, Gillian. "Education." In *The Cambridge Social History of Britain, 1750–1950,* vol. 3, ed. F.M.L. Thompson. Cambridge, U.K.: Cambridge University Press, 1990.

Taussig, Michael T. *The Devil and Commodity Fetishism in South America.* Chapel Hill: University of North Carolina Press, 1980.

Thom, Daniel E. "An Annotated Bibliography of the Erotica in the New York Public Library Research Collection." Master's thesis, City University of New York, 1983.

Thompson, E. P. *Customs in Common.* New York: New Press, 1991.

———. *The Making of the English Working Class.* London: Victor Gollancz, 1963.

Thompson, F.M.L., ed. *The Cambridge Social History of Britain, 1750–1950.* 3 vols. Cambridge, U.K.: Cambridge University Press, 1990.

Tidrick, Kathryn. *Empire and the English Character.* London: I. B. Taurus, 1992.

Tomlinson, John. *Cultural Imperialism: A Critical Introduction.* Baltimore: Johns Hopkins University Press, 1991.

Turner, James G. "The Properties of Libertinism." *Eighteenth-Century Life* 9, no. 3 (1985): 75–87.

Vance, Carole S. "Pleasure and Danger: Toward a Politics of Sexuality." In *Pleasure and Danger: Exploring Female Sexuality* , ed. Carole S. Vance. Boston: Routledge & Kegan Paul, 1984.

van Keuren, David Keith. "Human Science in Victorian Britain: Anthropology in Institutional and Disciplinary Formation, 1863–1908." Ph.D. diss, University of Pennsylvania, 1982; Ann Arbor, Mich: University Microfilms, 1982.

Wagner, Peter. *Eros Revived: Erotica of the Enlightenment in England and America.* London: Secker & Warburg, 1988.

Walkowitz, Judith. *City of Dreadful Delight: Narratives of Sexual Danger in Late Victorian London.* Chicago: University of Chicago Press, 1992.

———. *Prostitution and Victorian Society: Women, Class, and the State.* Cambridge, U. K.: Cambridge University Press, 1980.

Webb, R. K. *The British Working-Class Reader, 1790–1848.* London: George Allen & Unwin, 1955.

Weeks, Jeffrey. *Making Sexual History.* London: Polity Press, 2000.

———. *Sex, Politics, and Society: The Regulation of Sexuality since 1800.* London: Longman Group, 1981.

———. *Sexuality and Its Discontents.* London: Routledge & Kegan Paul, 1985.

Weintraub, Stanley. *Beardsley: A Biography.* New York: George Braziller, 1967.

Weiermair, Peter. *Wilhelm von Gloeden.* Cologne, Germany: Taschen, 1996.

Wilkins, Kay. "Andréa de Nerciat and the Libertine Tradition in Eighteenth-Century France." *Studies on Voltaire and the Eighteenth Century* 256 (1988): 225–235.

Williams, Raymond. *Culture and Society, 1780–1950.* New York: Columbia University Press, 1983.

Index

About the Author

LISA Z. SIGEL is an assistant professor of history at Millsaps College and a visiting lecturer at DePaul University. She did her graduate work at Carnegie Mellon University in the department of history and writes on sex, gender, and British history.